EXPLORATIONS IN ECONOMIC LIBERALISM

Also by Geoffrey E. Wood

FINANCIAL CRISES AND THE WORLD BANKING SYSTEM
(*editor with Forrest Capie*)

MACROECONOMIC POLICY AND ECONOMIC
INTERDEPENDENCE (*editor with Donald R. Hodgman*)

MONETARY AND EXCHANGE RATE POLICY (*editor with Donald
R. Hodgman*)

MONETARY ECONOMICS IN THE 1980s (*editor with Forrest Capie*)

UNREGULATED BANKING: CHAOS OR ORDER? (*editor with
Forrest Capie*)

Explorations in Economic Liberalism

The Wincott Lectures

Edited by

Geoffrey E. Wood
City University Business School
London

Foreword by

Lord Harris of High Cross

330.122
E96

 First published in Great Britain 1996 by
MACMILLAN PRESS LTD
Houndmills, Basingstoke, Hampshire RG21 6XS
and London
Companies and representatives
throughout the world

A catalogue record for this book is available
from the British Library.

ISBN 0–333–65739–X

 First published in the United States of America 1996 by
ST. MARTIN'S PRESS, INC.,
Scholarly and Reference Division,
175 Fifth Avenue,
New York, N.Y. 10010

ISBN 0–312–15997–8

Library of Congress Cataloging-in-Publication Data
Explorations in economic liberalism : the Wincott lectures / edited by
Geoffrey E. Wood.
p.   cm.
Includes bibliographical references and index.
ISBN 0–312–15977–8
1. Free enterprise.   2. Wincott, Harold.   I. Wincott, Harold.
II. Wood, Geoffrey Edward.
HB95.E97   1996
330.12'2—dc20   95–53930
                                                                  CIP

10   9   8   7   6   5   4   3   2   1
05   04   03   02   01   00   99   98   97   96

Printed and bound in Great Britain by
Antony Rowe Ltd, Chippenham, Wiltshire

Contents

Harold Wincott

Foreword:
Harold Wincott – Doyen of Financial Journalism

Ralph Harris

I am not hopeful of conveying fully to a younger generation the enduring place Harold Wincott earned in the postwar transformation of financial journalism. When I took up economics at Cambridge in 1945, few people outside the Square Mile and perhaps the financial communities scattered around the provinces made a habit of poring over the acres of anonymous, densely packed, columns headed 'City Editor', 'Financial Editor' or 'Our Own Correspondent'. A real scoop might justify 'from our special correspondent'.

By 1957, when the Institute of Economic Affairs set up its first office behind Throgmorton Street, some of the anonymity was being shed. In the next decade I had the good fortune to meet a veritable academy of City journalists with names already winning wide recognition among businessmen, politicians and even professional economists. Among the most celebrated in their day were Oscar Hobson, Paul Bareau, Manning Dacey, Richard Fry, Wilfred King, Maurice Green, followed later by William Clarke, Andrew Shonfield, Patrick Hutber, Nigel Lawson, Peter Jay, Christopher Fildes, and, of course, the everlasting Samuel Brittan. All of them shared a serious, even scholarly approach to the interpretation of current affairs. And with few exceptions, they also shared a broad commitment to market economy learned from close observation of the real world.

I believe none of these famous names would begrudge pride of place to Harold Wincott. Certainly, by the time of his death in 1969 at the age of 62, his weekly articles in *The Financial Times* had become something of a national institution. Unique among such a galaxy, this pre-eminence was achieved without the least claim to formal study, let alone university education. Indeed, his apprenticeship was altogether more practical.

Born in North London in 1906, he left Hornsey County School at 16. His father wanted him to go into the small family business of heraldic engravers, but through a fellow choir member, Harold got his first job as office boy in an accountant's firm. He then progressed through the stocks and shares department of an insurance office to become a statistician with a stock broker. Through the lucky chance of Wilfred King happening to be a slightly senior old-boy of Hornsey County as well as assistant editor of the *Financial News*, Harold got his opening in journalism on the sub-editor's table of the paper in 1930, working up to become chief sub. The following year, he married Joyce, who was the daughter of a printer and worked at the Bank of England. They formed a perfect match.

Having attracted the attention of Brendan Bracken, he was appointed editor of the *Investors Chronicle* in 1938 at little over the age of 30 and continued in the chair for 30 years, uninterrupted by war. After 1945 he added a sheaf of appointments as investment adviser to several blue-chip companies, a trade-union unit trust, and Provincial Insurance which remained his favourite as a private, family-managed company rare in the insurance business. In 1950, already known for his weekly column as 'Candidus' in the *Investors Chronicle*, he added a regular Tuesday column, under his own name in the *FT*, which continued to attract ever-widening fame until his untimely death at 62 in March 1969.

With that background, it went without saying that everything he wrote was grounded in a sure grasp and shrewd assessment of financial and economic affairs. He once described his painstaking fact-finding and analysis to be 'something like a squirrel gathering nuts for winter', never knowing when he would need to draw on the store. But that was only a beginning, to which he added luminous, yet unpretentious, prose enlivened by a humorous turn rare in exposition of the dismal science. Above all, he was remarkable for the powerful combination of courage and independence in the service of unwavering convictions. Thus did he come to trumpet, in and out of season, unfashionably ahead of his time, the moral and material benefits of dispersed initiative in competitive markets – what he called 'liberal capitalism' – as an essential buttress of the free society.

My favourite example of his fearless championing of unpopular causes was provoked by the unprecedented resignation in 1958 of Harold Macmillan's Chancellor of the Exchequer, Peter Thorneycroft, and his two Treasury ministers, Enoch Powell and Nigel Birch. The issue was the cabinet's refusal to cut government expenditure, preferring in the words of Lord Hailsham 'to adhere to our social policies'. Faced by what might now be seen as the last effort for 20 years to dethrone the Keynesian-collectivist consensus by halting inflationary finance, Wincott commented:

There you have it. Mr Thorneycroft's policy, if you like, makes him a hard-faced, hard money man. That makes two of us (at least).

Wincott's stand was certainly in sharp contrast to the characteristically weak, permissive defence of Macmillan by the leader writers elsewhere in what I thought was well-named the 'pink-un'. In characteristic style, combining trenchant analysis with homely analogy, he concluded:

> In the ultimate resort, if Mr Amory (the new Chancellor) is not to be as expendable as Mr Thorneycroft was, it is the attitude of mind in the Conservative Party which has got to change. For over six years now, that attitude has been the 'Dear-Mother-I-am-going-to-save-7s 6d-but-not-this-week' attitude. It still is. But the supply of weeks is running out.

Ten years later, the enduring nature of Wincott's contribution to generally ephemeral journalism was perhaps best caught by Lord (Lionel) Robbins, then both senior Professor at the LSE and chairman of *The Financial Times*:

> There is no working journalist who knows better how to pluck the day than Mr Wincott: the occasion of his utterances is almost always intensely contemporaneous. But none know better how to invest the discussion of the passing moment with the overtones of the permanent issues.*

A final measure of Harold Wincott's wide following might especially impress fellow economists. When Graham Hutton and I, encouraged by Lionel Robbins and Peter Scott of Provincial Insurance, launched an appeal fund to commemorate his example, our target of £100 000 (equal to well over half a million today) was fully subscribed from individual readers and corporate admirers within a few months. As a result, since 1969 the Wincott Foundation has been able to perpetuate his memory and example through modest research grants, prestigious annual awards for financial journalism and a distinguished series of lectures from which the present selection is taken. Mrs Joyce Wincott and my fellow Trustees join me in hoping that all who share our admiration of Harold Wincott will welcome this volume as a fitting tribute to the doyen of financial journalists.

Lord Harris of High Cross

* Foreword to a selection of Harold Wincott's articles from *The Financial Times*, reprinted as *The Business of Capitalism*, IEA, 1968.

Notes on the Contributors

Jagdish Bhagwati, Arthur Lehman Professor of Economics and Professor of Political Science at Columbia University, New York, Cambridge, studied at MIT and Oxford, returning to India in 1961 as Professor of Economics at the Indian Statistical Institute. He returned to MIT in 1968, leaving it twelve years later as the Ford International Professor of Economics to join Columbia. Professor Bhagwati has also served as Economic Policy Adviser to the Director-General, GATT (1991–93). Among his recent books are *Protectionism, The World Trading System at Risk* and *India in Transition*. Professor Bhagwati also writes frequently for *The New York Times, The Wall Street Journal* and *The Financial Times*, and reviews for *The New Republic*.

Milton Friedman taught from 1946 to 1977 at the University of Chicago, where in 1962 he became the Paul Snowden Russell Distinguished Service Professor of Economics. Milton Friedman is now Senior Research Fellow at the Hoover Institution of Stanford University. He has taught at universities throughout the world, from Cambridge to Tokyo. He has also been on the research staff of the National Bureau of Economic Research. Professor Friedman was awarded the 1976 Nobel Prize in Economic Sciences. Among his best-known books are *Essays in Positive Economics, Studies in the Quantity Theory of Money, A Theory of the Consumption Function, Capitalism and Freedom, A Monetary History of the United States, 1867–1960* (with Anna J. Schwartz), and *The Optimum Quantity of Money*.

F. A. Hayek was Director of the Austrian Institute for Economics Research, 1927–31, and Lecturer in Economics at the University of Vienna, 1929–31. He was (1931–50) Tooke Professor of Economic Science and Statistics, University of London (1950–62), Professor of Social and Moral Science, University of Chicago, and (1962–68) Professor of Economics, University of Freiburg. He was awarded the Nobel Memorial Prize in Economic Sciences in 1974. Professor Hayek's most important publications include *Monetary Theory and the Trade Cycle, The Pure Theory of Capital, The Road to Serfdom, Individualism and Economic Order, The Counter-Revolution of Science* and *The Constitution of Liberty*. He died in 1992.

Deepak Lal is Professor Emeritus of Political Economy at University College, London, and James S. Coleman Professor of International Development Studies, University of California, Los Angeles. He has been Lecturer, Jesus College, and Christ Church, Oxford. He has served as a consultant to the ILO, UNCTAD, OECD, UNIDO, the World Bank, and the ministries of planning in South Korea and Sri Lanka. Professor Lal is the author of numerous books, including *Wells and Welfare, Methods of Project Analysis, Appraising Foreign Investment in Developing Countries, Unemployment and Wage Inflation in Industrial Economies,* and *Prices for Planning.*

J. E. Meade taught at Oxford, London and Cambridge Universities, and in 1977 won the Nobel Prize for Economic Sciences. From 1937 to 1940 he was an official of the League of Nations and author of *The World Economic Surveys* for those years. From 1940 to 1947 he was first a member, and later Director, of the Economic Section of the Cabinet Office. His books include *An Introduction to Economic Analysis and Policy, Planning and the Price Mechanism, Problems of Economic Union, Efficiency, Equality and the Ownership of Property* and *The Theory of Indicative Planning.* He died in 1995.

Sir Alan Peacock was Professor of Economics and Head of the Department of Economics at the University of York at its foundation in 1962. From 1973 to 1976 he was seconded as Chief Economic Adviser to the Department of Trade and Industry. His books include *Income Redistribution and Social Policy* and *Classics in the Theory of Public Finance.* From 1978 to 1983 he was successively Professor of Economics, Principal and Vice-Chancellor at the University of Birmingham. Since 1987 he has been Research Professor in Public Finances, Heriot-Watt University. He was a member of the Arts Council from 1986 to 1992.

Lord Robbins became Professor of Economics in 1929. Among many honours, he was created a Life Peer in 1959 and a Companion of Honour in 1968. Lord Robbins' books include *An Essay on the Nature and Significance of Economic Science, The Economic Causes of War, The Economic Problem in Peace and War, Politics and Economics, The Evolution of Modern Economic Theory, Autobiography of an Economist,* and *Money, Trade and International Relations.* He died in 1984.

Anna J. Schwartz has been a member of the research staff of the National Bureau of Economic Research for many years. The classic study to arise out of her work was her publication with Milton Friedman of *A Monetary History of the United States, 1867–1960*. She was a co-author with Milton Friedman of *Monetary Statistics of the United States* and *Monetary Trends in the United States and the United Kingdom: Their Relation to Income, Prices and Interest Rates, 1867–1957*.

George J. Stigler, winner of the 1982 Nobel Prize for Economic Science, was for many years the Charles R. Walgreen Professor of American Institutions and Director of the Walgreen Foundation in the Graduate Business School at the University of Chicago from 1958. He also taught at Iowa State University and the Universities of Minnesota, Brown and Columbia and at the London School of Economics.

Sir Alan Walters has been Professor of Political Economy at the Johns Hopkins University, Baltimore, Maryland since 1976. He has taught at the University of Birmingham and the London School of Economics (where he was the Cassel Professor of Economics from 1968 to 1976). His books include *Growth without Development, The Economics of Road User Charges*, and *An Introduction to Econometrics*. Since 1991 he has been Vice-Chairman and Director of the AIG Trading Group. Between 1981 and 1984 he was Economic Adviser to the Prime Minister.

Introduction

Geoffrey E. Wood

Harold Wincott, in whose honour the lectures published in this volume were delivered, was never an economic policy-maker in the sense of one who works in a government ministry or in a central bank. But by his commentaries on economic and financial affairs he influenced the intellectual climate in which decisions were made. Like Harold Wincott, none of the authors of the lectures printed in this volume made a career in government; a good number, indeed, only worked in government in time of war, and some never worked there at all. But all – even George Stigler, who remarked on one occasion that he did not wish to change the world but only to understand it – have profoundly influenced both policy and the intellectual climate in which it is made.

This brief introduction to the essays in this volume aims to place the papers in their historical context and sketch the influence they have had, and offers a few conjectures as to how they may have influence in the future. The lectures are discussed in the order of the volume, with the occasional cross-reference.

MILTON FRIEDMAN (1970) – 'THE COUNTER-REVOLUTION IN MONETARY THEORY'

It has over the past few years become more and more widely recognised that monetary policy is important. Without monetary control, economic instability and, according to whether monetary conditions are too tight or too easy, deflation or inflation will result. It is in considerable part thanks to the efforts of Milton Friedman, the first Wincott lecturer, that these propositions, not always generally accepted in the second half of this century, are now both widely acknowledged and in many countries the basis for policy.

In his lecture Professor Friedman first describes how some key propositions concerning the role of money in the economy were set out by Irving Fisher; in particular the relationship of rough proportionality between growth in money and in prices, the distinction between real and nominal interest rates, and the distinction between anticipated and unanticipated inflation. He then shows how following the views of Keynes in the *General Theory* (although not, Professor Friedman emphasises, in the *Tract on Monetary Reform*) the role of money was diminished by the claim that money's velocity of circulation fluctuates and offsets variations in the supply of money. Monetary policy thus lost its influence on economic activity, and was supplemented in importance by the component of total spending which is independent of current income – by what is known in the textbooks as autonomous spending. This is largely said to comprise private investment and government expenditure.

That change was the 'Revolution'. The 'Counter-Revolution' of the lecture's title was the overthrowing of that revolution by a vast body of evidence, much of it due to Friedman himself and to his joint work with Anna Schwartz (another Wincott lecturer). Their work led to a reinterpretation of the Great Depression, showing it to be primarily the result of failures of monetary policy. But that dramatic episode is not the only item of evidence. Professor Friedman in this lecture quotes several others, including two striking examples from the USA in 1966 and in 1968, when monetary and fiscal policy sought to drive the economy in opposite directions simultaneously, and monetary policy won both battles.

There is a wealth of material here from which, even 25 years after the lecture was given, both economists and policy-makers could learn. There is an explanation of why once inflation is started it is usually hard to stop. There is explanation of why interest rates are a poor guide to whether monetary policy is tight or easy. And, of the greatest importance, there is emphasis on how little we know of the details of an economy's workings, and why, therefore, monetary policy should be guided by simple rules rather than by efforts to direct precisely the course of the economy.

The paper is a masterly – and very readable – review of history of economic thought, economic history, and economic theory, and draws out the implications of all three for the conduct of policy. The ideas set out in it have influenced policy in countries as far apart geographically as New Zealand and the UK, and by governments of almost the full range of political persuasions.

JAMES MEADE (1971) – 'WAGES AND PRICES IN A MIXED ECONOMY'

Monetary policy can, as Milton Friedman had argued, control and end inflation. But because people's expectations of inflation tend to lag behind actual inflation performance, there can be rises – perhaps substantial rises – in unemployment during the process. In addition, as a result of, for example, legislation which confers some degree of monopoly power on trade unions, negotiated wage bargains may create substantial levels of unemployment even when prices have been stabilised for some time and lagging expectations are no longer exacerbating wage claims and consequently unemployment. These are the problems Professor Meade sets out to address.

The historical background against which he wrote is summarised in the first table of his lecture. Inflation had almost doubled (from 6.5 per cent p.a.) in the five years he surveyed; and unemployment had a little less than doubled (from 1.53 per cent) over the same period. The relative scale of one of the problems he examined was plainly different from that now confronting Britain's economy; but the reconciliation of stable prices with a satisfactorily low unemployment level is still a major economic problem. What solutions does Professor Meade propose?

He first very carefully considers whether inflation is a problem worth bothering about. After all, he notes, if it is 'anticipated' (to use his term in this context) then all prices and wages rise together, and no one appears to suffer.[1] But inflation, he says, can also be 'expensive' – when for one reason or another, 'the various groups in the community are so acting as to make demands on real resources that . . . it is impossible to fulfil'.

Such an inflation, he argues, is worth stopping. His concern is not so much how to do that but rather how to achieve *both* stable prices and a high level of employment. For these, two conditions must be satisfied.

> First, the government must be able by fiscal and monetary policies to keep total money expenditures at the level necessary to provide a market for the full-employment capacity level of output at uninflated money prices; and second, the wage-price fixing processes must be such as to ensure, at this full-employment, capacity level of real activity, both that money wage-rates are not pushed up more quickly than output per head is growing and also that profit margins are stabilised.

The problem he addresses is concerned with the second of these two conditions:

the problem of restraining the wage-price fixing processes so as to avoid, or at least much reduce, price inflation at full-employment levels of output.

The solution is in principle a straightforward one. If any union makes a wage claim above a certain percentage, that union loses various forms of protection.[2] These normally confer on the union's members greater bargaining power than they would possess in the open market. Removing the protection thus makes it harder for the union to price some other workers out of jobs.

Similar restraints are also, of course, surely necessary to prevent monopolistic price setting. Here, Professor Meade suggests a strengthened monopolies commission. But he does not rely only on bureaucracy: he also turns the market to his advantage.

Companies should be encouraged to distribute profits. 'If the finance of capital development from ploughed back funds was heavily discouraged by taxation, companies would have to compete on the open capital market for new funds, which would promote competition in favour of the most promising new enterprises.'

Further, and touching upon the subject of the final lecture in this volume, Professor Meade advocates free trade. 'But far and away the most effective way of promoting competition and curbing monopolistic pressures would be to admit the free import of goods from all foreign sources....'.

Not all Professor Meade's proposals have been adopted. The world has gradually shuffled, sometimes forward, sometimes back but on balance forward, towards free trade. The powers of the unions have in Britain been attacked although not by the methods he advocated. The results are not perhaps very striking; but if one compares unemployment in Britain with the still higher levels in some countries where such powers have been not reduced but even perhaps augmented, it seems clear that something has been gained.

FRIEDRICH HAYEK (1973) – 'ECONOMIC FREEDOM AND REPRESENTATIVE GOVERNMENT'

Monopoly power also concerned Friedrich Hayek, in his Wincott Lecture. His concern was that to ensure it retains its majority a government will 'buy the support of particular groups by the promise of special advantages'. How can this be tackled?

Hayek suggests a return to the principles expressed by the classical theorists of representative government – that the legislature should limit itself to passing laws, 'in the sense of general rules of just conduct equally applicable to all citizens'.

This, Hayek argues, is necessary to prevent the rise of groups with protected monopolies, which cause inflationary pressure and unemployment (as Meade discussed), and also inhibit the growth and change of economies.

Having thus defined the problem, Hayek, via an examination of the nature of law and the various forms legislation can take, sets out a proposal which would separate the governing body from the legislating body. Hayek acknowledges that the proposal is a 'utopian construction'. His argument in support of setting out such a scheme is provided by David Hume in his essay on 'The Idea of a Perfect Commonwealth'.

> In all cases, it must be advantageous to know what is the most perfect in the kind, that we may be able to bring any real constitution or form of government as near it as possible, by such gentle alterations and innovations as may not give too great a disturbance to society.

No such scheme of government has as yet been adopted. But more and more economists, commentators, and politicians have become aware of, and concerned about, the dangerous powers of special interest groups. Progress is being made.

LORD ROBBINS (1974) 'ASPECTS OF POSTWAR ECONOMIC POLICY'

Robbins, too, was concerned with unemployment and inflation. His aim was to review how post-1950 British economic policy had led to accelerating inflation, rising unemployment, and in addition, ensured that 'our purchases from abroad are sustained at their present volume only by unprecedented borrowing from abroad'. Lord Robbins of course put the problem in context. He pointed out that income per head had in real terms grown by some 60 per cent between 1951 and 1971. But this compared badly with many other countries in the same period. Why?

A variety of factors is examined briefly and incisively. High marginal taxation reduced work effort, as it did both the incentive and the ability to save. Then there was policy towards industry. Nationalisation produced problems – not perhaps inevitably, but certainly in practice. There was the 'politicisation and bureaucratisation of general policy regarding investment and price policy'. We are all familiar with examples. Prices of nationalised industries were kept low to restrain the price index. Investment was frequently deferred to reduce public expenditure's growth so as to allow tax reductions – undesirable not because tax reductions are undesirable, but because they were financed by investment cuts on the sole grounds that the majority of voters would in the short run not notice their consequences.

Restrictive practices were damaging; indeed, 'The mismanagement of money apart, I regard restrictive practices as perhaps the most serious of our current problems.' There are laws against such practices by business. Why, Robbins asked, should they not apply also to trade unions and professional associations? Strikes must of course be allowed in a free society – so long as (echoing Professor Meade) 'those who withhold labour are made to bear the full consequences of their action'.

Again like Professor Meade, Lord Robbins was concerned with the harm that inflation did, and considered how inflation could be stopped. He was unequivocal: 'there can be many initial causes. But they are all subject to one underlying condition, that the supply of money or the credit base – call it what you will – is allowed to increase so as to permit their operation'. He thus in different terms echoed the famous observation of Milton Friedman's Wincott Lecture, 'inflation is always and everywhere a monetary phenomenon'.

Why was there the lack of will to restrain money growth and thus inflation? He suggests that it resulted from the 'blanket pledge to maintain a high level of employment' to which the experience of the 1930s gave rise. First, he observed, there are statistical ambiguities with the term full employment. Second, there was no reference to wages in that pledge; and 'claims for increases which exceed the increase in productivity in general will certainly produce unemployment unless there is a corresponding inflation'.[3]

He rejected incomes policies of the types so far tried as no more than temporary aids. We should, he maintained, avoid 'unemployment due to positive deflation' (i.e. to a falling general level of prices). But we should reduce the rate of increase of money, and thereby maintain a stable price level on average over time. The principle behind his recommendations has certainly been adopted by several governments since he wrote; let us hope that performance improves with practice.

ALAN PEACOCK (1976) – 'THE CREDIBILITY OF LIBERAL ECONOMICS'

Alan Peacock's basic position is that 'traditional liberal political economy' is well founded. His concern is not to defend it, but rather to consider why 'an eclectic body of economic thought with a long and honorable tradition', a body which was at one time popular and widely accepted, is now 'fighting for survival in political and governmental, if not in academic, circles'.

Alan Peacock follows the economist's approach of considering both supply and demand. Supply has been constricted, he suggests, by the changed incentives facing academic economists. The display of mathematical and statistical skills is valued. There is nothing wrong with that; but, as Professor Peacock notes, the display is to a considerable extent valued purely as display. Whether it is accompanied by 'imaginative insight into the workings of the economic system' is seen as less important. Second, there is 'welfare economics', a branch of the subject which, *inter alia*, analyses 'market failure'. Too often, the standard recommendation for market failure is government intervention – without regard for the fact that such intervention is costly and seldom perfect. There is a 'curious blend of often penetrating observation of the workings of the market system with an astonishingly naive view of the political and bureaucratic process'.

So much for supply. Why demand has not corrected this situation is Professor Peacock's next topic. He suggests lack of demand is the result of holding a utopian view of society – of being unwilling to recognise that resources are scarce, and that these scarce resources must be allocated among competing uses. His agenda then starts with trying to enlighten and persuade policy-makers and commentators. But he does not stop there. He suggests that attempts to persuade and advance the level of economic understanding of the population as a whole are worthwhile, and in addition urges consideration of political reforms such as that advocated by Friedrich Hayek in a previous lecture (Chapter 3 of this volume). These, he suggests, will be necessary preconditions for carrying out the kind of liberal economic programme that will ultimately bring great benefits.

ALAN WALTERS (1977) – 'ECONOMISTS AND THE BRITISH ECONOMY'

Like Lord Robbins before him, Alan Walters was concerned with the performance of the British economy since the 1950s. His approach, however, was to examine the theories which had influenced economic policy, to set out how experience had falsified them, and to discuss what should replace them.

The notion that there was a stable relationship between the level of unemployment and the rate of inflation – a stable 'Phillips curve' – had, he argued, gone. Money mattered for inflation. And, of great importance, 'no model, whether monetary or Keynesian, could foretell accurately the performance of the economy over the next two years'. In the course of his lecture, Alan Walters developed these points by discussion of both theory and evidence. Consumption (and savings) behaved in the 1970s quite differently from any forecast. In particular, in 1974–75 consumption fell dramatically, and not just in Britain but in a good part of the Western world. Some forecasters had predicted a small fall, and some a rise; none had predicted a large fall. The supposed stability of the consumption function, the relationship between consumption and income, is 'one of the props of conventional macroeconomics'. The episode, despite much rationalisation after the event, had knocked away that prop, at least in so far as it supposedly assisted forecasting. Essentially the same was true of investment; it too completely failed to behave as forecast. Another aid to forecasting was thus knocked away.

Alan Walters then turned to wages. Were these rigid in money terms? Was there even, as (the then) Sir John Hicks had claimed, a floor to real wages? The evidence rejected both conjectures.

Continuing with his attack on the possibility of short-term forecasting, and thus on 'fine tuning', Alan Walters then reviewed how expectations are formed. As he pointed out, people do not 'simply extrapolate their past experience into the future'. Rather they form their expectations taking account of all available information, including information about the behaviour of the authorities. In such circumstances, policy should be guided by rules; for only then can stability of private sector behaviour be expected.

After a brief review of how, despite its falsification, simplified Keynesianism continued to guide economic policy,[4] Alan Walters concludes by offering his own policy proposals. They are in two parts. First there is a technical one; money should grow at a steady rate.

This would prevent 'some of the most wild swings (in economic policy)'. Reverting finally to themes of previous lecturers, Alan Walters concludes by first discussing briefly why false ideas persist, and secondly by suggesting, rather pessimistically, that demand will call forth some new 'economic Messiah'.

GEORGE J. STIGLER (1982) – 'THE PLEASURES AND PAINS OF MODERN CAPITALISM'

In his lecture George Stigler focused on 'the fundamental organisational unit of capitalism'. That unit is the business firm, and he examined the fortunes of the business sector. His evidence is drawn from the United Sates, but the analytical approach is widely applicable.

He starts from the presumption that all consumers benefit from an efficient economy – even those dependent on welfare, for the more efficient the economy the more there is to distribute. Why, then, are there so many controls on business despite there surely being an apparently enormous interest group which opposes them? His answer is that business is selectively *in favour* of controls – controls which limit competition. These controls are the 'pleasures' of his lecture's title. What are the pains?

'The pains of modern capitalism have the same source as the pleasures.' The pains, too, arise from regulation. They arise not from the power of consumer groups, but from the spillover effects of regulation. One industry is hurt by the regulation which benefits another. 'If steel is protected, steel-users must pay higher prices. . . .'.

Which have won on balance? The pleasures or the pains? By examining returns to equities, Stigler, noting that these have declined, concludes that the pains have won. This is of course striking empirical support for the concerns voiced by other Wincott lecturers, most notably Alan Peacock. What in Stigler's view is the outlook? It is not, despite his own evidence, too bleak. There are thriving unregulated industries. These will help. But there must also be an effort to lighten the regulatory regime. Economists can argue in favour of this. But they must show that business on balance loses by regulation. Only then can regulation's most powerful defenders be turned to being its opponents.

DEEPAK LAL (1989) – 'THE LIMITS OF INTERNATIONAL COOPERATION'

Whether or not due to the influence of the various Wincott lecturers – and in some cases the evidence of influence is indisputable – *dirigisme* retreated in the 1970s and 1980s. Economies relied increasingly on markets and less on planning. But as Deepak Lal observed at the start of his lecture, there was also a paradox. While economic liberalism was gaining ground in domestic policy, 'in many aspects of thought and action in international economic relationships, there [seemed] to be a reincarnation of the "Dirigiste Dogma"'.

Deepak Lal in his lecture examined two aspects of this; plans for international coordination of macroeconomic and exchange rate policies, and the 'acceptance of establishing . . . an International Green Economic Order'.

The analytical basis of his paper is a discussion of the theory of externalities. These are the 'uncompensated side-effects [i.e. uncompensated by perpetrators] of a producers' or consumers' activity on other economic agents'. Externalities are then classified into four types.[5]

Making use of this fourfold classification, Deepak Lal argues that only some externalities may require government action to correct market inefficiencies. Many externalities change the allocation of resources between individuals, but do not disturb the efficiency of that allocation.

This analysis is first applied to 'international policy coordination'. Professor Lal shows here that the arguments for such coordination are flawed. Uncoordinated action produces different outcomes from coordinated action (or, rather, from coordinated action's hypothetical ideal outcomes; government is not perfect). But the outcomes of uncoordinated actions are *efficient*; arguments for coordination are in effect generally arguments for redistribution.

After reviewing, and similarly rejecting, other arguments for policy coordination at the macroeconomic level, Professor Lal turns to 'International Environmental Externalities'. Here, he urges 'we must look at the facts, and ask what the rational response to them should be'. What are the facts? First, neither global warming nor global freezing is likely. Second, if we look at past ranges of temperature variation, we find such variations in the future would not destroy, or even harm, the world as a whole. Rather they would shift the places where productive and profitable agriculture is possible. Prospective changes in world climate have distributional effects on income; they do not destroy the possibility of life. Some groups understandably would not like this distributional effect; but the desire of one part of the world to preserve its present supremacy in one activity is not a strong foundation for international regulation.

Professor Lal concludes that international arguments for planning are just as flawed as the domestic arguments. There is no basis whatsoever for establishing a global managed economy just as national ones are collapsing.

ANNA J. SCHWARTZ (1992) – 'DO CURRENCY BOARDS HAVE A FUTURE?'

In her lecture Anna Schwartz considered a possible solution to a basic economic problem facing some Eastern European (and also some other) economies. They wish to move to a functioning market system, but before such a market system, with its set of continuously changing relative prices, can function well, it requires a monetary system with a money reasonably stable in value. Without such a money there is no unit in which prices can be quoted and economies would soon revert to the inefficiencies of barter. To introduce such a money quickly, some authors have proposed that these economies base their monetary system on 'currency boards'.

These are systems under which one country fixes the value of its currency rigidly to that of another. It holds complete reserve backing in assets denominated in the currency of the other country for all the money it issues. In consequence, the country with the currency board imports the monetary policy of the other country; its currency is then as stable as that to which it is anchored. The scheme seems appealing – indeed, it is close to seeming a miracle cure for monetary disorders.

One should in general be sceptical of such cures. Anna Schwartz shows this case is no exception. After explaining in detail what currency boards were, she discusses some examples of how they operated. Two factors were of particular importance. First, the currency to which the board chose to link had to be stable. Second, the currency to which the board linked had to be issued by a country with which the currency board country did a substantial part of its foreign trade. This was necessary to prevent sharp fluctuations in the price of its internationally traded goods relative to goods in general. (The second factor was what led some countries in the British Empire to link not to sterling but to the US dollar.)

Today it would be hard to find a suitable anchor for a currency board. No country now has a stable, rule-based monetary system such as the gold standard provided, and the increased diversification of trade means that few countries any longer have a dominant trading partner.

But it was not for these reasons that currency boards declined. (Those few currency boards which remain are significantly different from the traditional form.) Dr Schwartz summarises the reasons for their decline as follows: the end of belief in the legitimacy of Empire; acceptance of the belief that currency boards hampered development in the countries that used them; and the fact that the boards did not permit discretionary monetary policy. She shows the second to be wrong and the third a blessing rather than a handicap. Nevertheless, for such fallacious reasons, which were widely endorsed, currency boards died.

In the final section of her paper, Anna Schwartz considers whether they can be revived. She is doubtful that they can. Despite their apparent intellectual appeal, currency boards are not, Dr Schwartz concludes, 'the wave of the future'.

It is notable that one of the reasons they are not is that governments, although becoming more market orientated in their economic policies, are not yet, by and large at any rate, willing to commit themselves to the classic liberal prescription of guiding policy by pre-announced rules.

JAGDISH BHAGWATI (1994) – 'FREE TRADE "FAIRNESS" AND THE NEW PROTECTIONISM: REFLECTIONS ON AN AGENDA FOR THE WORLD TRADE ORGANISATION'

Professor Bhagwati first argues that increased trade and investment flows, producing an increasingly interdependent world, will lead to mutual gains for every country that participates. This claim, he noted, was once rejected by many developing economies, who feared the consequences of trade with developed countries. They have put aside that fear, but now the developed countries fear trade with the underdeveloped. This fear, Professor Bhagwati argues, is as unfounded as the one it has replaced. He shows that the balance of evidence is inconsistent with the claim that trade with developing countries has harmed the developed by, in the United States, depressing the relative earnings of the unskilled, and in Europe (where wages are less flexible) increasing unemployment. These phenomena – which are real enough – are the product of other influences.

He then examines other arguments for protection – notably environmental protection and labour standards. Neither of these arguments is well founded. Countries having different standards for environmental protection is exactly like them having different endowments of natural resources. Neither difference can justify protection.[6] As for labour standards, Professor Bhagwati notes first that 'The notion that labour standards can be universalised, like human rights such as liberty and *habeas corpus*, simply by calling them "labour rights" ignores the difficulty of making any easy equation between culture-specific labour standards and universal "human rights".' He illustrates this by some comparisons which show that in many instances, different labour standards are just different, neither (except from the nation's own perspective) better nor worse. He argues, too, that even the apparently clear-cut issue of child labour is not straightforward.

He then turns from arguments for protection to arguments for regional free trade. Professor Bhagwati argues that while these have advantages in particular areas, in general worldwide free trade is preferable. He concludes with some observations on the World Trade Organisation which replaced GATT, and some aspects of it which might help produce that desirable goal.

CONCLUDING OVERVIEW

The lectures reprinted here range over many topics. But regardless of the aspect of economics which was the main subject, in every case two themes emerge. These are the importance of guiding economic policy by a clear, announced and credible set of rules; and the importance of keeping in check monopolistic, regulatory, and bureaucratic forces which hamper economic change and growth.

These two themes are central to the economic liberalism that Harold Wincott espoused. The remarkable lectures in this volume have greatly advanced acceptance of these ideas, and have already influenced policy. As time passes, and it becomes increasingly clear how important to economic prosperity are these apparently simple and certainly non-technical recommendations, their influence will surely spread still further.

NOTES

1. Such inflation would perhaps not be treated so kindly now. First because it appears to be a very rare animal; and second because recent studies (e.g. Barro, 1995) have found that even low rates of inflation harm growth.
2. As Professor Meade points out, there would have to be a mechanism for establishing how big the wage claim actually was. This is necessary because different sides to a wage dispute often disagree about the size of both the initial claim and the ultimate award.
3. Workers are sometimes urged to seek increases equal to their increases in productivity. This neglects that the increases in output per head may reflect, for example, capital accumulation. And it also neglects the possibility of a changing balance of demand and supply for different types of worker. Robbins was of course not concerned with productivity at that disaggregate level. His concern was that *average* wages not outstrip *average* productivity for the economy as a whole.
4. In his lecture Milton Friedman provides a brief sketch of why what is called Keynesianism is both simplified and, *inter alia*, unlikely to be what Keynes would have maintained had he lived on until the 1970s.
5. The origins of the classifications are given in Professor Lal's paper.
6. The only qualification to this is when the different environmental standards have spillover effects of a particular type. This possibility was examined in detail, and rejected, by Deepak Lal in his Wincott Lecture.

Foreword by Lord Robbins to Chapter 1

Chapter 1 was originally delivered as a lecture, the first of a series designed to commemorate a remarkable man. The late Harold Wincott was a financial journalist of unique standing in his generation. He combined wide knowledge of affairs, acute technical insight, attractive expositional style and warm feelings of humanity in a way which made him loved and respected by all who came in contact with him or had acquaintance with his writings. It is adequate testimony of this regard that, when he died in 1968 at the early age of 62, some of his friends, wishing to keep his memory green, succeeded in collecting some hundred thousand pounds, a memorial which it is safe to say has no parallel in the history of journalism in this country. The Trustees who administer this fund decided, rightly in my opinion, that one use which would have pleased Harold Wincott was the financing of a period, perhaps an annual, lecture of high academic quality on subjects which fell within his own multifarious range of interests.

It would be otiose to prolong this Foreword by any detailed description of Milton Friedman and his qualifications. The Trustees of the Wincott Fund were certainly fortunate in securing for the inauguration of their enterprise one of the foremost names among professional economists. Doubtless many of the propositions and causes for which Professor Friedman has stood are controversial. But even his severest detractors have never denied his technical eminence as an analytical economist or his importance in the free exchange of ideas characteristic of the present state of the subject. Even if you disagree with what he says, to listen to him or to read him is an intellectual stimulus of a rare variety. It makes you want to go on thinking.

Professor Friedman's contributions to monetary history and monetary theory are of course already available in many publications, of which his massive *Monetary History of the United States* and *The Optimum Quantity of Money*, are conspicuous examples. The present chapter, however, must be specially welcome to all who are interested in these subjects in that it embodies, with certain simplifications, a general conspectus of his position on the general value of the quantity theory of money, both as a guide to the understanding of financial

1

phenomena and as furnishing prescriptions on practical policy. In regard especially to the latter, I fancy that some at least of his English readers will be surprised – though perhaps they should not be – at the extreme moderation of his claims. Whether it is right or wrong, the essence of the Friedmanite prescription for the conduct of monetary policy is simply that an even rate of expansion is more likely to be an aid to general economic stability than more sophisticated attempts at fine tuning which might be suggested by other points of view. Whatever one's attitude to this recommendation – and I personally would confess to a spot more eclecticism than Professor Friedman would regard as respectable – I have no doubt at all that this is a position which deserves very serious consideration indeed.

ROBBINS

1 The Counter-Revolution in Monetary Theory[1]

Milton Friedman

It was a great pleasure to be honoured with being the first of the Harold Wincott lecturers, partly because economics owes so much to the work that has been done on this island. Coming back to Britain, as I am fortunate enough to be able to do from time to time, always means coming back to a warm circle of friends or friendly enemies.

I am going to discuss primarily a scientific development that has little ideological or political content. This development nonetheless has great relevance to governmental policy because it bears on the likely effects of particular kinds of governmental policy regardless of what party conducts the policy and for what purpose.

A counter-revolution must be preceded by two stages: an initial position from which there was a revolution, and the revolution. In order to set the stage, I would like first to make a few remarks about the initial position and the revolution.

It is convenient to have names to describe these positions. The initial position I shall call the quantity theory of money and associate it largely with the name of an American economist, Irving Fisher, although it is a doctrine to which many prominent English economists also made contributions. The revolution was made by Keynes in the 1930s. Keynes himself was a quantity theorist, so that his revolution was from, as it were, within the governing body. Keynes's name is the obvious name to attach to the revolution. The counter revolution also needs a name and perhaps the one most widely used in referring to it is 'the Chicago School'. More recently, however, it has been given a name which is less lovely but which has become so attached to it that I find it hard to avoid using it. That name is 'monetarism' because of the renewed emphasis on the role of the quantity of money.

A counter-revolution, whether in politics or in science, never restores the initial situation. It always produces a situation that has some similarity to the initial one but is also strongly influenced by the intervening revolution. That is certainly true of monetarism, which has

3

benefited much from Keynes's work. Indeed I may say, as have so many others since there is no way of contradicting it, that if Keynes were alive today he would no doubt be at the forefront of the counter-revolution. You must never judge a master by his disciples.

IRVING FISHER AND THE QUANTITY THEORY

Let me then start briefly to set the stage with the initial position, the quantity theory of money as developed primarily by Irving Fisher who is to my mind by far the greatest American economist. He was also an extraordinarily interesting and eccentric man. Indeed, I suspect that his professional reputation suffered during his life because he was not only an economist but also involved in many other activities, including being one of the leading members of the American prohibitionist party. He interviewed all potential presidential candidates for something like 30 years to find out what their position was on the subject of alcohol. His best-selling book, which has been translated into the largest number of languages, is not about economics at all but about health. It is about how to eat and keep healthy and is entitled *How to Live* (written jointly with Dr E. L. Fisk). But even that book is a tribute to his science. When he was a young man in his early thirties, he contracted tuberculosis, was given a year to live by his physicians, went out to the Far West where the air was good and proceeded to immerse himself in the study of health and methods of eating and so on. If we may judge the success of his scientific work by its results, he lived to the age of 80. He was also a leading statistician, developed the theory of index numbers, worked in mathematics, economics and utility theory and had time enough besides to invent the Kardex filing system, the familiar system in which one little envelope flaps on another, so you can pull out a flat drawer to see what is in it. He founded what is now Remington-Rand Corporation in order to produce and distribute his invention. As you can see, he was a man of very wide interests and ability.

MV = PT

The basic idea of the quantity theory, that there is a relation between the quantity of money on the one hand and prices on the other, is surely one of the oldest ideas in economics. It goes back thousands of years. But it is one thing to express this idea in general terms. It is another thing to introduce system into the relation between money on the one hand and prices and other magnitudes on the other. What Irving Fisher did was to analyse the relationship in far greater detail than had ever been done earlier. He developed and popularised what has come to be known as the quantity equation: $MV = PT$, money multiplied by velocity equals prices multiplied by the volume of transactions. This is an equation that every college student of economics used to have to learn, then for a time did not, and now, as the counter-revolution has progressed, must again learn. Fisher not only presented this equation, he also applied it in a variety of contexts. He once wrote a famous article interpreting the business cycle as the 'dance of the dollar', in which he argued that fluctuations in economic activity were primarily a reflection of changes in the quantity of money. Perhaps even more pertinent to the present day, he analysed in detail the relation between inflation on the one hand and interest rates on the other. His first book on this subject, *Appreciation and Interest*, published in 1896, can be read today with profit and is immediately applicable to today's conditions.

In that work, Fisher made a distinction which again is something that went out of favour and has now come back into common use, namely the distinction between the nominal interest rate in pounds per year per hundred pounds and the real interest rate, i.e. corrected for the effect of changing prices. If you lend someone £100 today and in 12 months receive back £106, and if in the meantime prices rise by 6 per cent then your £106 will be worth no more than your £100 today. The nominal interest rate is 6 per cent, but the real interest rate is zero. This distinction between the nominal interest rate and the real interest rate is of the utmost importance in understanding the effects of monetary policy as well as the behaviour of interest rates. Fisher also distinguished sharply between the actual real rate, the rate realised after the event, and the anticipated real rate that lenders expected to receive or borrowers expected to pay. No one would lend money at 6 per cent if he expected prices to rise by 6 per cent during the year. If he did lend at 6 per cent, it must have been because he expected prices to rise by less than 6 per cent: the realised real rate was less than the anticipated real rate. This distinction between the actual real rate and the anticipated real rate is of the greatest importance today in understanding the course of events. It explains why inflation is so stubborn once it has become embedded, because as inflation accelerates, people come to expect it. They come to build the expected inflation into the interest rates that they are willing to pay as borrowers or that they demand as lenders.

Wide Consensus

Up to, let us say, the year 1930, Irving Fisher's analysis was widely accepted. In monetary theory, that analysis was taken to mean that in the quantity equation MV = PT the term for velocity could be regarded as highly stable, that it could be taken as determined independently of the other terms in the equation, and that as a result changes in the quantity of money would be reflected either in prices or in output. It was also widely taken for granted that short-term fluctuations in the economy reflected changes in the quantity of money, or in the terms and conditions under which credit was available. It was taken for granted that the trend of prices over any considerable period reflected the behaviour of the quantity of money over that period.

In economic policy, it was widely accepted that monetary policy was the primary instrument available for stabilising the economy. Moreover, it was accepted that monetary policy should be operated largely through a combination of two blades of a scissors, the one blade being what in the USA is called 'discount rate' and in Britain is called 'Bank rate', the other blade being open-market operations, the purchase and sale of government securities.

That was more or less the initial doctrinal position prior to the Keynesian revolution. It was a position that was widely shared. Keynes's *A Tract on Monetary Reform*,[2] which I believe remains to this day one of his best books, reflects the consensus just described.

THE KEYNESIAN REVOLUTION

Then came the Keynesian revolution. What produced that revolution was the course of events. My colleague, George Stigler, in discussing the history of thought, has often argued that major changes within a discipline come from inside the discipline and are not produced by the impact of outside events. He may well be right in general. But in this particular instance I believe the basic source of the revolution and of the reaction against the quantity theory of money was a historical event, namely the great contraction or depression. In the United Kingdom, the contraction started in 1925 when Britain went back on gold at the prewar parity and ended in 1931 when Britain went off gold. In the United States, the contraction started in 1929 and ended when the USA went off gold in early 1933. In both countries, economic conditions were depressed for years after the contraction itself had ended and an expansion had begun.

Wrong Lessons from the Great Depression

The Great Depression shattered the acceptance of the quantity theory of money because it was widely interpreted as demonstrating that monetary policy was ineffective, at least against a decline in business. All sorts of aphorisms were coined that are still with us, to indicate why it was that providing monetary ease would not necessarily lead to economic expansion, such as 'You can lead a horse to water but you can't make him drink' or 'Monetary policy is like a string: you can pull on it but you can't push on it', and doubtless there are many more.

As it happens, this interpretation of the depression was completely wrong. It turns out, as I shall point out more fully below, that on re-examination, the depression is a tragic testament to the effectiveness of monetary policy, not a demonstration of its impotence. But what mattered for the world of ideas was not what was true but what was believed to be true. And it was believed at the time that monetary policy had been tried and had been found wanting.

In part that view reflected the natural tendency for the monetary authorities to blame other forces for the terrible economic events that were occurring. The people who run monetary policy are human beings, even as you and I, and a common human characteristic is that if anything bad happens it is somebody else's fault. In the course of collaborating on a book on the monetary history of the United States, I had the dismal task of reading through 50 years of annual reports of the Federal Reserve Board. The only element that lightened that dreary task was the cyclical oscillation in the power attributed to monetary policy by the system. In good years the report would read 'Thanks to the excellent monetary policy of the Federal Reserve . . .'. In bad years the report would read 'Despite the excellent policy of the Federal Reserve . . .', and it would go on to point out that monetary policy really was, after all, very weak and other forces so much stronger.

The monetary authorities proclaimed that they were pursuing easy money policies when in fact they were not and their protestations were largely accepted. Hence Keynes, along with many others, concluded that monetary policy had been tried and found wanting. In contrast to most others, he offered an alternative analysis to explain why the depression had occurred and to indicate a way of ameliorating the situation.

Keynes's Critique of the Quantity Theory

Keynes did not deny Irving Fisher's quantity equation. What Keynes said was something different. He said that, while of course MV equals PT, velocity, instead of being highly stable, is highly adaptable. If the quantity of money goes up, he said, what will happen is simply that the velocity of circulation of money will go down and nothing will happen on the other side of the equation to either prices or output. Correspondingly, if something pushes the right-hand side of the equation, PT or income, up without an increase in the quantity of money, all that will happen will be that velocity will rise. In other words, he said, velocity is a will-of-the-wisp. It can move one way or the other in response to changes either in the quantity of money or in income. The quantity of money is therefore of minor importance. (Since I am trying to cover highly technical material very briefly, I am leaving out many qualifications that are required for a full understanding of either Fisher or Keynes. I do want to stress that the statements I am making are simplifications and are not to be taken as a full exposition of any of the theories.)

What matters, said Keynes, is not the quantity of money. What matters is the part of total spending which is independent of current income, what has come to be called autonomous spending and to be identified in practice largely with investment by business and expenditures by government.

Keynes thereby directed attention away from the role of money and its relation to the flow of income and toward the relation between two flows of income, that which corresponds to autonomous spending and that which corresponds to induced spending. Moreover, he said, in the modern world, prices are highly rigid while quantities can change readily. When for whatever reason autonomous spending changes, the resulting change in income will manifest itself primarily in output and only secondarily and only after long lags in prices. Prices are determined by costs consisting mostly of wages, and wages are determined by the accident of past history.

The great contraction, he said, was the result of a collapse of demand for investment which in turn reflected a collapse of productive opportunities to use capital. Thus the engine and the motor of the great contraction was a collapse of investment transformed into a collapse of income by the multiplier process.

The Implications for Policy

This doctrine had far-reaching implications for economic policy. It meant that monetary policy was of little importance. Its only role was to keep interest rates down, both to reduce the pressure on the government budget in paying interest on its debts, and also because it might have a tiny bit of stimulating effect on investment. From this implication of the doctrine came the cheap money policy which was tried in country after country following the Second World War.

A second implication of the doctrine was that the major reliance for economic stabilisation could not be on monetary policy, as the quantity theorists had thought, but must be on fiscal policy, that is, on varying the rate of government spending and taxing.

A third implication was that inflation is largely to be interpreted as a cost-push phenomenon. It follows, although Keynes himself did not draw this conclusion from his doctrine, that the way to counteract inflation is through an incomes policy. If costs determine prices and costs are historically determined, then the way to stop any rise in prices is to stop the rise in costs.

These views became widely accepted by economists at large both as theory and as implications for policy. It is hard now at this distance in time to recognise how widely they were accepted. Let me just give you one quotation which could be multiplied many-fold, to give you the flavour of the views at the end of the Second World War. Parenthetically, acceptance of these views continued until more recently in Britain than in the United States. I quote from John H. Williams, who was a Professor of Economics at Harvard University, a principal advisor to the Federal Reserve Bank of New York, and widely regarded as an anti-Keynesian. In 1945 he wrote: 'I have long believed that the quantity of money by itself has a permissive rather than a positive effect on prices and production'. And in the sentence I want to stress he wrote: 'I can see no prospect of a revival of general monetary control in the post-war period'. That was a very sweeping statement, and one that obviously proved very far indeed from the mark.

The high point in the United States of the application of Keynesian ideas to economic policy probably came with the new economists of the Kennedy administration. Their finest hour was the tax cut of 1964 which was premised entirely on the principles that I have been describing.

Having sketched briefly the initial stage of the quantity theory, and the revolutionary stage of the Keynesian theory, I come now to the monetarist counter-revolution.

THE COUNTER-REVOLUTION

As so often happens, just about the time that Keynes's ideas were being triumphant in practice, they were losing their hold on the minds of scholars in the academies. A number of factors contributed to a change of attitude towards the Keynesian doctrine. One was the experience immediately after the Second World War. On the basis of the Keynesian analysis, economists and others expected the war to be followed by another great depression. With our present experience of over two decades of inflation behind us it is hard to recognise that this was the sentiment of the times. But alike in the United States, in Great Britain and in many other countries, the dominant view was that, once the Second World War ended, once the pump-priming and government spending for military purposes ended, there would be an enormous economic collapse because of the scarcity of investment opportunities that had been given the blame for the Great Depression. Massive unemployment and massive deflation were the bugaboos of the time. As you all know, that did not happen. The problem after the war turned out to be inflation rather than deflation.

A second postwar experience that was important was the failure of cheap money policies. In Britain, Chancellor Dalton tried to follow the Keynesian policy of keeping interest rates very low. As you all know, he was unable to do so and had to give up. The same thing happened in the United States. The Federal Reserve System followed a policy of pegging bond prices, trying to keep interest rates down. It finally gave up in 1953 after the Treasury–Federal Reserve Accord of 1951 laid the groundwork for setting interest rates free. In country after country, wherever the cheap money policy was tried, it led to inflation and had to be abandoned. In no country was inflation contained until orthodox monetary policy was employed. Germany was one example in 1948; Italy shortly after; Britain and the United States later yet.

Reconsideration of the Great Depression

Another important element that contributed to a questioning of the Keynesian doctrine was a re-examination of monetary history and particularly of the Great Depression. When the evidence was examined in detail it turned out that bad monetary policy had to be given a very large share of the blame. In the United States, there was a reduction in the quantity of money by a third from 1929 to 1933. This reduction in the quantity of money clearly made the depression much longer and more severe than it otherwise would have been. Moreover, and equally important, it turned out that the reduction in the quantity of money was not a consequence of the unwillingness of horses to drink. It was not a consequence of being unable to push on a string. It was a direct consequence of the policies followed by the Federal Reserve system.

From 1930 to 1933, a series of bank runs and bank failures were permitted to run their course because the Federal Reserve failed to provide liquidity for the banking system, which was one of the main functions the designers of the Federal Reserve system intended it to perform. Banks failed because the public at large, fearful for the safety of their deposits, tried to convert their deposits into currency. In a fractional reserve system, it is literally impossible for all depositors to do that unless there is some source of additional currency. The Federal Reserve system was established in 1913 in response to the banking panic of 1907 primarily to provide additional liquidity at a time of pressure on banks. In 1930–33, the system failed to do so and it failed to do so despite the fact that there were many people in the system who were calling upon it to do so and who recognised that this was its correct function.

It was widely asserted at the time that the decline in the quantity of money was a consequence of the lack of willing borrowers. Perhaps the most decisive bit of evidence against that interpretation is that many banks failed because of a decline in the price of government securities. Indeed, it turned out that many banks that had made bad private loans came through much better than banks that had been cautious and had bought large amounts of Treasury and municipal securities for secondary liquidity. The reason was that there was a market for the government securities and hence when bank examiners came around to check on the banks, they had to mark down the price of the governments to the market value. However, there was no market for bad loans, and therefore they were carried on the books at face value. As a result, many careful, conservative banks failed.

The quantity of money fell by a third and roughly a third of all banks failed. This is itself a fascinating story and one that I can only touch on. The important point for our purposes is that it is crystal clear that at all times during the contraction, the Federal Reserve had it within its power to prevent the decline in the quantity of money and to produce an increase. Monetary policy had not been tried and found wanting. It had not been tried. Or, alternatively, it had been tried perversely. It had been used to force an incredible deflation on the American economy and on the rest of the world. If Keynes had known the facts about the Great Depression as we now know them, he could not have interpreted that episode as he did.

Wider Evidence

Another scholarly element that contributed to a reaction against the Keynesian doctrine and to the emergence of the new doctrine was extensive empirical analysis of the relation between the quantity of money on the one hand, and income, prices and interest rates on the other. Perhaps the simplest way for me to suggest why this was relevant is to recall that an essential element of the Keynesian doctrine was the passivity of velocity. If money rose, velocity would decline. Empirically, however, it turns out that the movements of velocity tend to reinforce those of money instead of to offset them. When the quantity of money declined by a third from 1929 to 1933 in the United States, velocity declined also. When the quantity of money rises rapidly in almost any country, velocity also rises rapidly. Far from velocity offsetting the movements of the quantity of money, it reinforces them.

I cannot go into the whole body of scientific work that has been done. I can only say that there has arisen an extensive literature concerned with exploring these relations which has demonstrated very clearly the existence of a consistent relation between changes in the quantity of money and changes in other economic magnitudes of a very different kind from that which Keynes assumed to exist.

The final blow, at least in the United States, to the Keynesian orthodoxy was a number of dramatic episodes in our recent domestic experience. These episodes centred on two key issues. The first was whether the behaviour of the quantity of money or rates of interest is a better criterion to use in conducting monetary policy. You have had a curious combination in this area of central bankers harking back to the real bills doctrine of the early nineteenth century on the one hand, and Keynesians on the other, who alike agreed that the behaviour of interest rates was the relevant criterion for the conduct of monetary policy. By contrast, the new interpretation is that interest rates are a misleading index of policy and that central bankers should look rather at the quantity of money. The second key issue was the relative role of fiscal policy and of monetary policy. By fiscal policy, I mean changes in government spending and taxing, holding the quantity of money constant. By monetary policy, I mean changes in the quantity of money, holding government spending and taxing constant.

Fiscal versus Monetary Policy

The problem in discussing the relative roles of fiscal policy and monetary policy is primarily to keep them separate, because in practice they operate jointly most of the time. Ordinarily if a government raises its spending without raising taxes, that is, if it incurs a deficit in order to be expansionary, it will finance some of the deficit by printing money. Conversely if it runs a surplus, it will use part of that surplus to retire money. But from an analytical point of view, and from the point of view of getting at the issue that concerns the counter-revolution, it is important to consider fiscal policy and monetary policy separately, to consider each operating by itself. The Keynesians regarded as a clear implication of their position the proposition that fiscal policy by itself is important in affecting the level of income, that a large deficit would have essentially the same expansionary influence on the economy whether it was financed by borrowing from the public or by printing money.

The 'monetarists' rejected this proposition and maintained that fiscal policy by itself is largely ineffective, that what matters is what happens to the quantity of money. Off-hand that seems like an utterly silly idea. It seems absurd to say that if the government increases its expenditures without increasing taxes, that may not by itself be expansionary. Such a policy obviously puts income into the hands of the people to whom the government pays out its expenditures without taking any extra funds out of the hands of the taxpayers. Is that not obviously expansionary or inflationary? Up to that point, yes, but that is only half the story. We have to ask where the government gets the extra funds it spends. If the government prints money to meet its bills, that is monetary policy and we are trying to look at fiscal policy by itself. If the government gets the funds by borrowing from the public, then those people who lend the funds to the government have less to spend or to lend to others. The effect of the higher government expenditures may simply be higher spending by government and those who receive government funds and lower spending by those who lend to government or by those to whom lenders would have loaned the money instead. To discover any net effect on total spending, one must go to a more sophisticated level – to differences in the behaviour of the two groups of people or to effects of government borrowing on interest rates. There is no first-order effect.

Evidence from US 'Experiments'

The critical first test on both these key issues came in the USA in 1966. There was fear of developing inflation and in the spring of 1966 the Federal Reserve Board, belatedly, stepped very hard on the brake. I say 'stepped very hard' because the record on the Federal Reserve over 50 years is that it has almost invariably acted too much too late. Almost always it has waited too long before acting and then acted too strongly. In 1966, the result was a combination of a very tight monetary policy, under which the quantity of money did not grow at all during the final nine months of the year, and a very expansive fiscal policy. So you had a nice experiment. Which was going to dominate? The tight money policy or the easy fiscal policy? The Keynesians in general argued that the easy fiscal policy was going to dominate and therefore predicted continued rapid expansion in 1967. The monetarists argued that monetary policy would dominate, and so it turned out. There was a definite slowing down in the rate of growth of economic activity in the first half of 1967, following the tight money policy of 1966. When, in early 1967, the Federal Reserve reversed its policy and started to print money like mad, about six or nine months later, after the usual lag, income recovered and a rapid expansion in economic activity followed. Quite clearly, monetary policy had dominated fiscal policy in that encounter.

A still more dramatic example came in 1968 and from 1968 to the present. In the summer of 1968, under the influence of the Council of Economic Advisers and at the recommendation of President Johnson, Congress enacted a surtax of 10 per cent on income. It was enacted in order to fight the inflation which was then accelerating. The believers in the Keynesian view were so persuaded of the potency of this weapon that they were afraid of 'overkill'. They thought the tax increase might be too much and might stop the economy in its tracks. They persuaded the Federal Reserve system, or I should rather say that the Federal Reserve system was of the same view. Unfortunately for the United States, but fortunately for scientific knowledge, the Federal Reserve accordingly decided that it had best offset the overkill effects of fiscal policy by expanding the quantity of money rapidly. Once again, we had a beautiful controlled experiment with fiscal policy extremely tight and monetary policy extremely easy. Once again, there was a contrast between two sets of predictions. The Keynesians or fiscalists argued that the surtax would produce a sharp slow-down in the first half of 1969 at the latest while the monetarists argued that the rapid growth in the quantity of money would more than offset the fiscal effects, so that there would be a continued inflationary boom in the first half of 1969. Again, the monetarists proved correct. Then, in December 1968, the Federal Reserve Board did move to tighten money in the sense of slowing down the rate of growth of the quantity of money and that was followed after the appropriate interval by a slow-down in the economy. This test, I may say, is still in process, but up to now it again seems to be confirming the greater importance of the monetary than of the fiscal effect.

'This is where I came in'

One swallow does not make a spring. My own belief in the greater importance of monetary policy does not rest on these dramatic episodes. It rests on the experience of hundreds of years and of many countries. These episodes of the past few years illustrate that effect; they do not demonstrate it. Nonetheless, the public at large cannot be expected to follow the great masses of statistics. One dramatic episode is far more potent in influencing public opinion than a pile of well-digested, but less dramatic, episodes. The result in the USA at any rate has been a drastic shift in opinion, both professional and lay.

This shift, so far as I can detect, has been greater in the United States than in the United Kingdom. As a result, I have had in the UK the sensation that one has in a continuous cinema at the point where one says 'Oh, this is where I came in'. The debate about monetary effects in Britain is pursuing the identical course that it pursued in the United States about five or so years ago. I am sure that the same thing must have happened in the 1930s. When the British economists wandered over to the farther shores among their less cultivated American brethren, bringing to them the message of Keynes, they must have felt, as I have felt coming to these shores in the opposite direction, that this was where they came in. I am sure they then encountered the same objections that they had encountered in Britain five years earlier. And so it is today. Criticism of the monetary doctrines in this country today is at the naive, unsophisticated level we encountered in the USA about five or more years ago.

Thanks to the very able and active group of economists in this country who are currently working on the monetary statistics, and perhaps even more to the effect which the course of events will have, I suspect that the developments in this country will continue to imitate those in the United States. Not only in this area, but in other areas as well, I have had the experience of initially being in a small minority and have had the opportunity to observe the scenario that unfolds as an idea gains wider acceptance. There is a standard pattern. When anybody threatens an orthodox position, the first reaction is to ignore the interloper. The less said about him the better. But if he begins to win a hearing and gets annoying, the second reaction is to ridicule him, make fun of him as an extremist, a foolish fellow who has these silly ideas. After that stage passes the next, and the most important, stage is to put on his clothes. You adopt for your own his views, and then attribute to him a caricature of those views saying, 'He's an extremist, one of those fellows who says only money matters – everybody knows that sort. Of course money does matter, but . . .'.

KEY PROPOSITIONS OF MONETARISM

Let me finally describe the state to which the counter-revolution has come by listing systematically the central propositions of monetarism.

1. There is a consistent though not precise relation between the rate of growth of the quantity of money and the rate of growth of nominal income. (By nominal income, I mean income measured in pounds sterling or in dollars or in francs, not real income, income measured in real goods.) That is, whether the amount of money in existence is growing by 3 per cent a year, 5 per cent a year or 10 per cent a year will have a significant effect on how fast nominal income grows. If the quantity of money grows rapidly, so will nominal income; and conversely.

2. This relation is not obvious to the naked eye largely because it takes time for changes in monetary growth to affect income and how long it takes is itself variable. The rate of monetary growth today is not very closely related to the rate of income growth today. Today's income growth depends on what has been happening to money in the past. What happens to money today affects what is going to happen to income in the future.

3. On the average, a change in the rate of monetary growth produces a change in the rate of growth of nominal income about six to nine months later. This is an average that does not hold in every individual case. Sometimes the delay is longer, sometimes shorter. But I have been astounded at how regularly an average delay of six to nine months is found under widely different conditions. I have studied the

data for Japan, for India, for Israel, for the United States. Some of our students have studied it for Canada and for a number of South American countries. Whichever country you take, you generally get a delay of around six to nine months. How clear-cut the evidence for the delay is depends on how much variation there is in the quantity of money. The Japanese data have been particularly valuable because the Bank of Japan was very obliging for some 15 years from 1948 to 1963 and produced very wide movements in the rate of change in the quantity of money. As a result, there is no ambiguity in dating when it reached the top and when it reached the bottom. Unfortunately for science, in 1963 they discovered monetarism and they started to increase the quantity of money at a fairly stable rate and now we are not able to get much more information from the Japanese experience.

4. The changed rate of growth of nominal income typically shows up first in output and hardly at all in prices. If the rate of monetary growth is reduced, then about six to nine months later the rate of growth of nominal income and also of physical output will decline. However, the rate of price rise will be affected very little. There will be downward pressure on prices only as a gap emerges between actual and potential output.

5. On the average, the effect on prices comes about six to nine months after the effect on income and output, so the total delay between a change in monetary growth and a change in the rate of inflation averages something like 12–18 months. That is why it is a long road to hoe to stop an inflation that has been allowed to start. It cannot be stopped overnight.

6. Even after allowance for the delay in the effect of monetary growth, the relation is far from perfect. There's many a slip 'twixt the monetary change and the income change.

7. In the short run, which may be as much as five or ten years, monetary changes affect primarily output. Over decades, on the other hand, the rate of monetary growth affects primarily prices. What happens to output depends on real factors: the enterprise, ingenuity and industry of the people; the extent of thrift; the structure of industry and government; the relations among nations, and so on.

8. It follows from the propositions I have so far stated that *inflation is always and everywhere a monetary phenomenon* in the sense that it is and can be produced only by a more rapid increase in the quantity

of money than in output. However, there are many different possible reasons for monetary growth, including gold discoveries, financing of government spending, and financing of private spending.

9. Government spending may or may not be inflationary. It clearly will be inflationary if it is financed by creating money, that is, by printing currency or creating bank deposits. If it is financed by taxes or by borrowing from the public, the main effect is that the government spends the funds instead of the taxpayer or instead of the lender or instead of the person who would otherwise have borrowed the funds. Fiscal policy is extremely important in determining what fraction of total national income is spent by government and who bears the burden of that expenditure. By itself, it is not important for inflation. (This is the proposition about fiscal and monetary policy that I discussed earlier.)

10. One of the most difficult things to explain in simple fashion is the way in which a change in the quantity of money affects income. Generally, the initial effect is not on income at all, but on the prices of existing assets, bonds, equities, houses, and other physical capital. This effect, the liquidity effect stressed by Keynes, is an effect on the balance-sheet, not on the income account. An increased rate of monetary growth, whether produced through open-market operations or in other ways, raises the amount of cash that people and businesses have relative to other assets. The holders of the now excess cash will try to adjust their portfolios by buying other assets. But one man's spending is another man's receipts. All the people together cannot change the amount of cash all hold – only the monetary authorities can do that. However, as people *attempt* to change their cash balances, the effect spreads from one asset to another. This tends to raise the prices of assets and to reduce interest rates, which encourages spending to produce new assets and also encourages spending on current services rather than on purchasing existing assets. That is how the initial effect on balance-sheets gets translated into an effect on income and spending. The difference in this area between the monetarists and the Keynesians is not on the nature of the process, but on the range of assets considered. The Keynesians tend to concentrate on a narrow range of marketable assets and recorded interest rates. The monetarists insist that a far wider range of assets and of interest rates must be taken into account. They give importance to such assets as durable and even semi-durable consumer goods, structures and other real property. As a result, they regard the market interest rates stressed by the Keynesians as only a small part of the total spectrum of rates that are relevant.

11. One important feature of this mechanism is that a change in monetary growth affects interest rates in one direction at first but in the opposite direction later on. More rapid monetary growth at first tends to lower interest rates. But later on, as it raises spending and stimulates price inflation, it also produces a rise in the demand for loans which will tend to raise interest rates. In addition, rising prices introduce a discrepancy between real and nominal interest rates. That is why world-wide interest rates are highest in the countries that have had the most rapid rise in the quantity of money and also in prices – countries like Brazil, Chile or Korea. In the opposite direction, a slower rate of monetary growth at first raises interest rates but later on, as it reduces spending and price inflation, lowers interest rates. That is why world-wide interest rates are lowest in countries that *have had* the slowest rate of growth in the quantity of money – countries like Switzerland and Germany.

This two-edged relation between money and interest rates explains why monetarists insist that interest rates are a highly misleading guide to monetary policy. This is one respect in which the monetarist doctrines have already had a significant effect on US policy. The Federal Reserve in January 1970 shifted from primary reliance on 'money market conditions' (i.e. interest rates) as a criterion of policy to primary reliance on 'monetary aggregates' (i.e. the quantity of money).

The relations between money and yields on assets (interest rates and stock market earnings – price ratios) are even lower than between money and nominal income. Apparently, factors other than monetary growth play an extremely important part. Needless to say, we do not know in detail what they are, but that they are important we know from the many movements in interest rates and stock market prices which cannot readily be connected with movements in the quantity of money.

CONCLUDING CAUTIONS

These propositions clearly imply both that monetary policy is important and that the important feature of monetary policy is its effect on the quantity of money rather than on bank credit or total credit or interest rates. They also imply that wide swings in the rate of change of the quantity of money are destabilising and should be avoided. But beyond this, differing implications are drawn.

Some monetarists conclude that deliberate changes in the rate of monetary growth by the authorities can be useful to offset other forces making for instability, provided they are gradual and take into account the lags involved. They favour fine tuning, using changes in the quantity of money as the instrument of policy. Other monetarists, including myself, conclude that our present understanding of the relation between money, prices and output is so meagre, that there is so much leeway in these relations, that such discretionary changes do more harm than good. We believe that an automatic policy under which the quantity of money would grow at a steady rate – month-in, month-out, year-in, year-out – would provide a stable monetary framework for economic growth without itself being a source of instability and disturbance.

One of the most widespread misunderstandings of the monetarist position is the belief that this prescription of a stable rate of growth in the quantity of money derives from our confidence in a rigid connection between monetary change and economic change. The situation is quite the opposite. If I really believed in a precise, rigid, mechanical connection between money and income, if also I thought that I knew what it was and if I thought that the central bank shared that knowledge with me, which is an even larger 'if', I would then say that we should use the knowledge to offset other forces making for instability. However, I do not believe any of these 'ifs' to be true. On the average, there is a close relation between changes in the quantity of money and the subsequent course of national income. But economic policy must deal with the individual case, not the average. In any one case, there is much slippage. It is precisely this leeway, this looseness in the relation, this lack of a mechanical one-to-one correspondence between changes in money and in income that is the primary reason why I have long favoured for the USA a quasi-automatic monetary policy under which the quantity of money would grow at a steady rate of 4 or 5 per cent per year, month-in, month-out. (The desirable rate of growth will differ from country to country depending on the trends in output and money-holding propensities.)

There is a great deal of evidence from the past of attempts by monetary authorities to do better. The verdict is very clear. The attempts by monetary authorities to do better have done far more harm than good. The actions by the monetary authorities have been an important source of instability. As I have already indicated, the actions of the US monetary authorities were responsible for the 1929–33 catastrophe. They were responsible equally for the recent acceleration of inflation in the USA. That is why I have been and remain strongly opposed to discretionary monetary policy – at least until such time as we demonstrably know enough to limit discretion by more sophisticated rules than the steady-rate-of-growth rule I have suggested. That is why I have come to stress the danger of assigning too much weight to monetary policy. Just as I believe that Keynes's disciples went further than he himself would have gone, so I think there is a danger that people who find that a few good predictions have been made by using monetary aggregates will try to carry that relationship further than it can go. In 1967 I wrote:

> We are in danger of assigning to monetary policy a larger role than it can perform, in danger of asking it to accomplish tasks that it cannot achieve and, as a result, in danger of preventing it from making the contribution that it is capable of making.[3]

A steady rate of monetary growth at a moderate level can provide a framework under which a country can have little inflation and much growth. It will not produce perfect stability; it will not produce heaven on earth; but it can make an important contribution to a stable economic society.

NOTES

1. I chose this title because I once used it for a talk at the London School of Economics. At that time, I was predicting. Now, I am reporting.
2. Macmillan, London, 1923.
3. Milton Friedman, 'The Role of Monetary Policy', Presidential Address to the American Economic Association, 29 December, 1967: *American Economic Review*, March 1968 (reprinted in *The Optimum Quantity of Money and Other Essays*, Aldine Publishing, New York, 1969, pp. 95–110 – quotation from p. 99).

2 Wages and Prices in a Mixed Economy[1]

James E. Meade

INTRODUCTION

I need not dwell on the fact that we find ourselves not merely in an inflationary situation, but in a situation in which the rate of inflation has itself recently been rising rapidly and has been combined with an exceptionally high level of unemployment. This 'stagflation' is illustrated in Table 2.1.[2]

Table 2.1 Inflation and unemployment, 1966–71

	1966	1967	1968	1969	1970	1971 (1st Qtr.)
Percentage rise in						
(i) Weekly money earnings[a]	6.5	3.3	8.1	7.8	12.0	12.7[b]
(ii) Retail Prices	3.9	2.5	4.7	5.4	6.4	8.6[b]
Percentage of employees unemployed[a]	1.53	2.40	2.43	2.42	2.62	2.97

[a] Seasonally adjusted.
[b] Increase over corresponding period in 1970.

Since 1966 there has been a marked rise both in the level of unemployment and in the rates of inflation of wages and prices.

INFLATION: 'ANTICIPATED' AND 'EXPLOSIVE'

But should not the stagnation trouble us much more than the inflation? Perhaps price stability does not matter. After all money is but a veil and it is from the enjoyment of a large output of real goods and ser-

22

vices that the real standard of living arises. There is undoubtedly a very large element of truth in this assertion; and before one embarks on the rather formidable task of trying to remodel society so as to make full employment compatible with price stability, it is worthwhile asking what, if any, is the real disadvantage or danger in price inflation.

For this purpose it is useful, I think, to distinguish between two types of inflationary situation, which I will call 'anticipated' and 'explosive' inflation. By an anticipated inflation I mean a situation in which the future upward movement of the general level of prices is fully and accurately foreseen and is taken into account in all private and public contracts and other financial arrangements. The well-known distributional inequities of inflation would cease to exist because no one would be on a fixed money income; the old-age pensioner would have a money income which would rise in line with the cost of living.

Nor need there be any balance-of-payments problem. If the fully anticipated rate of inflation in the United Kingdom was 1 per cent per annum higher than the fully anticipated rate of inflation in the United States, then the sterling exchange rate would have to be depreciated in terms of dollars by 1 per cent per annum in order to keep sterling and dollar prices in line with each other. But if both inflations were fully anticipated, this would not present any insuperable problem. This need not lead to any speculative capital movements. The rate of interest would, of course, have to be, 1 per cent per annum higher in the UK than in the USA so that any gain on the exchanges by moving from sterling to dollars would be offset by loss of interest.

Nor need this external need for a higher rate of interest in the UK present any fundamental internal domestic problem. A fully anticipated 1 per cent per annum rise in all prices raises the yield on capital investment by 1 per cent per annum because it presents a 1 per cent per annum capital gain on all real capital goods. To maintain the same domestic relationship between the supply and demand for funds for investment, the money rate of interest must therefore be raised by 1 per cent per annum, if money prices are all known to be rising by 1 per cent per annum.

This situation could, however, give rise to a domestic liquidity problem. It is conceivable that the future movements of the general level of prices (i.e. a specified price index) is sufficiently accurately foreseen for one to be able to talk of a fully anticipated inflation; but this would not imply that the future movement of every individual price was precisely foreseen. Particular uncertainties will persist and people will wish to hold liquid fund's in order to meet unanticipated events. But if because of a rapid rate of price inflation the rate of interest on money loans is, say, 15 per cent per annum and if at the same time the rate of interest on liquid balances of money is zero, there will be a heavy cost in remaining liquid. This could lead to real economic inefficiency; economic decision-makers would, simply because of the monetary inflation, not be willing to preserve those socially desirable defences against uncertainties and risks which in a non-inflationary situation the holding of money balances would provide.

Cancelling-out the Disadvantage of 'Anticipated' Inflation

This disadvantage of anticipated inflation could itself be removed by the payment of a rate of interest on money balances equal to the anticipated rate of increase of prices. So far as deposit money is concerned, this presents no insuperable problem. It is a more difficult institutional problem to arrange for a rate of interest to be earned on the notes and coin which one carries round in one's pocket or holds in one's till. The retailer would be tempted not to hold much change; and you and I would be tempted not to have much cash in our pockets. There would be real inconveniences in shopping and one might even find oneself stranded without one's bus fare. But this, which is I think the only insuperable disadvantage of a fully anticipated inflation, is in my opinion a rather minor matter.

Problems of 'Explosive' Inflation

The situation is totally different when one considers what I have called 'explosive' inflation, which arises in a monetary economy when the various groups in the community are so acting as to make demands on real resources that, for one reason or another, it is impossible to fulfil. Let me give an example. Suppose output per man-hour to be rising by 3 per cent per annum; and suppose that wage-earners are demanding increases in wage-rates designed to raise their real take-home pay by 4 per cent per annum. It is possible that for a short time this gap can be closed by reductions in taxation or by a squeeze on profit margins. But at some point prices must start rising by 1 per cent per annum (the difference between wage per man and output per man) unless profits are first to be reduced to zero and then turned into ever-increasing losses. But when prices and also the cost of living start rising by 1 per cent per annum, wage-earners must demand wage rises of 5 per cent per annum in order to obtain a rise in real income (take-home pay) of

4 per cent per annum. But now prices and so the cost of living will start to rise by 2 per cent per annum (the difference between the increase of 5 per cent per annum in wage per man and the 3 per cent per annum increase in output per man). Wage-earners will now demand wage increases of 6 per cent per annum in order to achieve a real increase of 4 per cent per annum; this will however cause the cost of living to go up by 3 instead of 2 per cent per annum; and so on in an explosive inflationary spiral. You cannot get more than a pint out of a pint pot. The attempt to do so must lead to an ever-increasing rate of inflation, the actual rate always being higher than the anticipated rate.

An analogous situation can arise if each of two groups in society is trying to get a share of the national income which is incompatible with the share demanded by the other group. Consider two groups of workers, group 'A' and group 'B', each of which considers that it is right and proper that it should receive a differential 10 per cent above the other. Both start with a wage of 100: 'A' then demands 110 to restore what it considers to be the proper differential. 'B' then demands 10 per cent above that figure, namely 121, in order to restore what it considers to be the proper differential. 'A' then demands 10 per cent above that, namely 132.1; and so on in an infinite series. Moreover, as soon as 'A' in its demands seeks not merely 10 per cent more than the present level of 'B', but 10 per cent more than what 'B' will get in the future given the past experience of the rate of rise in the earnings of 'B', the percentage rate of inflation will explode; the rate of rise will become more and more rapid as both groups add their impossible, because incompatible, demands on to the past rate of inflation. If 'A' is trying to leap-frog over B's back at the very same moment that 'B' is leap-frogging over A's back, not only is the sky the limit, but both players will shoot off into the empyrean at an ever-increasing speed.

Money will have ceased to be a reliable counter or *numeraire* for useful trading calculations. It will have become involved in a set of very real incompatibilities, the removal of which presents the basic anti-inflationary task.

CONDITIONS FOR FULL EMPLOYMENT WITHOUT INFLATION

I conclude that it is worth real effort to understand and to take steps to control such an inflation. There has in the past been considerable dispute about some aspects of the mechanism of this inflationary process. I do not intend in this chapter to devote much time to the details of controversies about the relative importance of demand-pull versus cost-push influences on wage-rates and prices. But certain broad aspects of the mechanics of the inflationary process – aspects which are, I think, luckily fairly obvious and widely accepted – are essential for my present purpose. The national income measured in terms of money or, what with appropriate definitions comes to the same thing, the money value of the nation's production, depends upon two things: the real quantities of goods and services produced, and the money prices at which these goods and services are valued. Money prices and costs are directly determined by wage bargains, by the decisions of manufacturers as to what profit margins to charge, and similar decisions in individual markets. The quantities of goods and services produced are subject to upper limits set by the full employment of labour or the capacity use of capital equipment; but below these limits the quantities which can be sold at any given prices and thus the quantities of labour employed and of other inputs purchased by manufacturers will depend upon the total amount of money expenditures by consumers on consumption goods and services, by the government on public services of various kinds, by producers on investment in additional capital equipment, and by foreigners on the country's exports.

The total level of these money expenditures can undoubtedly be greatly influenced by governmental fiscal and monetary policies. Conscious and calculated demand control has, indeed, become a familiar and accepted feature of governmental policy since the general acceptance of Keynesian ideas at the end of the Second World War. I assume the possibility of effective demand control for the purpose of this lecture without discussing at all how it may be achieved.

Fiscal and Monetary Policies: Same Intention

I would, however, like to digress for one moment to emphasise that while fiscal and monetary policies may differ in important ways in their effects on different elements of total money expenditure, they are nevertheless both methods of influencing total money expenditure, i.e. the total money demand for goods and service. Those who see some magical effect on prices to be derived from a control of the supply of money other than through its effect on money demands for goods and services are surely chasing a will o' the wisp. Those economists who place their bets on monetary policy have, of course, always believed that changes in the supply of money operated through their effects on the money demand for goods and services, as can be seen from Professor Milton Friedman's exposition in the 1970 Wincott lecture on *The Counter Revolution in Monetary Theory*.[3] We may agree then that both fiscal policy and monetary policy can affect inflation only by influencing money demands for goods and services, and any resulting restraints on money demands may in both cases *either* restrain the volume of real output which is sold at unchanged prices *or* restrain the prices charged for the same quantities of output *or* cause partly the one effect and partly the other. There is, however, no obvious reason to believe that fiscal policy and monetary policy will differ in any essential way in their relative effects on prices and outputs.

The complete inflationary process thus depends on two rather separate sets of processes:

(i) the processes by which money wage-rates and prices are determined, and,

(ii) the processes by which total money expenditures are determined.

There are, of course, most important inter-relationships between these two sets of processes, and it is in the assessment of these inter-relationships that difficulties arise in the full analysis of the inflationary process. Thus a controlled restriction of total money expenditures would almost certainly not leave the course of money wages and prices totally unaffected and exert its full effect solely on the quantities of goods and services sold. Manufacturers, in fixing their profit margins, presumably pay some attention to the buoyancy of the markets in which they are selling their goods, and there is presumably at least some level of unemployment which would reduce the incentive of trade unions to insist on a given level of wage increases.

On the other hand, it is obvious that the total level of money expenditure may be affected by the level of money wages, since a rise in money wage-rates, if employment does not fall, will increase wage incomes, the prospect of which may well increase money expenditures on consumption goods. But the degree and speed of the effect of unemployment and excess capacity on wage- and price-fixing and the degree and speed of the effect of wages and prices on incomes and expenditures are both difficult matters to analyse and to measure. I do not intend to enter into these matters in this lecture.

Two Conditions for Non-Inflationary Full Employment

However, it is clear that in order to achieve full employment without price inflation, two separate conditions must be fulfilled:

first, the government must be able by fiscal and monetary policies to keep total money expenditures at the level necessary to provide a market for the full-employment capacity level of output at uninflated money prices; and

second, the wage-price fixing processes must be such as to ensure, at this full-employment, capacity level of real activity, both that money wage-rates are not pushed up more quickly than output per head is growing and also that profit margins are stabilised.

In this chapter I shall assume that we do know broadly how to control the total level of money expenditures at whatever level we desire. It is with the second of these two conditions that I wish to deal, namely the problem of restraining the wage-price fixing processes so as to avoid, or at least much reduce, price inflation at full-employment levels of output.

RECENT CHANGES IN THE LABOUR MARKET

Let me start with wage restraint which, as I shall argue later, is the basic problem. Until very recently it was possible to argue that a reasonably moderate restraint of total effective demand (such as to maintain the unemployment percentage at about $2\frac{1}{2}$ per cent) would damp down the labour market sufficiently to avoid an undue rate of inflation of money wage-rates. Professor Paish has shown very convincingly that for the years 1952–66 the level of demand for labour had a clear effect on the rate at which money wages were increased, the relationship being such that with an unemployment percentage of $2\frac{1}{2}$ one could expect an annual increase of incomes from employment of about 4 per cent per annum.[4]

But there has of recent years been a most dramatic and marked change. This can be seen clearly from Table 2.1, which shows that weekly wage-earnings rose in 1970 by 12 per cent, while the unemployment percentage was no less than 2.6 per cent. In 1970–71 the highest rates of rise of money wage-incomes have been combined not with the lowest, but with the highest, unemployment percentages since the end of the Second World War. Professor Paish has analysed this dramatic change. He reaches the conclusion that, whereas on the basis of the 1952–66 experience one would have expected the unemployment ruling between the middle of 1969 and the middle of 1970 to have been associated with an increase of 3.8 per cent in the money incomes earned from employment, in the result this increase in money earnings was no less than 13.7 per cent – some 10 points higher than one would have expected from previous experience.[5]

How can one explain this very dramatic increase in the amount of wage inflation associated with a given level of demand in the labour market? No one, I think, can at present give a confident answer to this question. There are many possible factors at work and very probably it is the combination of many different influences which has caused so large a change. I will do no more than to refer you to Professor Paish's analysis and to summarise briefly five possible influences.

Five Possible Influences on the Dramatic Rise in Earnings

(1) Theoretically one could explain the change if there had been a dramatic increase in structural unemployment, i.e. in unemployment that was highly concentrated in particular regions or occupations. Money wage-rates are much more easily pulled up by an excess demand for labour than they are pushed down by an excess supply of labour. If a given total of unemployment takes the form of a mass of unemployment in one particular market combined with a scarcity of labour elsewhere, the upward movement of wages where there is scarcity is likely to be rapid; and this is likely to be combined with little if any deflation of wage-rates where there is heavy unemployment. If the same total of unemployment were evenly spread over all labour markets, so that there was no scarcity of labour anywhere, the upward movement of wage-rates would almost certainly be much less marked.

There is not, however, any evidence of a dramatic increase in concentrated, structural unemployment sufficient to explain the dramatic change in the rate of wage inflation. We can dismiss this influence as an explanation. I have mentioned it at some length, however, because it does point one moral. An important element in any long-run policy designed to combine full employment with price stability should consist of policies to deal with structural unemployment: to bring new industries to depressed areas, to retrain unemployed workers, to enable unemployed workers to find houses to rent in regions of expanding demand, and to break down restrictive practices in the labour market which prevent workers in contracting occupations and industries from being admitted to work in more prosperous trades. For the less unemployment is concentrated in depressed, contracting regions and occupations, the lower will be the general level of unemployment needed to prevent an inflation of money wage-costs. But this has always been true; it is not a new phenomenon which will explain the sudden present intensification of the wage problem.

(2) There have in recent years been two very important changes in the labour market – namely, the institution of redundancy payments and of more generous income-related unemployment benefits – which have reduced the terrors of temporary forced unemployment. One likely result has been that in pressing wage claims trade unions and similar bodies have been less sensitive than before to any given level of unemployment among the workers concerned. This may well have exerted an appreciable influence, though it is difficult to imagine that it explains the whole of the change.

(3) A third influence may be found in the fact that the great recovery in the balance of payments after 1967 necessitated a reduction in the standard of living below what it would otherwise have been. In conditions of full employment you cannot import less and export more real goods and services without cutting down some forms of domestic consumption or other use of real resources. Higher prices of imports and higher direct and indirect taxes were among the necessary means which the then Chancellor of the Exchequer had the political courage to face. But wage-earners may not automatically accept lower incomes and higher prices without an attempt to restore the situation through more urgent demands for increased money wages. The real restraints on consumption after 1967 may well have intensified the pressures for increased money wage-incomes.

(4) This development may have made wage-earners more conscious of rises in the cost of living and more insistent that it is real wages rather than money wages in which they are interested. This in turn could well lead to an explosive inflationary situation of the kind which I outlined at the beginning of my lecture. Suppose that in a given situation a rise of 3 per cent per annum in the real wage-rate is what would correspond to the rise in the real productivity of labour. Suppose that last year the cost of living went up by 6 per cent. Suppose finally that workers demand a money wage increase of 10 per cent, because they aim at a rise in the real wage of 4 per cent (i.e. 10 per

cent rise in money wages minus 6 per cent to cover the rise in the cost of living = 4 per cent rise in the real wage, i.e. take-home pay). Then money wage-costs per unit of output will rise by 7 per cent (i.e. 10 per cent in the money wage-rate minus 3 per cent rise in output per head). Prices must be raised this year by 7 per cent instead of by last year's 6 per cent if profit margins are to be maintained. In this way a more-and-more definite and deliberate attempt to achieve an over-optimistic target of improvement in the real wage-rate by adding a precise figure to offset last year's rise in the cost of living can lead to a rapid acceleration of price, and so in turn of wage, inflation. I strongly suspect that something of this kind may have been happening.

(5) Any or all of the influences which I have already discussed may have initiated stronger pressure by trade unions and similar bodies for wage increases. Such pressures having resulted in a marked increase in the rate of rise of money wage-rates may have given individual trade unions an unexpected glimpse into the very large monopolistic powers which they possess for pushing money wage-rates up and which they have not fully exploited in the past. The consequence may have been a basic change in their attitudes. The order of magnitude of what is regarded as a reasonable annual claim may have been more or less permanently changed; and trade union leaders may have become much more acutely aware of their power to obtain concessions through the threat to disrupt basic economic activities.

PROPOSALS FOR RESTRAINING 'EXPLOSIVE' WAGE INFLATION

If it is really important to restrain this sort of explosive wage inflation and if it is impossible nowadays to do so merely by restricting the total demand for labour to a moderate and tolerable degree, what can be done about it?

(i) Full-Scale State Incomes Policy

One possibility is to attempt a full-scale governmental incomes policy, which involves, first, laying down criteria to determine the legitimacy of wage increases and, second, instituting some governmental machinery to see that these criteria are observed. This procedure in my opinion is neither desirable nor practicable. The criteria must cover such matters as productivity agreements, the treatment of very low wages, the correction of acute shortages of labour in particular markets, the maintenance of equitable differentials, and so on. The effective application of these criteria to basic rates and to overtime rates, to piece-rates and to hourly rates of wages for labour of different skills over a wide range of occupations and industries in a large number of firms in different localities would involve a most far-reaching incursion of governmental control into the whole of the private, free-enterprise sector of the economy. *This is in itself very undesirable*; and the experience of the valiant efforts of the now-defunct Prices and Incomes Board makes me wonder whether in any case so detailed and far-reaching an exercise is practicable.

(ii) Voluntary Incomes Policy

Another possibility is to work for what is known as a voluntary incomes policy, i.e. to hand over this same formidable task not to a governmental institution but to the joint decision of the TUC and the CBI. I believe this solution to be equally undesirable and equally impracticable. If it could be worked, it would mean that what were in essence public rules and regulations of the most far-reaching importance to the individual workers and employers concerned were determined by the decisions of two private monopolistic organisations in no way responsible to the democratically elected government. If the TUC and the CBI had the power over their members to make this solution possible, then in my opinion they would be usurping powers which properly belong to the government. Fortunately experience suggests that they do not possess the powers necessary to make this solution a practicable one.

I think we must squarely face the fact that trade unions *are* monopolistic organisations in which individuals have banded together to fix a price for what they are selling and that with the present rules and regulations these particular monopolistic bodies have too great a bargaining power.

This is, I know, largely for historical reasons a very emotive subject; and I want to make it clear from the outset that I am not just advocating trade-union bashing. It is true that a trade union is a monopolistic organisation. But even those who, like myself, would like to see as much freedom for private enterprise and trade as is feasible in modern conditions recognise that 'monopolistic' arrangements are often not merely inevitable, but even positively desirable. No one, I think, would suggest that transport by rail or the generation of electricity should be conducted by a very large number of small competing units. The fact that trade unions are monopolistic organisations does not automatically condemn them; and indeed they perform a number of very important, necessary functions. Many of their most important functions in representing the interests of the workers to the managers on many aspects of the conditions of their work and employment have nothing directly to do with wage-fixing. Moreover, where there would otherwise be a very large number of workers facing a very small number of employers, trade unions are needed to provide bargaining power in order to offset the monopsonistic, exploitative powers of the limited number of employers. Simple, straightforward trade-union bashing is not the answer. But this does not, of course, imply that there should be no social control over their activities. Indeed, in no other sphere of economic life does one consider it desirable that a monopolistic organisation should not be subject to social controls of one kind or another over such matters as the prices it charges or the amounts it supplies.

A Simple Scheme to Control Trade Unions' Bargaining Powers

I think that we must consider the possibility of some simple, practicable means of control over the bargaining powers of the trade unions; and I propose the following very simple scheme.

(1) The government lays down from time to time a 'norm' for the annual percentage rise in wage earnings. Let us speak of this norm as x per cent per annum; and I will discuss later the value of x.

(2) Any group of employers and employees would, however, be perfectly free to reach agreement on any wage or salary bargain, whether or not it implied a rise of earnings above the x per cent per annum norm.

(3) There would, however, be a recognised system of tribunals or courts to which, in the case of a trade dispute about wages or salaries, the matter could be referred in order to obtain a judgment as to whether the increase in pay which was claimed did or did not exceed the x per cent norm.

The functions of these wage tribunals or courts would be very limited, simply and solely to determine whether a particular pay claim would cause the earnings of the workers concerned to be more than x per cent higher than they were a year ago. Even so their task would not be an easy one. It may be remembered that the award of the Wilberforce Commission[6] in February 1971 after the December go-slow of the workers in the supply of electricity was claimed by some to represent a rise of some 20 per cent and by others to represent a rise of little over 10 per cent. The essential task of the tribunals would be to decide whether, taking into account such matters as fringe benefits and the probable effects on overtime, the cost to the employer of employing a given amount of the labour concerned would be raised by more than x per cent. Such a determination might take a little time; and the tribunals would have to be empowered to issue interim judgments which could later be revised by a final determination.

(4) If it were ruled by the tribunal that the pay claim under consideration exceeded the norm of x per cent, then, but only then, regulations would come into force to curb the bargaining power of the workers concerned in pressing the claim. The sort of regulations which might be appropriate would be: that any workers who went on strike in favour of the claim would lose any accumulated rights to redundancy payments in their existing jobs; that any supplementary benefits paid for the support of their wives and children would become a liability of the trade union that was supporting the strike or, failing that, would be treated as a debt of the individual worker concerned; and that the trade union would be liable to a tax on any strike benefits which it paid out to its members. On the other hand, there would be no curbing of trade unions' bargaining powers in respect of claims which did not exceed the x per cent norm.

The choice of an actual number for the x per cent norm would give the government an important new weapon for the management of the economy. In the present situation it would not be practicable to fix x immediately at a level which would avoid all further inflation. Acute problems of comparability during the transition to stability would arise, since some workers (group 'A') will have just received, say, a 15 per cent rise in pay, while another group of workers (group 'B') is caught by the new arrangement just before it has demanded its 15 per cent rise. To set a norm of 3 per cent in such conditions would be grossly unfair to group 'B'. Perhaps an initial norm of 10 per cent might be set.[7] Then, as the inflation tailed off, the norm could be reduced until some level compatible with general price stability was achieved. What this ultimate level should be would depend upon many things: the severity of the curbs imposed on those who pressed claims which exceeded the norm; the degree to which the government restricted total effective demand and thus maintained a restrictive pressure in the labour market; the extent to which restrictive practices in the various labour markets were controlled; and so on. The norm would merely provide the government with one extra dimension in its control of the economy.

SUPPLY AND DEMAND IN THE LABOUR MARKET

I hope that the general philosophy behind these proposals is clear. Free wage-bargaining would in general persist. Any wage agreed between workers and employers would be permissible. No strike or lock-out would be made illegal by these proposals. But there would be serious financial curbs on claims which are both excessive and resisted by employers.

Productivity Agreements

The result would be an absolute minimum of governmental intervention in labour markets. There would, for example, be no need to define legitimate productivity agreements in order to define a permitted exception to a norm for wage increases. Since any agreement reached willingly between employers and employed would be permitted, it would not matter whether or not it could be called a productivity agreement.

Wage Comparabilities

Similarly, the difficult – indeed, in my opinion, insoluble – problem of the definition by some governmental body of equity in the comparability of one wage with another would disappear. Comparability might well be taken into account, as it is now, in the determination of wages in a wage-bargain; but that would be a matter for the employers and employees concerned to determine. It is, however, an important negative merit of the proposals which I have put forward that they do not interfere arbitrarily with existing wage comparabilities. My proposals refer equally to all employees whether wage-earners or salaried professionals and whether in private or public employment. In my opinion it is manifestly unfair, and for that very reason I suspect ultimately impracticable, to try to contain inflation by government resistance to wage claims by public servants without any similar resistance to wage claims in the private sector. My proposals would apply equally in all sectors.

Labour Scarcities

In a similar way it would not be the duty of any governmental body to determine whether a specially high wage-rate might be offered to meet a scarcity of labour in a particular labour market. That also would be left to the free determination of the employers and employed in the market concerned. Successful, expanding employers would be free to offer any wage they liked to attract the labour they needed. Wage drift of that kind should not, and with my proposals would not, be frowned upon.

The proposals I have put forward thus have the merit that they in no way impede an upward movement of earnings in markets where there is an excess demand for labour relatively to earnings in markets where there is an excess supply of labour. The wage-rate is the price of labour; and in our sort of mixed economy prices have an important role to play in helping to achieve an efficient use of economic resources. A high market price for a particular resource ruling in a particular market where that resource is scarce will

(i) help to attract the resource to that market from other markets where it is in more plentiful supply; and
(ii) help to induce the users of that resource where it is scarce to economise in its use.

Both these influences are desirable in the interests of economic efficiency.

I do not wish to imply that the use of resources should simply be left in all cases to the free play of uncontrolled markets. Far from it. Let me take an example. I believe that the social costs of road transport are much higher than those of rail transport. Heavy taxation of road transport used to finance the carriage of heavy goods traffic by rail would in my view be much in the social interest. But after allowance is made for any such interventions and controls there will result a certain demand for railwaymen and a certain demand for road transport workers; and if the other state interventions are correct it will be economically efficient to meet these labour demands. Has the wage-rate a role to play here?

Labour a Special Case

Labour is, of course, a very special case, and there are many ways in which it should not be treated just like any other commodity. Men and women and children should be generously supported in childhood, sickness, unemployment, old-age, and other times of dependent need. Moreover, as I shall argue later, radical fiscal and similar measures outside the wage system should be taken to influence the distribution of income and wealth which should not be determined simply by the forces of supply and demand in the labour market. But if such fiscal measures are adequately developed, then relative wage-rates as between different skills, regions, occupations, industries, etc., can be used for the double purpose, first, to induce individual employers to economise in the use of labour where it is scarce and to make free use of it where it is plentiful, and, secondly, to attract labour from firms where it is in plentiful supply to firms where it is scarce.

In so far as labour cannot move easily between regions and occupations, the first of these functions is very important both for the maintenance of full employment and for ensuring the most economic use of available labour resources. If computer programmers are scarce, it is important that they should be used only on the most important and productive tasks; and a high cost for employing a computer programmer will help to cut out wasteful uses of scarce ability. If unskilled workers are available in large numbers in a particular market, it is important that useful tasks they could perform should not be made unprofitable by a high cost for the employment of such workers.

Promotion of Labour Mobility

But it is important to promote the movement of labour from uses of low to uses of high social productivity. It is probable that at present the incentive to move from a sector where pay is low to a sector where pay is high is less important than the incentive to move from a sector where there is unemployment to a sector where job opportunities are good.[8] But this does not, of course, automatically ensure the movement of labour from points of low to points of high productivity. Job opportunities for new entrants may be poor in a highly-paid occupation just because the cost of labour is maintained there at an artificially high level, and there may be a high unsatisfied demand for labour in another sector just because labour is cheap there. The more readily relative wages can be allowed to respond to true scarcities and surpluses of labour, the less likely are such situations to arise and the more nearly will opportunities for employment be equalised in all sectors. But the more nearly this position is realised, the more important will differences in pay become relatively to differences in job opportunities in attracting labour from depressed to prosperous occupations.

Reducing Restrictive Practices

But for this to happen one very important condition must be fulfilled. There must not be any extensive network of restrictions on the entry into particular labour markets. Limitation of entry to a trade to persons trained as apprentices, when the number of apprentices permitted to train is unnecessarily limited or the time and expense of apprenticeship are unduly extended; trade union insistence on pre-entry closed-shop arrangements, whereby only trade unionists may work in a particular sector of industry and the trade union itself limits the number who may join it; professional examination requirements which demand qualifications or time spent in training which are not essential for the proper performance of the professional service; all these and similar restrictive practices may make it impossible or unnecessarily difficult for people to move into a particular labour market. An exceptionally high rate of pay to such a group of workers may be needed to restrict the demand to the artificially restricted supply; but the high rate of pay is not needed to attract labour; indeed, it is paid solely because the labour which would be attracted is artificially excluded.

For this reason a proper set of policies for the control of wage inflation cannot be divorced from a proper set of policies for the removal of unnecessary restrictive practices in labour markets. I cannot in this lecture cover this aspect of the subject, which is a matter for legislation to amend the rules of trade unions and professional associations about the qualifications for employment on particular tasks. The recent Industrial Relations Act is, of course, highly relevant here in its banning of closed shops which might restrict the entry of new labour and in its insistence that a union should admit all persons who are reasonably qualified for the trade in question.

The difficult problem here is, of course, the definition of what qualifications are reasonably needed for a particular job. In many cases where the employer is a business concern which is technically quite capable of judging for itself what skill is necessary and whether any particular applicant has in one way or another acquired that skill, there is really in effect little need for any systematic process of definition of the required skill and for the exclusion of those without that skill. But in some jobs these simple conditions are not fulfilled. This may be the case with certain industrial skills. It is certainly the case with specific professional skills where the 'employer' (for example, the citizen in ill-health or in conflict with the law) needs the services of a professional person (for example, a doctor or lawyer) who is highly trained in tech-

niques which the 'employer' does not begin to understand. Some system for an independent determination of the necessary skills and for
an independent judgment on who has and who has not acquired those
skills is necessary in cases of this kind. The machinery for this purpose will inevitably depend very largely upon the opinions of the professionals concerned: doctors will know more about the requirements
of medical knowledge and lawyers more about the requirements of
legal knowledge than anyone else. But even doctors and lawyers are
human and will not want their position to be undermined by an avoid-
able inflation of their numbers. It would seem that the final decision
on professional qualifications must not be left to the closed guild of
the existing professionals. Some independent body must decide, relying, however, inevitably very largely on the advice of the professionals.

A CRITICAL LOOK AT THE PROPOSALS

I fear that I have been tempted to stray somewhat from my main theme.
The central point is simply that the proposals I have put forward for
the curbing of wage inflation do nothing to impede the movement of
relative wages in response to the true relative scarcities of labour in
different markets. Any wage-rate freely agreed between employer and
employed is permissible.

(i) Ineffective against Inflation?

But may not this very fact mean that my proposals will be ineffective
as an anti-inflationary device? It can be argued that there will always
be some important sectors where, to maintain smooth relations with
the workers, employers will be willing to grant excessive inflationary
wage increases and where these increases will set the tone for excessive claims elsewhere to maintain existing differentials and comparabilities.

I do not think that this need be a fatal flaw. Proposals of the kind I
have made for the curbing of inflationary wage increases are not, of
course, a panacea for all our evils. In particular they are no substitute
for monetary and fiscal policies which will properly prevent an excessive inflation of demand. The proposals I have made in this lecture will
increase the bargaining power with which employers can resist excessive wage claims; they must be combined with a control of total money
demand which means that, over the whole range of economic activity,
producers do not find it easy simply to pass on higher money costs in

charging higher money prices without losing sales.

Consider one recent example, namely the wage settlement by Ford in April 1971 involving a 16 per cent rise in pay for two successive years which was widely considered to set an unfortunate inflationary pattern. It must be remembered that this wage increase was not given readily, but only after a seven-week strike. Suppose that a 10 per cent norm had been ruling and that the strikers had known that they would lose all their accumulated rights to redundancy payments if they struck for more than this. Suppose that the trade unions concerned had known that they would incur a liability for all supplementary benefits paid to the workers' families and, say, a 100 per cent tax on any strike pay they distributed. Suppose further that the Industrial Relations Act had been in force, ensuring that Ford could employ any labour[9] which was available. Suppose finally, as I shall later propose, that Ford had had to compete with foreign cars imported free of all duty. Would it not have been likely that the dispute would have been settled for a rate of rise of wages that did not exceed the ruling 10 per cent norm and did not, therefore, bring into operation the curbs I have suggested?

(ii) No Help for Low-Paid Workers?

That my proposals allow wide freedom for wage flexibility on supply-demand grounds may give rise to another type of criticism, namely that they do nothing to discriminate in favour of exceptionally rapid rises for exceptionally low wage-earners. I believe myself to have a strong egalitarian philosophy, and yet I would reject this criticism. Wage-rates, like all prices, have a dual effect. If they are set on supply-demand principles they can help to ensure that the most effective use is made of the available labour; but at the same time they are a major determinant of the distribution of income. The best arrangement, in my view, is to allow the market wage-rate charged to the employer of labour to be set on supply-demand principles to ensure that employers economise in scarce types of labour and make full use of plentiful types of labour, and then to modify, very radically if necessary, the resulting distribution of income by means of fiscal policies of one kind or another.

The removal of restrictive devices which maintain high earnings in particular professional or industrial occupations by limiting entry to those occupations will itself do something to raise wages in lower-paid outside occupations. It will make it more possible for low-paid persons to move into high-paid jobs; and this will not only help those who do move but, by reducing the supply of labour in the low-paid occupations, will improve the position of those who are left behind.

Trade Unions' Role in Income Redistribution

Upward pressure by trade union action on money wage-rates in general is not an effective means for redistributing income as between the general body of wages on the one hand and the general body of incomes from property on the other. Experience suggests that the result is in the main merely an inflation of money prices as profit margins are restored or, if prices cannot be raised, some increase in the general level of unemployment. This does not, however, mean that trade unions never have any role to play in improving distribution. Particular groups of workers may, of course, be being sweated or exploited because unorganised competitive workers without monopolistic bargaining power are being employed by a set of tightly organised, monopsonistic employers. In such circumstances the organisation of workers' interests through a trade union or some form of government wage council is the answer. But even when all monopsonistic exploitation has been removed, a low wage may be needed in some labour markets in order to give scope for the full employment of the labour available in that market. In such conditions the imposition of a substantially higher minimum wage or the exceptional pushing up of the wage-rate on the grounds of equalising this particularly low wage-rate with the higher earnings available to other workers may well lead to the unemployment of the less-qualified workers. Far better in my opinion is to have some system for the subsidisation of low incomes rather than to impose a minimum wage-rate or otherwise artificially to 'jack-up' the wage-rates of well-organised (but nevertheless low-paid) workers.

Redistributional Devices

There are a wide range of fiscal devices for the redistribution of income and wealth. They include such measures as the reform of death duties and of the laws of inheritance designed to produce a much greater equality of inherited property; specially favourable opportunities for the accumulation of property by those who are less well-off; the progressive taxation of high incomes and the direct subsidisation of low incomes; the bringing into the tax net of exempt incomes, such as the Schedule 'A' value of owner-occupied houses, so that property owners may not receive substantial slices of tax-free income; the development

of social benefits and of educational and other opportunities for upward mobility; and so on. I would advocate a radical development on
these lines; and if such a development were achieved *pari passu* with
the reform of wage-fixing institutions on the lines I have advocated, it
would perhaps help to make the application of the supply-demand principle to wages politically more acceptable.

BRINGING PROFITS AND PRICES INTO THE NET

There remains one further fundamental matter which I must discuss. I
have so far spoken solely about the determination of *rates of pay*, i.e.,
of wages and salaries. But should not the same principles be applied
to other forms of income and, in particular, to profits and profit margins?

I agree wholeheartedly that just as some social control of the kind
which I have outlined is necessary over the exercise of monopolistic
bargaining power of trade unions and similar professional organisations, so some social control is needed over the exercise of monopolistic power by the producers and sellers of commodities. In addition
I would argue that, just as in the case of wages and salaries, any further redistribution of income and wealth should be a matter for fiscal
and similar policies and not for wage and price control. Thus the curbing
of monopolistic powers by producers of products will help to restrain
profit margins; but if a further move in the direction of redistribution
of income is required from rich to poor this should be achieved by
progressive taxation and similar fiscal devices and not by additional
direct controls over selling prices or profit margins.

Up to this point, I would agree, the case for social control over
prices or profit margins is on all fours with the case for social control
over wages and salaries. But the methods of application of control
must be quite different in the two cases and for this reason the two
sets of problems should be tackled by two different sets of institutions. This does not, of course, imply that they should not be tackled
simultaneously and with equal vigour.

The reason why different methods of attack are appropriate is simple.
The sort of wage bargains which may need social control are typically
those that take place between a monopolistic organisation on the supply side (namely, a trade union) and a monopsonistic organisation on
the demand side (namely, an employers' association or a large-scale
single employer) – what economists call a case of bilateral monopoly.
Such a case can be handled by my suggestion for taking steps to regu-

late the bargaining strength of the parties in this bilateral bargain. But this is not at all the typical situation in a case of a monopolistic sale of a product. A large-scale manufacturer of cars does not strike a bargain over the price of cars with a consumers' association, or with one large-scale consumer. There are many independent, unorganised consumers facing the large-scale monopolistic seller. This situation cannot be controlled by measures designed to affect bargaining strengths on one side or the other.

Curbing Producers' Monopolies

But measures can be taken to curb monopolistic action by producers and to encourage price competition among them. First, there are the measures designed to curb the growth of monopoly power by restricting mergers, combines, and similar developments and measures designed to outlaw restrictive practices by producers. I cannot here discuss these measures which we associate with the work of the Monopolies Commission and with the operation of the Restrictive Practices Act. It would, however, be possible for these measures to be supplemented by more specific controls over certain prices. Detailed governmental control over all selling prices is, in my opinion, impracticable and undesirable for just the same reasons which I argued earlier in the case of detailed governmental control over all wages and salaries. But there is much to be said in favour of a system of the following kind. An official council might be set up with the specific duty of bringing complaints to government departments who would be empowered to refer to the Monopolies Commission the question whether in a particular case a particular producer was charging prices which represented undesirable monopolistic profit margins. If such were ruled to be the case, the producer in question could be required to reduce his prices accordingly.

There are other less direct ways of preventing monopolistic abuses and encouraging competition. I will mention two controversial possibilities. First, the present arrangements whereby undistributed profits are taxed less heavily than distributed profits should be reversed. If the finance of capital development from ploughed-back funds was heavily discouraged by taxation, companies would have to compete on the open capital market for new funds, which would promote competition in favour of the most promising new enterprises. Second, the discouragement of advertising through the taxation of advertisement expenditures, the removal of advertising from television, and so on, could induce producers to compete more by charging lower prices rather than by spending money on advertising, much of which is designed to build up the monopolistic market power of the producer by 'bamboozling' the consumer into thinking that there is something unique about a particular brand.

FREE IMPORTS MOST EFFECTIVE WEAPON

But far and away the most effective way of promoting competition and curbing monopolistic powers would be to admit the free import of goods from all foreign sources; and this would also make producers who had to face foreign competition more willing to resist inflationary wage-claims.

Alternative Roads to Free Imports

This possibility opens up the whole question of our financial and economic relations with the rest of the world. Membership of the European Economic Community would, of course, open us up to the direct competition of the manufactures of Germany, France, Italy, and the Benelux countries. A North American Free Trade Area or a unilateral move back to our ancient and honourable free trade policy would be even more effective from this point of view.[10]

But whatever form it takes, free importation raises basic problems of the mechanism for maintaining equilibrium in our balance of payments. There must be some effective means other than import restriction for us to combine full employment at home with a balanced balance of payments. One method would be to allow the exchange rate to vary so as to reconcile our own domestic policies for the control of demand and the regulation of wage inflation with the needs of external economic and financial conditions; and this is the method which I would myself advocate.

Wages in a Monetary Union

There is, however, serious talk of the EEC developing into a monetary union in which there would not only be free trade between the members, but in which the members would share a common money or, at least, operate a system of rigidly and immutably fixed exchange rates. If we are seriously to contemplate such a possibility, I suggest that there are three basic necessary conditions, all of which must be simultaneously satisfied.

First, the members of the monetary union must have an effective joint monetary and fiscal policy to stabilise total monetary demand within the monetary union as a whole. If recessions of total demand within the monetary union as a whole were a real possibility, the adjustments of cost-price structures in the UK necessary to reconcile full employment with a balanced balance of payments might be altogether too large to be manageable.

Second, the members of the monetary union must be assured in one way or another of extensive currency reserves to finance substantial imbalances in the balance of payments, since relative cost-price adjustments between the members will undoubtedly be necessary from time to time and cannot be expected to operate very quickly.

Finally, membership of a free-trade monetary union would make some governmental control over the degree of wage-cost inflation in the UK absolutely essential. Without it we would be continually subject to the risk that we should have to face prolonged periods of unemployment and low levels of economic activity in the interests of balance-of-payments equilibrium. Whether or not these particular proposals would be sufficient for this purpose is a question which only experience of them could answer.

NOTE ON THE MEASUREMENT OF INFLUENCES AFFECTING THE ALLOCATION OF LABOUR

Recent investigations[11] have suggested that differences in wage-earnings play a relatively small part in attracting labour from one occupation to another. It is implied that labour is re-allocated among occupations rather by the fact that jobs are offered in expanding sectors while unemployment rules in contracting sectors. The basic method of these investigations is to compare over a series of years (i) the rise in earnings, and (ii) the increase in employment in various sectors, in order to see whether exceptionally high increases in pay have been associated with exceptionally high increases in the labour available. The result has in general been to find (1) that changes in employment have been very great relatively to changes in pay and (2) that there is little if any positive correlation between rises in pay and rises in employment.

If changes in employment were due solely to changes in the demand

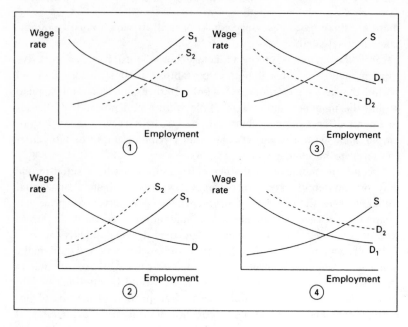

Figure 2.1

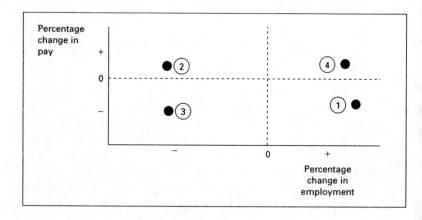

Figure 2.2

for the various products of labour, the absence of a positive correlation between wage increases and increases in numbers employed would imply that relative wages played a small part and that some other mechanism (such as unemployment in contracting industries and good job opportunities in expanding industries) had been the main factor leading to the movement of labour.

But suppose that there have also been important changes on the supply side in various labour markets. (And there have in fact been at least some very important changes of this kind, such as the increase in the supply of white-collar workers due to the expansion of educational opportunities or the reduction in the supply of coal-miners because of the abnormal age-distribution of coal-miners after the Second World War.) Then one would expect to find relative pay declining where employment had been increased because of the increased supply of labour, and pay increasing where employment had declined because of the scarcity of the supply of labour.

Consider an economy in which there were changes over a period of time in the four sectors.

In sector (I) the supply of labour at any given pay has fallen; in sector (2) the supply of labour has risen; in sector (3) the demand for labour has fallen; and in sector (4) the demand has risen. In all cases both supply and demand are very sensitive to changes in pay. The scatter diagram between percentage changes in employment and percentage changes in pay would be as in Fig. 2.2.

The movements of employment would be very large compared with movements in pay and there would be no correlation between the two. Yet supplies of labour and demands for labour are both very sensitive to relative changes in pay, and we need not rely on any other mechanism to explain the reallocation of labour.

This Note is not intended to deny the great importance of relative job opportunities. It is merely maintained that in the absence of any distinction between the importance of shifts on the demand side and shifts on the supply side in labour markets, the method used does not provide any conclusive evidence of the unimportance of relative pay as such in attracting labour.

It is strange that those who put so much emphasis on job opportunities have not made the direct comparison between relative levels of unemployment (and/or of vacancies) and relative expansions of the labour supply in various sectors. To what extent is there exceptionally low unemployment in contracting occupations (because workers are moving elsewhere and the supply is diminished) rather than exceptionally high unemployment (which is driving workers to seek jobs elsewhere)? It would be interesting to know.

NOTES

1. I am greatly indebted to Professor E. H. Phelps Brown, Sir Alexander Cairncross, Mr John Gratwick, Mr Graham Hutton, Mr L. F. Neal, Professor W. B. Reddaway, Professor B. C. Roberts and Mr Z. A. Silberston for extensive comments on an early draft of the lecture on which this chapter is based. As a result I greatly simplified the positive proposals which I put forward and to which, of course, I commit no one but myself.
2. Taken from Tables XVIII and XX of Professor F. W. Paish, *Rise and Fall of Incomes Policy,* Hobart Paper 47, IEA, second edition, July 1971.
3. See Chapter 1 above.
4. F. W. Paish, op. cit.
5. F. W. Paish, op. cit., p. 70.
6. *Report of a Court of Inquiry into a Dispute: Electricity Supply Industry,* Cmnd 4594, HMSO, London, February 1971.
7. Professor Reddaway has suggested to me that the norm might take the form of, say, 30 per cent over the last three years rather than of 10 per cent over the last year. That is to say, the curbs on bargaining power would be applied if a current wage claim would cause wage-earnings this year to be more than 30 per cent in excess of what they were three years ago rather than if it would cause wage-earnings to be more than 10 per cent in excess of what they were one year ago. Such a rule would certainly ease the problem of fairness in the transitional period and might well be a more acceptable form for the long run as well.
8. The evidence for this conclusion is highly persuasive but not conclusive. See the final section of this chapter.
9. The wage claim made by the Ford workers was based largely on a demand for comparability with the earnings of workers in car manufacture in the Midlands. But has this any more force than comparability between the earnings of Ford workers and the earnings of workers with similar qualifications in and around Dagenham? The pay of Ford workers might be low relatively to that of other workers in the Midlands but high relatively to that of other workers in and around Dagenham. What is the correct comparability? Suppose that in the absence of artificial restrictions the other workers in and around Dagenham could readily and effectively change their occupations to that of car manufacture, but that the geographical movement of car workers from Dagenham to the Midlands was difficult and expensive. There would be a large available supply of workers seeking employment at Ford; and the rate of rise of wages there should be restrained. But if occupational mobility between other workers and car manufacture in and around Dagenham were truly difficult and expensive, while regional mobility for car workers were easy and cheap,

suitable labour for Ford at Dagenham would become scarce and an exceptional wage-rise would be appropriate.

10. I have given a more detailed analysis for and against these alternatives in *UK, Commonwealth & Common Market: A Reappraisal*, Hobart Paper 17, IEA, third edition, January 1971.

11. W. B. Reddaway, 'Wage Flexibility and the Distribution of Labour', *Lloyds Bank Review*, 1959; Report by an Expert Group for the OECD, *Wages and Labour Mobility*, OECD, 1965.

3 Economic Freedom and Representative Government

F. A. Hayek

THE SEEDS OF DESTRUCTION

Thirty years ago I wrote a book[1] which, in a manner which many regarded as unduly alarmist, described the dangers that the then visible collectivist tendencies created for personal freedom. I am glad that these fears so far have not materialised, but I do not think this has proved me wrong. In the first instance I did not, as many misunderstood me, contend that if government interfered at all with economic affairs it was bound to go the whole way to a totalitarian system. I was trying to argue rather what in more homely terms is expressed by saying 'if you don't mend your principles you will go to the devil'.

Postwar Revival: The 'Great Prosperity'

In the event developments since the war, in Britain as well as in the rest of the Western world, have gone much less in the direction which the prevalent collectivist doctrines seemed to suggest was likely. Indeed, the first 20 years after the war saw a revival of a free market economy much stronger than even its most enthusiastic supporters could have hoped. Although I like to think that those who worked for this consummation in the intellectual sphere, such as Harold Wincott, have contributed to it, I do not overrate what intellectual debate can achieve. At least as important were probably the experiences of Germany, relying on a market economy, rapidly becoming the strongest economic power of Europe – and to some extent the practical efforts for a removal of the obstacles to international trade, such as GATT and perhaps in some measure the intentions if not the practice of the EEC.

The result was the Great Prosperity of the last 20 to 25 years which, I fear, will in the future appear as an event as unique as the Great Depression of the 1930s now appears to us. To me at least it seems clear that, until six or eight years ago, this prosperity was due entirely to the freeing of the spontaneous forces of the economic system and not, as in the later years, to inflation. Since this is today often forgotten I may perhaps remind you that, in the most remarkable burst of prosperity of this period, that of the German Federal Republic, the average annual rise of prices remained below 2 per cent until 1966.

I believe that even this modest rate of inflation would not have been necessary to secure the prosperity, and indeed that we should all today have better prospects of continuing prosperity if we had been content with what was achieved without inflation and had not attempted to stimulate it further by an expansionist credit policy. Instead such a policy has created a situation in which it is thought necessary to impose controls which will destroy the main foundations of the prosperity, namely the functioning market. Indeed the measures supposedly necessary to combat inflation – as if inflation were something which attacks us and not something which we create – threaten to destroy the free economy in the near future.

Inflation: The Threat to Freedom

We find ourselves in the paradoxical situation that, after a period during which the market economy has been more successful than ever before in rapidly raising living standards in the Western world, the prospects of its continuance even for the next few years must appear slight. I have indeed never felt so pessimistic about the chances of preserving a functioning market economy as I do at this moment – and this means also of the prospects of preserving a free political order. Although the threat to free institutions now comes from a source different from that with which I was concerned 30 years ago, it has become even more acute than it was then.

That a systematically pursued incomes policy means the suspension of the price mechanism and before long the replacement of the market by a centrally directed economy seems to me beyond doubt. I cannot here discuss the ways in which we may still avoid this course, or the chances that we may still do so. Although I regard it as at this time the chief duty of every economist to fight inflation – and to explain, why a repressed inflation is even worse than an open inflation – I am here concerned with another task. As I see it, inflation has merely speeded up the process of the destruction of the market economy which has been going on for other reasons, and brought much nearer the moment when, seeing the economic, political and moral consequences of a centrally directed economy, we shall have to think how we can re-establish a market economy on a firmer and more durable basis.

THE DANGER OF UNLIMITED GOVERNMENT

For some time I have been convinced that it is not only the deliberate attempts of the various kinds of collectivists to replace the market economy by a planned system, nor the consequences of the new monetary policies, which threaten to destroy the market economy: the political institutions prevailing in the Western world necessarily produce a drift in this direction which can be halted or prevented only by changing these institutions. I have belatedly come to agree with Joseph Schumpeter who 30 years ago argued[2] that there was an irreconcilable conflict between democracy and capitalism – except that it is not democracy as such but the particular forms of democratic organisation, now regarded as the only possible forms of democracy, which will produce a progressive expansion of governmental control of economic life even if the majority of the people wish to preserve a market economy.

Majority Rule and Special Interests

The reason is that it is now generally taken for granted that in a democracy the powers of the majority must be unlimited, and that a government with unlimited powers will be forced, to secure the continued support of a majority, to use its unlimited powers in the service of special interests – such groups as particular traders, the inhabitants of particular regions, etc. We shall see this most clearly if we consider the situation in a community in which the mass of the people are in favour of a market order and against government direction, but, as will normally happen, most of the groups wish an exception to be made in their favour. In such conditions a political party hoping to achieve and maintain power will have little choice but to use its powers to buy the support of particular groups. They will do so not because the majority is interventionist, but because the ruling party would not retain a majority if it did not buy the support of particular groups by the promise of special advantages. This means in practice that even a statesman wholly devoted to the common interest of all the citizens will be under the constant necessity of satisfying special interests, because only thus will he be able to retain the support of a majority which he needs to achieve what is really important to him.

The root of the evil is thus the unlimited power of the legislature in modern democracies, a power which the majority will be constantly forced to use in a manner that most of its members may not desire. What we call the will of the majority is thus really an artefact of the existing institutions, and particularly of the omnipotence of the sovereign legislature, which by the mechanics of the political process will be driven to do things that most of its members do not really want, simply because there are no formal limits to its powers.

It is widely believed that this omnipotence of the representative legislature is a necessary attribute of democracy because the will of the representative assembly could be limited only by placing another will above it. Legal positivism, the most influential current theory of jurisprudence, particularly represents this sovereignty of the legislature as logically necessary. This, however, was by no means the view of the classical theorists of representative government. John Locke made it very clear that in a free state even the power of the legislative body should be limited in a definite manner, namely to the passing of laws in the specific sense of general rules of just conduct equally applicable to all citizens. That all coercion would be legitimate only if it meant the application of general rules of law in this sense became the basic principle of liberalism. For Locke, and for the later theorists of Whiggism and the separation of powers, it was not so much the source from which the laws originated as their character of general rules of just conduct equally applicable to all which justified their coercive application.

What is Law?

This older liberal conception of the necessary limitation of all power by requiring the legislature to commit itself to general rules has, in the course of the last century, been replaced gradually and almost imperceptibly by the altogether different though not incompatible conception that it was the approval of the majority which was the only and sufficient restraint on legislation. And the older conception was not only forgotten but no longer even understood. It was thought that any substantive limitation of the legislative power was unnecessary once this power was placed in the hands of the majority, because approval by it was regarded as an adequate test of justice. In practice this majority opinion usually represents no more than the result of bargaining rather than a genuine agreement on principles. Even the concept of the arbitrariness which democratic government was supposed to prevent changed its content: its opposite was no longer the general rules equally applicable to all but the approval of a command by the majority – as if a majority might not treat a minority arbitrarily.

THE FUNDAMENTAL PRINCIPLE

Today it is rarely understood that the limitation of all coercion to the enforcement of general rules of just conduct was the fundamental principle of classical liberalism, or, I would almost say, its definition of liberty. This is largely a consequence of the fact that the substantive (or 'material') conception of law (as distinguished from a purely formal one) which underlies it, and which alone gives a clear meaning to such ideas as that of the separation of powers, of the rule of law or of a government under the law, had been rarely stated explicitly but merely tacitly presupposed by most of the classical writers. There are few passages in their seventeenth- and eighteenth-century writings in which they explicitly say what they mean by 'law'. Many uses of the term, however, make sense only if it is interpreted to mean exclusively general rules of just conduct and not every expression of the will of the duly authorised representative body.

Tyranny of Majorities

Though the older conception of law survives in limited connections, it is certainly no longer generally understood, and in consequence has ceased to be an effective limit on legislation. While in the theoretical concept of the separation of powers the legislature derived its authority from the circumstance that it committed itself to general rules and was supposed to impose only general rules, there are now no limits on what a legislature may command and so claim to be 'law'. While its power was thus once supposed to be limited not by a superior will but by a generally recognised principle, there are now no limits whatever. There is therefore also no reason why the coalitions of organised interests on which the governing majorities rest should not discriminate against any widely disliked group. Differences in wealth, education, tradition, religion, language or race may today become the cause of differential treatment on the pretext of a pretended principle of social justice or of public necessity. Once such discrimination is recognised as legitimate, all the safeguards of individual freedom of the liberal tradition are gone. If it is assumed that whatever the majority decides is just, even if what it lays down is not a general rule, but aims at affecting particular people, it would be expecting too much to believe that a sense of justice will restrain the caprice of the majority: in any group it is soon believed that what is desired by the group is just. And since the theoreticians of democracy have for over a hundred years taught the majorities that whatever they desire is just, we must not be surprised if the majorities no longer even ask whether what they decide is just. Legal positivism has powerfully contributed to this development by its contention that law is not dependent on justice but determines what is just.

Mirage of 'Social Justice'

Unfortunately, we have not only failed to impose upon legislatures the limitations inherent in the necessity of committing themselves to general rules. We have also charged them with tasks which they can perform only if they are not thus limited but are free to use coercion in the discriminatory manner that is required to assure benefits to particular people or groups. This they are constantly asked to do in the name of what is called social or distributive justice, a conception which has largely taken the place of the justice of individual action. It requires that not the individuals but 'society' be just in determining the share of individuals in the social product; and in order to realise any particular distribution of the social product regarded as just it is necessary that government directs individuals in what they must do.

Indeed, in a market economy in which no single person or group determines who gets what, and the shares of individuals always depend on many circumstances which nobody could have foreseen, the whole conception of social or distributive justice is empty and meaningless; and there will therefore never exist agreement on what is just in this sense. I am not sure that the concept has a definite meaning even in a centrally directed economy, or that in such a system people would ever agree on what distribution is just. I am certain, however, that nothing has done so much to destroy the juridical safeguards of individual freedom as the striving after this mirage of social justice. An adequate treatment of the topic would indeed presuppose a careful dissection of this ideal which almost everybody seems to believe to have a definite meaning but which proves more completely devoid of such meaning the more one thinks about it. But my main concern here, is what we have to do, if we ever again get a chance, to stop those tendencies inherent in the existing political systems which drive us towards a totalitarian order.

Compatibility of Collective Wants

Before I turn to this main problem, I should correct a widespread misunderstanding. The basic principle of the liberal tradition, that all the coercive action of government must be limited to the enforcement of general rules of just conduct, does not preclude government from rendering many other services for which, except for raising the necessary finance, it need not rely on coercion. It is true that in the nineteenth century a deep and not wholly unjustified distrust of government often made liberals wish to restrain government much more narrowly. But even then, of course, certain collective wants were recognised which only an agency possessing the power of taxation could satisfy. I am the last person to deny that increased wealth and the increased density of population have enlarged the number of collective needs which government can and should satisfy. Such government services are entirely compatible with liberal principles so long as,

> *firstly*, government does not claim a monopoly and new methods of rendering services through the market (e.g. in some now covered by social insurance) are not prevented;
> *secondly*, the means are raised by taxation on uniform principles and taxation is not used as an instrument for the redistribution of income; and,
> *thirdly*, the wants satisfied are collective wants of the community as a whole and not merely collective wants of particular groups.

Not every collective want deserves to be satisfied: the desire of the small bootmakers to be protected against the competition of the factories is also a collective need of the bootmakers, but clearly not one which in a liberal economic system could be satisfied.

Nineteenth-century liberalism in general attempted to keep the growth of these service activities of government in check by entrusting them to local rather than central government in the hope that competition between the local authorities would control their extent. I cannot consider here how far this principle had to be abandoned and mention it only as another part of the traditional liberal doctrine whose rationale is no longer understood.

I had to consider these points to make it clear that those checks on government activity refer only to its powers of coercion but not to the necessary services we today expect government to render to the citizens.

I hope that what I have said so far has made it clear that the task we shall have to perform if we are to re-establish and preserve a free society is in the first instance an intellectual task: it presupposes that we not only recover conceptions which we have largely lost and which must once again become generally understood, but also that we design new institutional safeguards which will prevent a repetition of the process

of gradual erosion of the safeguards which the theory of liberal constitutionalism had meant to provide.

THE SEPARATION OF POWERS

The device to which the theorists of liberal constitutionalism had looked
to guarantee individual liberty and the prevention of all arbitrariness
was the separation of powers. If the legislature laid down only general
rules equally applicable to all and the executive could use coercion
only to enforce obedience to these general rules, personal liberty would
indeed be secure. This presupposes, however, that the legislature is
confined to laying down such general rules. But, instead of confining
parliament to making laws in this sense, we have given it unlimited
power simply by calling 'law' everything which it proclaims: a legislature is now not a body that makes laws; a law is whatever is re-
solved by a legislature.

This state of affairs was brought about by the loss of the old meaning of 'law' and by the desire to make government democratic by
placing the direction and control of government in the hands of the
legislatures, which are in consequence constantly called upon to order
all sorts of specific actions – to issue commands which are called laws,
although in character they are wholly different from those laws to the
production of which the theory of the separation of powers had intended to confine the legislatures.

The Concept of 'Lawyer's Law'

Although the task of designing and establishing new institutions must
appear difficult and almost hopeless, the task of reviving and making
once more generally understood a lost concept for which we no longer
have even an unambiguous name is perhaps even more difficult. It is a
task which in this case has to be achieved in the face of the contrary
teaching of the dominant school of jurisprudence. I will try briefly to
state the essential characteristics of laws in this specific narrow sense
of the term before I turn to the institutional arrangements which would
secure that the task of making such laws be really separated from the
tasks of governing.

A good way is to consider the peculiar properties which judge-made
law possesses of necessity, while they belong to the products of legislatures in general only in so far as these have endeavoured to emulate

judge-made law. It is no accident that this concept of law has been preserved much longer in the common-law countries whereas it was rarely understood in countries which relied wholly on statute law.

This law consists essentially of what used to be known as 'lawyer's law' – which is and can be applied by courts of justice and to which the agencies of government are as much subject as are private persons. Since this judge-made law arises out of the settlement of disputes, it relates solely to the relations of acting persons towards one another and does not control an individual's actions which do not affect others. It defines the protected domains of each person with which others are prohibited from interfering. The aim is to prevent conflicts between people who do not act under central direction but on their own initiative, pursuing their own ends on the basis of their own knowledge.

These rules must thus apply in circumstances which nobody can foresee and must therefore be designed to cover a maximum number of future instances. This determines what is commonly but not very helpfully described as their 'abstract' character, by which is meant that they are intended to apply in the same manner to all situations in which certain generic factors are present and not only to particular designated persons, groups, places, times, etc. They do not prescribe to the individuals specific tasks or ends of their actions, but aim at making it possible for them so mutually to adjust their plans that each will have a good chance of achieving his aims. The delimitation of the personal domains which achieve this purpose is of course determined chiefly by the law of property, contract, and torts, and the penal laws which protect 'life, liberty and property'.

Limits to Coercion

An individual who is bound to obey only such rules of just conduct as I have called these rules of law in this narrow sense is free in the sense that he is not legally subject to anybody's commands, that within known limits he can choose the means and ends of his activities. But where everybody is free in this sense each is thrown into a process which nobody controls and the outcome of which for each is in large measure unpredictable. Freedom and risk are thus inseparable. Nor can it be claimed that the magnitude of each individual's share of the national income, dependent on so many circumstances which nobody knows, will be just. But nor can these shares meaningfully be described as unjust. We must be content if we can prevent them from being affected by unjust actions. We can of course in a free society provide a floor below which nobody need fall, by providing outside the market for all some insurance against misfortune. There is indeed much we can do to improve the framework within which the market will operate beneficially. But we cannot in such a society make the distribution of incomes correspond to some standard of social or distributive justice, and attempts to do so are likely to destroy the market order.

But if, to preserve individual freedom, we must confine coercion to the enforcement of general rules of just conduct, how can we prevent legislatures from authorising coercion to secure particular benefits for particular groups – especially a legislature organised on party lines where the governing majority frequently will be a majority only because it promises such special benefits to some groups? The truth is of course that the so-called legislatures have *never* been confined to making laws in this narrow sense, although the theory of the separation of powers tacitly assumed that they were. And since it has come to be accepted that not only legislation but also the direction of current government activities should be in the hands of the representatives of the majority, the direction of government has become the chief task of the legislatures. This has had the effect not only of entirely obliterating the distinction between laws in the sense of general rules of just conduct and laws in the sense of specific commands, but also of organising the legislatures not in the manner most suitable for making laws in the classical sense but in the manner required for efficient government, that is above all, on party lines.

Representative Government Driven to Serve Sectional Interests

Now, I believe we are right in wanting both legislation in the old sense and current government to be conducted democratically. But it seems to me it was a fatal error, though historically probably inevitable, to entrust these two distinct tasks to the same representative assembly. This makes the distinction between legislation and government, and thereby also the observance of the principles of the rule of law and of a government under the law, practically impossible. Though it may secure that every act of government has the approval of the representative assembly, it does not protect the citizens against discretionary coercion. Indeed, a representative assembly organised in the manner necessary for efficient government, and not restrained by some general laws it cannot alter, is bound to be driven to use its powers to satisfy the demands of sectional interests.

It is no accident that most of the classical theorists of representative government and of the separation of powers disliked the party system and hoped that a division of the legislature on party lines could be avoided. They did so because they conceived of the legislatures as concerned with the making of laws in the narrow sense, and believed that there could exist on the rules of just conduct a prevalent common opinion independent of particular interests. But it cannot be denied that democratic *government* requires the support of an organised body of representatives, which we call parties, committed to a programme of action, and a similarly organised opposition which offers an alternative government.

Separate Legislative Assembly

It would seem the obvious solution of this difficulty to have two distinct representative assemblies with different tasks, one a true legislative body and the other concerned with government proper, i.e. everything except the making of laws in the narrow sense. And it is at least not inconceivable that such a system might have developed in Britain if at the time when the House of Commons with the exclusive power over money bills achieved in effect sole control of government, the House of Lords, as the supreme court of justice, had obtained the sole right to develop the law in the narrow sense. But such a development was of course not possible so long as the House of Lords represented not the people at large but a class.

On reflection, however, one realises that little would be gained by merely having two representative assemblies instead of one if they were elected and organised on the same principles and therefore also had the same composition. They would be driven by the same circumstances which govern the decisions of modern parliaments and acting in collusion would probably produce the same sort of authorisation for whatever the government of the day wished to do. Even if we assume that the legislative chamber (as distinguished from the governmental one) were restricted by the constitution to passing laws in the narrow sense of general rules of just conduct, and this restriction were made effective through the control by a constitutional court, little would probably be achieved so long as the legislative assembly were under the same necessity of satisfying the demands of particular groups which force the hands of the governing majorities in today's parliaments.

Specific Interests and Permanent Principles

While for the governmental assemblies we should want something more or less of the same kind as the existing parliaments, whose organisation and manner of proceeding have indeed been shaped by the needs of governing rather than the making of laws, something very different would be needed for the legislative assembly. We should want an assembly not concerned with the particular needs of particular groups but rather with the general permanent principles on which the activities of the community were to be ordered. Its members and its resolutions should represent not specific groups and their particular desires but the prevailing opinion on what kind of conduct was just and what kind was not. In laying down rules to be valid for long periods ahead this assembly should be 'representative of', or reproduce a sort of cross-section of, the prevailing opinions on right and wrong; its members should not be the spokesmen of particular interests, or express the 'will' of any particular section of the population on any specific measure of government. They should be men and women trusted and respected for the traits of character they had shown in the ordinary business of life, and not dependent on the approval of particular groups of electors. And they should be wholly exempt from the party discipline necessary to keep a governing team together, but evidently undesirable in the body which lays down the rules that limit the powers of government.

Membership of Legislative Assembly

Such a legislative assembly could be achieved if, *first*, its members were elected for long periods, *secondly*, they were not eligible for re-election after the end of the period, and, *thirdly*, to secure a continuous renewal of the body in accord with gradually changing opinions among the electorate, its members were not all elected at the same time but a constant fraction of their number replaced every year as their mandate expired; or, in other words, if they were elected, for instance, for fifteen years and one-fifteenth of their number replaced every year. It would further seem to me expedient to provide that at each election the representatives should be chosen by and from only one age-group so that every citizen would vote only once in his life, say in his fortieth year, for a representative chosen from his age-group.

The result would be an assembly composed of persons between their fortieth and their fifty-fifth year, elected after they had opportunity to prove their ability in ordinary life (and, incidentally, of an average

age somewhat below that of contemporary parliaments). It would probably be desirable to disqualify those who had occupied positions in the governmental assembly or other political or party organisations and it would also be necessary to assure to those elected for the period after their retirement some dignified, paid and pensionable position, such as lay-judge or the like.

The advantage of an election by age-groups, and at an age at which the individuals could have proved themselves in ordinary life, would be that in general a person's contemporaries are the best judges of his character and ability; and that among the relatively small numbers participating in each election the candidates would be more likely to be personally known to the voters and chosen according to the personal esteem in which they were held by the voters – especially if, as would seem likely and deserve encouragement, the anticipation of this common task led to the formation of clubs of the age-groups for the discussion of public affairs.

ADVANTAGES OF LEGISLATIVE SEPARATION

The purpose of all this would of course be to create a legislature which was not subservient to government and did not produce whatever laws government wanted for the achievement of its momentary purposes, but rather which with the law laid down the permanent limits to the coercive powers of government – limits within which government had to move and which even the democratically elected governmental assembly could not overstep. While the latter assembly would be entirely free in determining the organisation of government, the use to be made of the means placed at the disposal of government and the character of the services to be rendered by government, it would itself possess no coercive powers over the individual citizens. Such powers, including the power to raise by taxation the means for financing the services rendered by government, would extend only to the enforcement of the rules of just conduct laid down by the legislative assembly. Against any overstepping of these limits by government (or the governmental assembly) there would be open an appeal to a constitutional court which would be competent in the case of conflict between the legislature proper and the governmental bodies.

A further desirable effect of such an arrangement would be that the legislature would for once have enough time for its proper task. This is important because in modern times legislatures frequently have left the regulation of matters which might have been effected by general rules of law to administrative orders and even administrative discretion simply because they were so busy with their governmental tasks that they had neither time for nor interest in making law proper. It is also a task which requires expert knowledge which a long-serving representative might acquire but is not likely to be possessed by a busy politician anxious for results which he can show his constituents before the next election. It is a curious consequence of giving the representative assembly unlimited power that it has largely ceased to be the chief determining agent in shaping the law proper, but has left this task more and more to the bureaucracy.

I will not here pursue further the details of this Utopia – though I must confess that I have found fascinating and instructive the exploration of the new opportunities offered by contemplating the possibility of separating the truly legislative assembly from the governmental body. If the reader rightly asks what the purpose of such a Utopian construction can be if by calling it thus I admit that I do not believe it can be realised in the foreseeable future, I can answer in the words of David Hume in his essay on 'The Idea of a Perfect Commonwealth', that

in all cases, it must be advantageous to know what is the most perfect in the kind, that we may be able to bring any real constitution or form of government as near it as possible, by such gentle alterations and innovations as may not give too great a disturbance to society.

NOTES

1. *The Roads to Serfdom*, Routledge, London, 1944.
2. *Capitalism, Socialism and Democracy*, Allen & Unwin, London, 1943 (Unwin University Books, No. 28, 3rd edn, 1950).

4 Aspects of Postwar Economic Policy

Lord Robbins

INTRODUCTION

I want to discuss some aspects of the policies of the last three decades which have contributed to the anxious position in which we now find ourselves, with our money rapidly depreciating in value, our purchases from abroad sustained at their present volume only by unprecedented borrowing from abroad and, at the same time, our domestic economic activity faced with contraction.

I hope that with my phrase 'policies which have contributed' I have indicated implicitly the limitation of this objective. But perhaps I had better say in so many words that it will not be my contention that *all* our present troubles are of our own making. If all our policies since the war had been above reproach there would certainly have been many adverse circumstances which we should have had to contend with, the aftermath of the supreme effort of the mobilisation of the war economy, the growth of competition in third markets, the operation of the oil cartel, from time to time adverse turns in the terms of trade, and so on.

Nor would I wish to suggest that ours are the only difficulties in an otherwise prosperous and carefree Western world – others have their problems too. But it is my conviction that some at least of ours – and I should say a substantial part – would not be nearly so acute had our policies and conceptions of policy been different.

A GENERAL PERSPECTIVE

Before launching on this analysis, it is important to establish a general perspective. Our situation at the present time is grievous and humiliating: that the Federal Republic of Germany, part of an entity utterly defeated in the last war, with its cities partially obliterated, its industry disrupted, and its financial system in ruins, should now be the strongest economic power in Western Europe, with an income per head considerably exceeding our own, bringing support and succour to a depressed area like Italy, while we are going round cap in hand for loans to prevent an utter collapse of sterling: that surely is a circumstance which gives ground for serious thought and apprehension. But, if we take the period as a whole, it cannot be said to have been one of impoverishment for the inhabitants of this island. From 1951 to 1971 income per head increased at an average rate of some $2\frac{1}{2}$ per cent per annum. So that over the whole period the improvement was more than 60 per cent which, if not nearly so high as in many places elsewhere, at least in earlier days would have been regarded as gratifying.

Now averages do not tell us everything. And while I have no doubt that common observation bears out these indications of the solid improvement in the position of the common lot of the majority in this country – the increase of all sorts of amenities, travel, amusement, transport, clothing, and so on – I have equally no doubt that this has been accompanied by a relative impoverishment of many members of the upper-income brackets due to the increased price of services. When I was a young don in the 1920s, with an income of not much more than £800 a year, my wife and I could afford one maid living in and another coming in most days of the week. Nowadays with an income, even deflated by the ordinary cost-of-living index, substantially above that figure, we consider ourselves lucky to have occasional help. And this, in little, is what has been happening in many quarters, while the average has been advancing – a circumstance not frequently alluded to by propagandists of the egalitarian tendency. I hasten to say that I see nothing to grizzle about in all this. In the absence of inflation, the scarcity of domestic services is probably the best rough indication of comparative wealth: in the USA it is conspicuous; in large parts of Asia it is almost negligible. If we believe in increased power over nature and the consequent increase in wealth per head, this is one of the aspects of that process which we have to get used to.

Grounds for Disquiet

I draw attention to this brighter side of our recent history to make sure that it has a proper place in our present perspective, not in order to encourage any smugness about the past or to dispel present anxieties. For if we look at what has been happening elsewhere, there are indeed grounds for disquiet. I have alluded already to the comparison with Federal Germany. But this is not a unique circumstance. If we take as our yardstick GNP per head, so far as the Western world is concerned, we find that, in the last thirty or so years, we have slipped from a position eclipsed only by North America and Sweden, to one in which we are now well down the league tables, still somewhat ahead of Italy and Greece, but yearly being more and more outdistanced by most of the others.

Now military power apart – which in a frighteningly disordered world is still quite important – I would see no need to worry about this, if it were the result of a conscious decision to prefer leisure and the amenities of contemplation to material advancement. As Ricardo pointed out,

it is not the province of the Political Economist to advise – he is to tell you how to become rich – but he is not to tell you to prefer riches to indolence or indolence to riches.

But we know that in fact this is not the main cause of the difference. It is probably true that the representative worker in this country would prefer a somewhat lower income to what he would get now if he were prepared to work the hours of a hundred years ago, or what he could get if he were prepared to work as strenuously as some of his competitors now work elsewhere. But we know that in practice when there are reductions of hours, there is, in general, no lowering of absolute earnings: and cases of deliberate surrender of material well-being for the opportunity of increased contemplation or recreation are the exception rather than the rule. We tend to be discontented that our productivity is not better, but we are not willing to adopt policies which would remedy this defect.

Moreover, in the last few years this decline in our relative rate of growth has been accompanied by positive anxieties – a higher degree of inflation than elsewhere, a worsening position of the balance of payments, quite apart from the misfortune due to the exactions of the oil cartel, and, at the present time, a virtual certainty that we cannot emancipate ourselves from these misfortunes save by measures involving some depression of activity and some, though not necessarily catastrophic, temporary decline in our standard of living. There certainly is a case for investigation.

THE BURDEN OF TAXATION

Let me begin with the so-called burden of taxation; and let me say at once that, in my judgement, this is an area in which the utmost caution is necessary in formulating any conclusions. Tax systems are complex: one kind of tax may be better or worse than another from the point of view of its effects on GNP. The same may be said of different kinds of expenditure. We can agree that we are heavily taxed and that it would be agreeable if any beneficial results which may accrue from government expenditure could be achieved by a less onerous budget. But we need to choose our words very carefully if, in diagnosing detrimental effects, we are to indicate the direction and weight of our condemnation.

Thus, if we take what is usually the chief target in this connection, the burden of heavy and highly progressive direct taxation – which is certainly our lot in this country – I certainly do not think that we have any demonstrable justification for wide-sweeping generalisations about the effects on the incentive to work. *A priori* we cannot predict the result on production of just any increase in direct taxation: over a considerable range the effect of an increased tax bill may cause a man to work harder to maintain his standard of life, or it may make him decide to be content with less and spend more hours in his garden or on the golf course – or perhaps even to live elsewhere. Thus there is some case for a good deal of agnosticism.

But good sense suggests that this can go too far. We should all agree that a marginal rate of tax at 100p in the pound would be likely to cause quite a number of people to moderate their efforts and their willingness to take risks; and I do not see why similar considerations should not hold if the marginal rates are such as they are now as regards high incomes from work. It is really rather ridiculous to admit that a rate of 100 per cent must have serious effects on incentive and to argue that anything less leaves the incentive unaffected. So my judgement is that we have indeed suffered in this way, particularly as regards keenness and initiative. But I confess I find it difficult to put an order of magnitude on the evil.

INCENTIVES, SAVING AND INVESTMENT

When we come to saving I have fewer inhibitions; and since a deficiency in the proportion of GNP devoted to investment is certainly one of the less disputable figures which are relevant to a survey of our comparatively indifferent performance, this is important. It is important, too, in relation to a matter which will eventually form one of the main features of my diagnosis – our difficulties in restraining inflation.

As regards the *incentive* to save, I suppose some reserve should be expressed concerning the effects of direct taxation on the lower groups of income and wealth. The advocates of the 'we don't know what happens' school of thought, who are sometimes to be found among professional economists, never tire of pointing to the possibility of what Dennis Robertson, recalling an obscure Victorian writer, called the Sargant Man[1] – the man who will save more if the return is less, in order to maintain the objective of a constant investment income. I suppose this has some counterpart in real life at what, for short, can be called non-sadistic levels of taxation. But when we get into the higher reaches, when we get to rates even considerably lower than 98 per cent – the sort of thing which makes Mr Healey laugh – the supposition of many Sargant men per hundred of the relevant age group becomes somewhat remote. Who is going to be tempted to save at the prospect of a 2 per cent residue of whatever return on investment is available? And although, since the war, there has been plenty of money illusion about – as for instance with small savers who have been deceived by fraudulent government propaganda to lend at negative or low real rates of interest – the temptation to save for accumulation *per se* has surely been substantially eroded in recent years so that the effect is not favourable.

Ability to Save Diminished

If now we turn from the *incentive* to the *ability* to save, the conclusion must be still more unequivocal. The effect of taxation is to diminish the ability to save: that proposition is self-evident. And, although we cannot judge the effects of this on aggregate investment until we know how the proceeds of taxation are used, it would certainly show a marked degree of naiveté to argue that, in this country in the years since the war, the expenditure of government has been such as to make the volume of net material investment larger than it would have been had the volume of private saving been larger. The only possible escape, for those who dislike this conclusion, would be to argue that investment in human capital has been so much increased by various welfare expenditures that productivity in general has not suffered. Of this I can only say that, if they are content with that sort of argument, they will be content with anything.

INDUSTRIAL POLICY

I now turn to what may be called industrial policy. You will see as I proceed, that some at least of the points which emerge will reach forward to the matters of finance and aggregate expenditure which will be the final feature of my survey. But, for the time being, I want to ask to what extent policy in regard to industrial structure and industrial relations has contributed to the comparative indifference of our performance since the war and its culmination in our present difficulties.

Look first at the organisation of industry. In the years since the war the area of state ownership and control has been widely extended. For good or bad, for our time at least, we are truly a mixed economy. With the nationalisation in some form or other of coal, gas, electricity, rail and air transport and iron and steel, we certainly present to the outside world a picture of a semi-socialist industrial structure; and there is, I know, a school of thought which is inclined to regard this – just like that – as the root of all our troubles. I can remember friends and acquaintances who, in the troubles of the second half of the 1940s when the great nationalisations were taking place, went about attributing our difficulties to 'all this socialism'.

I confess that I have always found this over-simple. I just do not believe that the main troubles with the balance of payments of those days were at all connected with the contemporary measures of nationalisation. If there have been difficulties arising from such policies – and I believe that there have been many – they developed later. Moreover it should be noted that there were some nationalisations – railways, gas and electricity conspicuously – which mainly substituted one form of collectivist control for others – although it may have been less effective, as I sometimes suspect. We must remember too that similar controls have existed elsewhere where the rate of growth has been superior and the apprehensions regarding the general equilibrium of the system have been less.

I have fewer reserves about the detrimental influences flowing from the nationalisation of coal and steel. In the former case doubtless there was a certain political inevitability about what happened; but the political influences since then have not been helpful. As for the buffeting about of iron and steel, I can see no excuses whatever, only political frivolity.

Mixed Economy: 'Source of Weakness'

In general, taking a broader view, I have little doubt that in various ways the degree of 'mixity' in our industrial structure has been a source of weakness. This for two reasons.

First, to use two ugly words, there is the politicalisation and bureaucratisation of general policy regarding investment and price policy. Granted the desirability in some connections of some control in this sphere, I cannot believe that the time of the able men, recruited for the most part from private enterprise, who control these great operations is really best spent in the virtually unending conferences and correspondence with ministers and higher civil servants which form such a large part of their activities. It is all very well to argue that the immunity from parliamentary questions on matters of detail, which is the convention in this respect, is any solution as regards these larger questions of policy. I submit that the onus of proof rests fairly and squarely with those who argue that the patterns of investment and price policy which have been imposed on our public corporations by politics and public service procedures have been anything but a drag on the productivity of the system as a whole.

My second reason for attributing some at least of the difficulties of these years to this aspect of the mixed element in our system relates to the extent to which it is vulnerable in regard to the settlement of wage bargaining and the conduct of employment policy. In regard to both these matters I think many serious difficulties have emerged which would not have been nearly so acute if the state had not been so extensively involved. This, however, is a question which I can more conveniently deal with later on in another context.

RESTRICTIVE PRACTICES

I now come to an area in which the issues are not so elusive, even if it is still not possible to reach quantitative conclusions: the field of industrial relations. This has two leading aspects, the prevalence of restrictive practices – demarcation of functions, limitations on entry into particular groups, for instance – and strikes about pay. Needless to say, the prevalence of restrictive practices is not unconnected with the desire to influence rates of pay – indeed control of recruitment, either by way of direct limitation of numbers or the enforcement of unnecessary length of apprenticeships, is probably the most effective way in which organised unions or professions can secure incomes much higher than would otherwise be the case. But the division has meaning and each aspect deserves separate comment.

As regards the first I am inclined to be dogmatic. So far as the organisation of production is concerned, I can think of no factor which is a greater drag on efficiency than the degree of restrictive practice prevalent in this country as compared with most places elsewhere. I refrain from giving actual examples from my own experience in business. But, if you take comparative figures of per capita employment in leading industries here and abroad I see no escape from the conclusion that a substantial area of industry in this country is greatly overmanned; and, when one has discounted all other causes, restriction of function and job reservation seem to me to play a leading part. This is one part of the field where, if the unbelievable were to take place, namely a spontaneous abandonment of such practices, it would be possible to conceive of a great and almost immediate increase in productivity – the kind of thing which some leading politicians appear to envisage when they combine a 25 per cent increase in money supply with an actual rate of growth not likely to be much more than 4 or 5 per cent. The mismanagement of money apart, I regard restrictive practices as perhaps the most serious of our current problems.

Controls Required

It may be asked: 'But where does policy come in in this context?' In the old days it used to be argued that job restriction and control of entry were due to the prevalence of unemployment. Once that is removed, it was said, all this will disappear. Well, there has not been much unemployment, except in special areas, in the last quarter of a century; but we have not seen much relaxation of restrictive practices. I therefore ask myself whether government action of a different sort is not called for. One of the significant – and welcome – changes in public policy since the war has been the introduction of law and an administrative and judicial apparatus for dealing with monopoly and restrictive practices in the control of industrial undertakings. I was not born yesterday; and I am not unaware that the question may sound naive, especially in our present position. But it is really not irrelevant to ask at least what are the logical and ethical reasons why trade unions and professional associations should be exempt in such respects? The virtual *absence* of control is surely a significant factor.

After the rather tough and downright line which I have just taken in regard to restrictive practices, you may be surprised to hear me say that the problems, both of the effects and of the desirable law regarding industrial disputes, are of much greater complexity. I imagine that we can all think of cases in which the effects of an industrial dispute might be catastrophic and the desirability of special legislation to prevent such a dispute incontestable. If, for instance, at some time in the future the entire supply of energy in a certain area were to derive from a single installation based on atomic fusion, it is surely clear that a walk-out on the part of the highly specialised staff could bring the affairs of the whole community to a standstill and that therefore a contract of engagement, similar to that of military service, would be appropriate, with very severe penalties for violation.

Fortunately for the world up to date, the development of techniques has not yet faced us with the necessity of such extreme measures as this. And it is my belief, which I think could be borne out by the examination of statistics, that, in the main, *up to quite recently*, the effects of strikes and such-like disturbances can be greatly exaggerated. Until the dock strike which helped to precipitate the devaluation of 1967, I would say that, in my lifetime, the only strike in this country to which the adjective 'disastrous' could be applied, as regards general repercussions on the health of the economy, was the coal strike of the middle-1920s, and we know that that was predominantly due to a flagrantly bad monetary policy which, by an over-valuation of the pound, created a position in which the mining industry, so dependent then on export sales, was suddenly confronted with a position in which the standard of living of the miners was seriously jeopardised.

Strikes and the Economy

Speaking generally, I would say that although strikes can be a terrible nuisance, yet the principle of liberty to withhold the supply of labour, if the terms offered are considered to be inadequate, is so important that, if the system of law and public finance is such that *those who withhold labour are made to bear the full consequences of their action and are precluded from violent interference with alternative sources of supply*, a free society should be prepared to put up with the occasional inconvenience which such action involves. Examination of the figures, from the middle of the last century until the end of the Second World War, does not suggest that strikes have greatly deflected the course of economic history. Save where there has existed tight sectional monopolies due to control of entry and such-like restrictions, most strikes have not done much more than confirm, as it were, the broad tendencies of demand and supply in the labour markets concerned. It is a mistake to regard the widespread rise in real earnings of the last hundred years as chiefly due to trade union action. It was due to general influences working for economic growth.

In recent years, however, the picture has become more complicated. The provisions of our form of welfare state have relieved trade union funds of some at least of the financial consequences of withdrawal of labour to an extent which has little parallel in the past or elsewhere. Furthermore, the existence of large areas of nationalised industry where the existence of what is believed to be a sort of 'widow's curse' in the shape of subsidies from the public purse, have made demands in that quarter much less related to conditions of profitability. In my judgement at least, this has played an appreciable part in the origin of the inflation on the cost side which has been the cause of so many difficulties in the last few years. But this brings me to the next stage of my argument.

GROWTH AND INFLATION

This is a section to which I attach critical importance in the interpretation of our misfortunes. The policies – or absence of policies – which I have been discussing hitherto would in any event have been some drag on efficiency. Their prevalence does much to explain the failure to achieve a higher rate of growth in the period under discussion. But in themselves they would not have led us to the troubles characteristic of the period. Given an appropriate match between aggregate expenditure and the value of the national product at constant, or slightly rising prices, we should have been left with growth figures probably better than those I quoted at the beginning – which were not too bad by historical comparison – and the recurrent external crises; and the present position in which we hover on the brink of a major economic and social catastrophe, would not have emerged. The central responsibility for the anxieties of this postwar period lies fairly and squarely with excess expenditure and inflation. Even the difficulties which are due to the activities of the oil cartel would be manageable if it were not for that.

Evils of Inflation

As is well known, the nature of the trouble is two-fold. If we were living in a closed community or in no important connection with the rest of the world, a fall in the purchasing power of money of the order of magnitude of recent experience would still be a grave evil. I will not dwell on the substantial impoverishment of all those who live on fixed incomes arising from savings – a class whose troubles are not likely to excite the compassion, though they may arouse the mirth, of some highly placed persons. Nor will I expatiate at length on the distortion of production planning, the cumulative inadequacy of working capital in a *milieu* where accountants still proceed on the assumption that governments will do their duty to maintain the stability of the value of money – one of the main causes of our present liquidity crisis. These and other embarrassments, although regarded until very recently as rather sophisticated refinements of outlook only indulged in by mere academics, are now very painfully obvious. But I do think it desirable to emphasise the cumulative effects of inflation on the solidarity and standards of society. The growth of class consciousness in a society where there is less division between the classes than ever before, the violence of labour disputes, the lapses from commercial and personal honesty which are there for all to see, derive largely from the casino-like atmosphere which rising prices engender. There is no better way of destroying the basis of free societies than the recent rates of inflation in Great Britain.

All this, as I have said, would occur in an isolated society. In the world of open international connections in which we live, there are further menacing possibilities. If the rate of inflation in any one area is larger than the rate of inflation elsewhere, then there are apt to arise difficulties with the balance of payments. Imports rise, exports are embarrassed. As the situation develops, reserves seem to be more and more inadequate and there arises the danger of withdrawals of foreign capital. With the kind of adverse balance which we are running at present, or even the balance which we should be running were we not mortgaging in advance future benefits from North Sea oil, the possibility of a situation in which there may be a real shortage of essential foods and raw materials, due to lack of foreign exchange, is no longer a figment of the imagination. And let me interpolate that that situation is not to be taken care of automatically by the floating exchange rate. In present circumstances a large downward fluctuation of sterling is more likely to accelerate the internal inflation, *via* the effects on the cost of living and wage bargains, than to restore some equilibrium relationship with the outside world.

CAUSES OF INFLATION

What are the causes of all this? To listen to the pronouncements of some at least of those who bear the main responsibility, one might imagine that they are of a completely impersonal and uncontrollable nature – a world disease, so to speak, as if some new influenza virus had appeared for which no adequate vaccine has been discovered, and therefore those who bear the burden of government are to be pitied rather than condemned. But this will not do. It may be that the temper of the times – whatever that means – is inflationary and that other nations have their problems too. But it is also true that the degree of inflation is not uniform and that the greater the degree of governmental prudence the less the damage. It is really no accident that the Federal Republic of Germany is now financially the strongest power in Europe and that we are (nearly) the weakest. Or must we make the assumption that we need to be defeated in two wars and have our economic structure in physical ruins, before our political leaders are in a position to do their duty in regard to the value of money?

The plain truth is that inflation is due to human action: it is not the product of some mysterious *Zeitgeist*. It may arise on the demand side as a result of budgetary deficits of the type of which we have had recent experience. It may arise on the same side, the side of demand, from an investment boom engendered by rates of interest radically below expectations of profit and financed by the creation of credit not matched by increases in the propensity to save – a state of affairs, as I have said earlier, which may easily be a possible consequence of the effects of taxation on the incentive and ability to save. It may arise on the cost side from demands by associations of producers involving claims on the real national product greatly exceeding the prospective or even possible increases in productivity.

One Underlying Condition

Thus there can be many initial causes. But they are all subject to one underlying condition, namely, *that the supply of money or the credit base – call it what you will – is allowed to increase so as to permit their operation.* This is obvious on the demand side: all plans for deficit financing and inflationary borrowing would have to be speedily modified if finance were not forthcoming. But it is true on the cost side too: if the money supply were inelastic in regard to excessive demands for higher earnings and prices, such movements would exhaust themselves in rising unemployment and the piling-up of stocks.

Thus the deciding control rests with those whose duty it is to provide reasonable stability in the value of money. I would not go all the way with those who, like Mr Powell, argue that *no* responsibility rests with those who make extravagant plans or claims. I can see what they mean but I find their use of words paradoxical. It is clear to me that the ultimate responsibility lies with government; and I am also clear that, from time to time and especially in recent years, our own governments have not lived up to this responsibility.

Spectre of the Thirties

Why has this happened? What intellectual influences have been at work? I would agree that some of the influences have not been intellectual; there have been unaccountable psychological blind-spots in some high quarters, not to mention elements of pure destructionism elsewhere. But, in the main, ours is still a reasonable and peaceful society; and, for errors of the kind which have been made in the last few years to be received with acquiescence or even support, there must have existed genuine misapprehensions and misunderstandings which have been an obstacle to more sensible policies.

I have no doubt that a naive belief that high-pressure demand is the best way to achieve growth has had something to do with it. But to understand the deeper causes I think we must go back some way. Our present troubles are, at least in part, an illustration of the chronic tendency to fight today's battles in terms of the tactics and strategy appropriate to those of yesterday; and much of the policy of the period since the war has been based on the analysis and presumptions applicable to the interwar period. Then, in the 1930s, the great evil was deflation; and many of us, including, I am sorry to say, myself, were apt to give exhortations to financial prudence which would only have been justified if the system had been working at a reasonably brisk level of activity. What was needed then, as we all see now in the light of historical statistics, was financial expansion rather than prudence, still less contraction. And, as this came to be realised and as expenditure on rearmament and the commencement of hostilities showed what powers lay in the hands of governments to increase employment and economic activity when starting from a collapsed position, a strong determination to use such power in the future to prevent a recurrence of the troubles of the 1930s became accepted policy among most men of good will. Add to this the belief, which was also widely prevalent, that the end of the war, after perhaps a brief flare-up in the shape of a re-stocking boom, would see a relapse into tendencies to stagnation if something were not done about it, and it is easy to see how, by the beginning of the postwar period, the maintenance of demand for labour had become a dominating influence on the conduct of policy. As is well known, the wartime coalition government here issued an agreed White Paper committing themselves to the maintenance of high levels of employment.[2]

Now in my judgement, there can be no possible objection to the intention so to manage things as to avoid contractions of aggregate expenditure such as we now know were the main cause of the magnitude of the depression of the 1930s. Having been on the wrong side in this respect at that time, I should be very sorry indeed if I gave the impression that what I am about to say implied any support for the view that when aggregate expenditure has collapsed, as it did then, there is no need for governments to do anything about it. But the blanket pledge to maintain a high level of employment involves ambiguities which I think have confused much thinking ever since.[3]

Statistical Ambiguity of 'Full Employment'

First, there is an ambiguity about the quantitative significance of the term 'full employment'. By all existing methods of measurement there can never be full employment, in the sense of zero unemployed, save in a completely immobilised society where there are no changes in supply and demand. But where there are shifts in the necessary deployment of the labour force, as in the deployment of an army, there will always be some people changing jobs who will be caught in the statistical net. There will also always be some seasonal unemployment and a certain number of unemployables included. Before the war, when the labour force of the UK was considerably smaller than it is now, Keynes warned that, when it was reduced to some half million, the problems of 'full employment' would present themselves. Even Beveridge, whose recommendation of a labour market in which demand always exceeded supply was a prize recommendation for non-stop inflation, thought that his policy *could* – hopefully – bring about an *average* unemployment of 3 per cent. Now, since the war, with occasional exceptions, the percentage here has usually been far below that figure. Yet such are present expectations of what is practicable and desirable that the actual figure has only to rise a decimal point or two and even the non-sensational press will give the matter banner headlines on the front page. I cannot resist a certain compassion for ministers, with whose attitudes I usually have a minimum of sympathy, when they have to manoeuvre within such exacting constraints.

Secondly, and this is even more important, the undertaking to maintain high levels of employment – just like that – involved no reference to rates of wages. Now, whatever may be thought of the effect on employment of lowering rates of wages – which is a highly controversial matter – there can really be no doubt at all that claims for increases which greatly exceed the increase in productivity in general will certainly produce unemployment unless there is a corresponding inflation of the credit base and prices to provide a matching increase of aggregate expenditure. I am quite sure that those who, during the war, declared a policy of preventing the unemployment which was due to a contraction of aggregate demand, had no intention whatever of guaranteeing just any rate of inflation which cost increases of this kind would make necessary, if the unqualified promise to maintain high levels of employment were to be fulfilled.

Flawed Guarantee

Yet failure to recognise the unreason of such a guarantee is surely one of the main causes of our recent troubles. Professor Phelps Brown has calculated[4] that, if all incomes over £3000 per annum were to be appropriated for redistribution, then, after adjustment for loss of tax revenue and supposing – which is unlikely – that there was no loss of production, there would remain a 5 per cent increase for the rest. No wonder that claims of many times that order of magnitude must give rise to either unemployment or inflation. Let me make myself quite clear on this point. I would be very sorry indeed to be thought to attribute *all* the inflation which has taken place since the war, to influences on the cost side. There have certainly been abundant influences on the demand side, too, in the shape of deliberate deficit financing and artificially low rates of interest. Nevertheless I am inclined to attribute much of our present difficulties to the response or the absence of a response to this kind of pressure – namely for increases of incomes not justified by general increases in production.

THE REMEDY

What then is the remedy? Many fellow economists whom I respect have long urged the desirability of a general policy of statutory control of incomes – with, of course, control of prices thrown in to mollify injured feelings. Only in this way, they contend, can we achieve stability in employment and stability in the value of money.

Now I frankly confess that I am sceptical of the long-run effectiveness of such policies, to say nothing of their compatibility with the fundamentals of a free society. All experience hitherto suggests that, after a short time, they break down. The freeze, which is the crudest form, rapidly breeds an overwhelming sense of injustice, especially on the part of those who have just been left out. More sophisticated experiments, with upper limits subject to exceptions and adjustments, may last longer; but hitherto they have broken on the unwillingness of employers and employed to be thus regimented in the demand for and supply of labour. Even if policies of this sort were ideologically acceptable – which they palpably are not to many very differing schools of thought – the sheer difficulty of judging *without market indications* what should be the appropriate rate for differing grades of ability and assiduity seems, at least hitherto, to defy the best efforts of administrative ingenuity. I do not believe that any suggestions that have yet been put forward, either as regards administrative organisation or technical criteria, begin to solve the long-term problem of viable incomes policies.

Incomes Policy: A Temporary Aid

This is not to say, however, that, as emergency measures, such policies are altogether to be dismissed. I do believe that, in emergencies such as that with which we have been confronted recently, there is a case to be made for *temporary* policies of this sort – not on the grounds that they can be made to last forever or that they guarantee social fairness and so on, but *simply that they may help to prevent more unemployment than is absolutely inevitable* if inflation is to be arrested.

Let me spell this out a little. If it be admitted, as it surely must be, that inflation is only to be checked by reduction of the excess of aggregate expenditure over the probable increase of production, then, if there continue to be claims for pay increases vastly greater than the GNP can carry without inflation, the reduction of the offending rate of increase must necessarily be accompanied by more unemployment than would have occurred if the claims had not been made. A check on excessive claims, therefore, crude though it be, may permit the imposition of the necessary fiscal and monetary restraints without causing as much dislocation as would otherwise take place. In a word, a temporary incomes policy of some kind or other is to be justified – if it is to be justified at all – in terms of its help in moderating the increase of unemployment, which in the absence of such restraint – or a similar restraint voluntarily imposed – must for a time be the inevitable result of an appreciable check to inflation.

I am sorry to say, however, this has not been the conception of the recent past. Until the position had become well nigh untenable, the government of 1970–74 pursued virtually inconsistent policies. Becoming convinced that something must be done about inflation, with some courage and in the face of many earlier failures, it imposed controls on incomes and prices. But at the same time, instead of using these controls as a means of mitigating the less agreeable consequences of the adoption of financial prudence, it went ahead with credit expansion and deficit budgeting on a scale unprecedented, I believe, in the peacetime history of this country. This was bound to frustrate the main justification of the policy. I do not say this by way of condemnation of intentions which were doubtless strictly honourable – we all live in glasshouses and should avoid throwing stones. But the moral of the episode deserves not to be forgotten.

Full Employment Cannot be Guaranteed

Where then are we to turn? I am quite clear as regards the ultimate objective, which I hope flows from what I have said already. The principle of employment policy is surely obvious. We should avoid the unemployment due to positive deflation – which, all writers on these subjects present please note, is not (repeat *not*) at all the same thing as reducing the *rate* of excess increase of money. But we should not guarantee the maintenance of employment whatever it costs in terms of inflation. The government should not fail to do what is necessary to maintain reasonably high rates of employment at incomes rising, roughly speaking, with the value of GNP at constant or slightly rising prices. But beyond that, it should be for individuals and groups of individuals to choose between this kind of stability and unemployment.

All this is easy enough to say – though it has taken a long time for some people to see it. But it is not so easy to achieve. I hope that nothing that I have said here will be taken as a recommendation for rash application of the brakes. To reduce the increase of the credit base from the, perhaps, 20 per cent excess at which it was running in 1973 to zero or even single figures within 12 months, in my judgement would be a grave over-reaction. We need policies more cautious and more complicated than that. But they are another story. All that I have tried to do here is to put certain policies of the past into what I hope is something like a true analytical and historical perspective. I am afraid it is a gloomy story. But in the truly deplorable situation in which we now find ourselves, we are lost if we do not learn from our mistakes.

NOTES

1. D. H. Robertson, *Utility and All That*, Allen & Unwin, London, 1952, p. 100.
2. *Employment Policy*, Cmd. 6527, HMSO, 1944.
3. In this connection I may be permitted to refer to my critique of Beveridge's *Full Employment in a Free Society*, entitled *Full Employment as an Objective*, written in 1949 and reprinted in *Money, Trade and International Relations*, Macmillan, London, 1971.
4. *Where Do Rises in Pay Come From?*, issued by Working Together, London, 1974.

5 The Credibility of Liberal Economics*

Alan Peacock

THE TASK

In 1836 at the close of an article in the *London Review* on 'Whether Political Economy is Useful', the protagonist of political economy, 'Mr B', whom James Mill uses to expound his views to 'Mr A', concludes with the resounding words:

> The people, therefore, in the legislature, void of knowledge, who say they distrust and despise political economy, make no presumption against the doctrines against which they vent only a senseless noise.... There is no branch of human knowledge more entitled to respect; and the men who affect to hold it in contempt afford indication only against themselves.[1]

Harold Wincott, I am sure, would have relished these words, believing as he did that politicians tended to avoid the main issues of economic policy not only through ignorance but also through funk. He used the dialogue as a technique of exposition very much in the manner of James Mill and, as Lord Robbins said of him, 'there is little that is alien to his lively eye and penetrating comment'.[2]

Stemming the Flood

While it is tempting to pursue this parallel in the British pamphleteering tradition, it is the contrast in the positions of James Mill and Harold Wincott which makes the theme of this chapter. One senses in Harold Wincott's later writings that he saw himself trying to stem a flood-tide of plausible but specious arguments attacking the market economy, whereas James Mill, like many of his sympathetic contemporaries, wrote as if on the crest of a wave.

In James Mill's time, the intellectual sons of Adam Smith were a close-knit fraternity, facing no professional rivals of their quality and influence in Britain. They had an effective propaganda machine in the form of the famous Reviews, such as the *Edinburgh* and the *Westminster*, and, with the possible exception of their controversial views on population, they were popular with the increasingly influential bourgeoisie and even with the radical politicians, for their attacks on what James Mill called 'regal and aristocratical servitude'. Even as late as 1872, it was to his son John Stuart Mill that Emily Davies, the first Mistress of Girton, wrote for a list of questions to be studied by her class in Political Economy.[3] (The imagination boggles at the thought of the present Mistress of that institution or, better still, the Principal of Newnham, Mrs Jean Floud, seeking such advice from, say, Milton Friedman.)

Today's intellectual descendants of the classical political economists – the liberals with a small 'l' – face a very different situation.

Wrong Motives

Consider our present preoccupation with trying to match our productive performance with the level of popular aspirations in growing real income, and add in the liberal prescription that the matching process must be compatible with maintaining individual freedom. It is widely assumed by those influential in policy discussion that liberal objectives are mutually incompatible anyway and that growth aspirations can be achieved only by much more (and not much less) economic planning associated with selective governmental intervention in the economy and further curtailment of individual freedom. It is further believed that liberals appeal to the wrong motives in emphasising the spur offered by material rewards within a competitive system, rather than by the call of 'patriotism' and close co-operation between the industrial 'estates of the realm' and government in the 'public interest'. In consequence their policy recommendations and the associated instruments, such as the reduction in high marginal rates of tax on earned income, the restoration of profitability in private industry, and the improvement in the allocation of capital through a properly working capital market in the private sector, are manifestations of mortal sin.

These attacks on traditional liberal political economy are misconceived, particularly those which brand both Classical economists and their heirs as rampant supporters of *laissez-faire*; but strong vested interests have been created in a mythology of liberal economic thought, especially among those who wish to remain protected from the rigours of market forces. Thus a Minister of the Crown whom I heard announce that he was 'deeply devoted to the distortion of the free market' may be emitting in James Mill's words 'a senseless noise' or be badly advised, but he is clearly far from being on the defensive.[4]

Though I must say something about a liberal view of our present troubles, I am more immediately concerned with how it has come about that what may fairly be described as an eclectic body of economic thought with a long and honourable tradition may now be fighting for survival in political and governmental, if not in academic, circles.

I am therefore in much the same position as my friend, Thomas Keir, a Minister, not of the Crown but of the Kirk, who writing 30 years ago did not question the tenets of his faith but sought 'to discover what impedes their acceptance'.[5] Only if we examine what he called 'the intellectual and emotional occasions of hesitancy' which confront liberal solutions to our present difficulties can we discover what are the best ways of removing doubt and making the voice of reason both welcome and influential.

THE BACKGROUND

I can obviously assume familiarity with the major propositions of liberal political economy and the kinds of attack which have been made on them. In offering some background to the present problem of maintaining and extending the credibility of liberal views, I need only refer to the contrast between the growth of the public sector and its influence on all aspects of our daily life and on liberal support for Adam Smith's 'system of natural liberty' which, though not laissez-fairist, associates the wholesale exercise of authority over the use of resources by the state as damaging to both individual freedom and economic progress.

Consider the present controversy over the size of the public sector. A good deal of the argument is concerned with the short-term problem of stabilisation. That problem is certainly made more difficult by the inability (or unwillingness?) of governments to control the size of the public deficit, and therefore the money supply and interest rates. It is also concerned with the general problem of re-allocating resources, as the Public Expenditure White Papers show, between public and private consumption and investment so that something like the long-term average investment/Gross Domestic Product ratio can be restored. I am not concerned here with this problem, except to say that it is easy to sympathise with any government trying to undo past mistakes which make budget adjustments of this kind so difficult today.

Immense Distortions

Less obvious but just as important are the immense distortions produced in the economy by a large, expanding, and highly centralised
public sector. Such distortions constrain individual initiative and therefore
reduce the efficiency with which resources are used. Such distortions
are compounded by the use of regulatory instruments on top of financial
controls whose effects often appear to cancel one another out.

(i) 'Motivation' Distortion

The first distortion might be called 'motivation' distortion. Let me give
an example. A private firm, in order to survive, must be able to make
a return on its capital which is at least as high as the return which
could be made by the alternative use of its capital funds. However, to
perform this operation now requires an important set of skills which
have increasingly less to do with satisfying the needs of current and
potential final consumers. An enormous amount of time and effort has
to be devoted to determining how and to what degree the actions of government are likely to determine the profitability, location and even the
products of business operations. The acquisition of investible funds is
becoming increasingly dependent on the decisions of a handful of civil
servants entrusted with the onerous and awesome task of administer-
ing grants and loans under the Industry Acts. The reputation of major
firms becomes more dependent on the public activities of its directors
as members of government bodies of all kinds. To be seen working
for the common good has some bearing on how a firm may be regarded when it comes to the negotiation of government support and
the award of government contracts.

One Hundred Acts to Track A whole panoply of measures as old as
the companies legislation of the nineteenth-century and as new as the
Employment Protection Act must be scrutinised in order for firms to
keep on the right side of government. It was recently estimated that a
public company has to keep track of at least 100 major Acts of Parliament to do so. The results of the augmentation of selective government intervention and further attempts to influence firms through
'planning agreements' add a new dimension to what must be regarded
as a major deterrent to the efficient operation of business, namely the
high opportunity cost of 'interface with government' alongside the
foregone alternative of concentrating on the job of producing what
customers want and meeting delivery dates.

(ii) Production 'Mix' Distortion

The second distortion relates to the production 'mix'. It seems in the nature of things that large, centralised government not directly subject to the discipline of the market generates both allocational inefficiency and production inefficiency – the wrong things produced at more than minimum average cost. The most dramatic example of misallocation is provided by the enormous expenditure on 'launching aid' for aerospace projects. Over a period of nearly 30 years from 1945 governments underwrote losses of at least £1.3 billion at 1974 prices. It would require a great feat of imagination to believe that the uncovenanted benefits, in the form of technological spin-off and national morale, given the alternative uses of resources, could make up the loss difference.[6] Latterly the policy of constraining the pricing and investment decisions of the nationalised fuel industries by government income redistribution objectives makes nonsense of any attempt to stimulate competitive conditions – an attempt which experience suggests is bound to fail – in the public corporation sector.

The mistakes of saddling a public corporation with vaguely defined social objectives, on top of even vaguer financial criteria, are repeated in the guidelines for the National Enterprise Board. If one wanted to be sure that the Board's role should conform to the main object of the current industrial strategy, it would seem sensible to judge its success in terms of the speed with which it could return convalescent industries to the private sector – subject to the strict condition that it should raise new capital not from government (i.e. taxpayers) but from reinvested profits and/or the capital market. This would at least give it a veneer of economic respectability.

(iii) Misallocation of Factor Inputs

It follows that the first two distortions imply a third – the misallocation of factor inputs. This misallocation is worsened by government legislation which perpetuates imperfections in the labour market and hinders labour mobility by a housing subsidy policy which does not even achieve its supposed objective of helping the poor. I want only to emphasise the special skills and ingenuity required in operating a system of economic controls, ranging from price and wage policies to micro-intervention in industry, not to speak of important social services, when the market is set aside as a method of allocation. It is no wonder therefore that the inevitable accompaniment of a large and growing public sector is the draining of skilled manpower into the bureaucratic machine – and one can't altogether blame those who have taken on the task of beating the market at its own game.[7] It is significant that the certainly unintended effect of the educational expansion of the late 1960s has been to man-up traditionally labour-intensive services in the non-market sector, where productivity gains must be relatively low.

One must be careful here for, in principle at least, there is no reason to believe that the technology of government services is invariably labour-intensive, but as they are not marketed, the usual spurs to technical innovation are lacking and permanent employment contracts instituted for other reasons make any process of change operate slowly.

Lack of Pressure for Change: Public Sector Influence

It would be easy to produce a compendium of statements by a wide cross-section of the community, public servants included, which would offer general support to this analysis. So the question remains why there is so little public pressure on politicians in Britain to make radical changes. One possible reason is lack of opportunity for individuals, as voters, to participate in the political process to anything like the extent available to voters in more decentralised democracies.

A more powerful reason is that the influence of the public sector is so widespread, and so important financially to individual households and firms, that the benefits of a reduction in its size to any given household seem uncertain. It might be generally agreed that the public sector should be reduced in size, but few have a direct interest in offering to forgo the advantages they derive from government services, subsidies, grants, etc. if others cannot be enjoined to do the same. Moreover, a double bargain has to be struck covering not only the amount and the form of cuts in public expenditure, but also the distribution of the resultant gains in the form of cuts in taxes. Even if there were no bargaining costs incurred in seeking agreement, and if there were much greater participation in the political process, there could be no guarantee that the desired result could be achieved.

This kind of problem is supposed to confront liberals with a difficult dilemma; for if large-scale, centralised, public action were the outcome of freely expressed choices, simulating as near as possible freedom of choice in competitive markets, why should liberals oppose them? The answer is simple but somehow mystifying to the mathematicians of fiscal politics. Liberal political economists will support those democratic systems and market systems which give full expression to individual choice but they do not necessarily have to like the results.

The dilemma of liberals does not lie in their dislike of some of the outcomes of a democratic system of choice which they themselves fought to introduce, but in how to persuade and certainly not to force the community to make choices which preserve their own freedom. But before considering a strategy of persuasion, I must examine why the credibility of liberal economics is called in question.

THE SUPPLY OF LIBERAL POLITICAL ECONOMY

The vigorous and critical examination of the political economy of government, and of suggestions for its reform, is therefore as important today as it was to Adam Smith in his famous attack on the Mercantile System.[8] It calls for a wide knowledge of the structure of society and of economic history, analytical skill and practical insight. If, as a result of such examination, the political economist finds himself nailing his colours to the liberal mast and becoming imbued with a crusading spirit, he faces the exhausting though exciting prospect of public disputation, and, in the present climate of opinion, the risk of being pilloried for his pains. The first impediment to the acceptance of liberal political economy therefore lies in the high opportunity cost attached to acquiring the necessary knowledge, skill and stamina to maintain the supply of ideas and policy recommendations.

The task I have outlined for an economist anxious to put forward his views on the state of society contrasts markedly with the role which academic economists assume in their daily lives. In the course of my academic lifetime, the economics journals have become incomprehensible to anyone except the cognoscenti. (I date the fateful moment when economists became members of an exclusive professional coterie from the day about 25 years ago when Tom Marshall, one of our most eminent sociologists, announced in the LSE common room that he had regretfully cancelled his subscription to the *Economic Journal*. He was prepared to accept that he might not understand most of the articles but the moment of truth came when he could not even decipher the meaning of the title 'Does the Matrix Multiplier Oscillate?'.)

No Protection against Ethical Bias

I do not wish to provide knocking copy for those who would jeer at these developments since marvellous and good things may come from the workshops of economics researchers which may be of ultimate benefit to mankind. However, the illusion that mathematical skill is a protection against the penetration of ethical bias and a complete substitute for imaginative insight into the workings of the economic system is widespread. Those of you who would seek inspiration and instruction from the normal staff and graduate seminars need to be warned that they are often arid, joyless affairs. A fashionable hypothesis is considered, reasons are given why it may be incomplete, an extra term may be added to the basic equation purporting to represent some behavioural characteristics of economic agents, a standard econometric testing procedure is deployed to show how the modified hypothesis stands up. There is then some discussion about the speaker's knowledge of the literature, about the quality of the data and the suitability of the tests, and above all the elegance of the model. Then everyone adjourns to the bar satisfied that the subject is still open and that fortunately the speaker has observed the proprieties of discourse by concluding that 'further research is needed' – hopefully to be financed by the SSRC!

This widely practised ritual is indicative of the motivation of the younger creative members of the economics profession. Though interested in the efficiency of the market they are largely immune from its immediate pressures; in such circumstances it is only natural that they should seek to maximise their reputation within their peer group rather than concern themselves with the training requirements of the employers of their students or with public enlightenment. Moreover, it is in their economic interests to do so provided they wish to remain in academic life, for their promotion prospects will be geared to what their universities and faculties consider important, notably the strength of publication in the top academic journals. In this situation why incur the time and energy costs of seeking to reform the world with the further prospect, for a liberal political economist, of retailing 'reactionary' ideas which embarrass one's academic colleagues?

Of course, I have exaggerated and must add two important qualifications to my argument. The first is that there are outstanding liberal members of the profession who combine a reputation as influential writers on policy matters with important contributions to the scientific development of economics but, following the predictions of their own analysis, they have an understandable tendency to emigrate! The comparative advantage they may have, together with other distinguished overseas economists, in supplying *us* with liberal ideas is more apparent than real. They are no longer in the line of fire.

How Welfare Economics has Changed

The second qualification is represented by the strong hold still exercised over a large section of the profession by the branch of the subject known as welfare economics. The tenets of its most fashionable version, going back to Pareto and Pigou, are considered as the foundation of 'sound' views on policy matters and are based on a number of propositions which might appear attractive to liberal economists. Ignoring finer points of interpretation,[9] it is initially assumed that individual welfare is what counts and that individuals are the best judges of their own welfare. From familiar assumptions of economic behaviour, prescriptions about the optimal production and the allocation of resources and sometimes the optimal distribution of resources are put forward which at first sight seem to imply strong support for a free market system with the government confining its activities to certain basic services, such as defence and law and order, for some transfer measures to remove major disparities in the distribution of income and wealth (though this usually requires further initial value and behavioural assumptions), and for measures which promote competition in factor and product markets.

It is interesting to observe that as welfare economics has developed it has tended to support more and more government intervention. Latter-day Pigovians continue to discover new examples of 'market failure'. Goods such as education are under provided by the market because producers cannot capture those benefits of supply which accrue to the community at large. Producers may impose costs on others, e.g. through pollution, which are not reflected in their costs of production. Cases where social benefits and costs diverge from private benefits and costs certainly abound, though the divergences may be very difficult to quantify; but the existence of market failure leads welfare economists all too readily to assume that there is an efficient and costless form of government action always at hand to rectify the market's deficiencies. The range of suggested action varies with each example of deficiency from elaborate tax and subsidy schemes to direct controls and public takeover of production as in the so-called 'natural monopoly' case. Seldom are the costs of the control methods themselves evaluated and the kinds of distortion inevitably associated with bureaucratic control, which I have already discussed, are conveniently forgotten.

Blend of Acuity and Naiveté

The curious idea that welfare economics is innocent of political judge-
ments, or at least is based on a set of value statements that only mo-
rons would oppose, is difficult to explain but, as Lord Robbins has
recently reminded us,[10] the notion displays a lack of sophistication in
marked contrast to the Classical economists. The fact remains that its
adherents appear to believe that they have made notable advances in
the field of public policy whereas what is normally found in their specu-
lations is a curious blend of often penetrating observation of the workings
of the market system with an astonishingly naive view of the political
and bureaucratic process. Moreover, in so far as the forms of government intervention are specified, one fortunate side-effect is support for
the generation of employment opportunities for economists!

THE EMOTIONAL RESISTANCE TO LIBERAL POLITICAL ECONOMY[11]

I now turn to the demand for liberal ideas in order to examine the
nature and if possible the extent of sales resistance, beginning first of
all with 'the emotional occasions of hesitancy'. This is a large and
treacherous field of inquiry and what I have to say can at most be
suggestive.

It is ironic that the most striking contemporary example of Keynes's
dictum that 'practical men ... are usually the slaves of some defunct
economist' is to be found in the influence of Keynes himself. We all
know that a rounded view of his work would lead one to be wary of
concluding that he believed capitalist economies would suffer from
long-run underemployment of resources, and would need large and continuous government deficits to raise output and employment. The fact
remains that these are the central ideas with which he is widely associated. Unfortunately these ideas gave strong encouragement to one
of the most influential fantasies among otherwise intelligent beings,
namely that the problem of scarce resources and the conflicts of choice
to which it gives rise are pure inventions.

Keynesianism and Utopia

The popular, highly vulgarised, version of Keynesianism – that the
problem of production has been solved by maintaining aggregate demand,

and that the only economic problem is distribution – is a marvellous tonic for those who have Utopian visions of society. To give only one example, Lewis Mumford in his famous book *The Culture of Cities*, on which generations of town planners have been reared, stated that

> Fortunately, our civilisation as a whole is now at a point technically where it is feasible to give the population as a whole that basis in good breeding and good nurture which has hitherto been the exclusive possession of aristocracies.[12]

Only appropriate distributional and allocational policies were needed to turn megalopolis into paradise because splendid housing and perceptive planning would produce moral regeneration alongside economic sufficiency.

There are copious examples which replicate Mumford's dream of gracious living coupled with transformation in the human character, the latest being associated with the bucolic paradises of radical economists in which market relations disappear and in the process peaceful cooperation will replace competition to produce a life of 'luxe, calme et volupté'.

The Obscene Heresy

The obscene heresy of liberal economists has been to continue to support two propositions derived from the teaching of our intellectual antecedents. The first, derived from Hume and Smith, is that human nature changes little. In Hume's words,

> men are not able radically to cure, either in themselves or others, that narrowness of soul which makes them prefer the present to the remote. They cannot change their natures. All they can do is to change their situation ...[13]

The second proposition points to the limits to change in man's situation imposed by the problem of scarce resources which have competing uses, that is to say, the rejection of the vulgarised, popular view of the Keynesian message of abundance. If we couple these two constraints, derived from introspection and empirical observation, with the liberal's preference for personal liberty – only restricted to the extent that is necessary to ensure adequate realisation of and access to its benefits for all – then pronouncement of the anathema by those who believe they know what is good for us is a sure thing, because the inevitable consequence of the liberal position is that there is no possibility of an orderly heaven on earth. At most, we approach a tolerable, perhaps almost comfortable, though certainly unstable existence, constantly having to adapt to changing economic circumstances, e.g. the energy crisis, threat from illiberal dictatorships, etc.

One might have interesting arguments with those who claim that economists exaggerate the constraints on resources and take a rather narrow view of the behavioural characteristics of human beings; and that they possibly underestimate the extent to which state action, through social services, can alter not only the economic and social situation of individuals but improve their behaviour. In a reasonable world, these matters can be decided by appeal to empirical observation and examination of the inferences drawn from such observations. At the very least, one can separate out questions of fact and logic from questions of value. Unfortunately, in areas where such debate is of vital public interest – for example, in social policy – there is all too often little opportunity for rational discourse with supporters of collective provision only of social services, such as health and education.

Ugly Allegation

I could offer countless examples of the sense of moral outrage which permeates the work of sociologists and social administrators when, with obvious distaste, they feel obliged to mention the hard facts of economic life. With some reluctance, for some of us knew him well and liked him, I single out as typical one quotation from a work of Richard Titmuss. In his book *Social Policy: An Introduction*, used throughout the length and breadth of this country as a textbook, he describes various models of social policy of which the one associated with liberalism is what he called 'Model A – The Residual Welfare Model':

> There are ... some social phenomena that may be studied with a certain degree of cold rational disinterestedness while never achieving the lack of involvement displayed by the mathematician analysing a quadratic equation. But this is not possible with the study of social policy or, to take another example, social deviation. ... One of the value assumptions, for instance, concealed in Model A – *The Residual Welfare Model of Social Policy* – is that the residual non-market sector (the public social policy sector) should concern itself with social deviants; the 'bad actuarial risks', those who are unwilling or unable to provide for their own needs – and the needs of their

families – through the normal mechanism of the market.

The definition of deviation means an aberration, turning from the right course, obliquity of conduct. Language is not a mere symbolic tool of communication. By describing someone as a deviant we express an attitude; we normally brand him and stigmatise him with our value-judgement . . . (p. 133).

There is a temptation to match this ugly allegation against liberal thinkers with angry polemic, rather in the manner of Ludwig von Mises's brilliant diagnosis of what he labelled the 'Fourier Complex'.[14] But the idea that liberal economists want to promote social conformity *in order* to isolate the morally delinquent and deviant poor is manifestly absurd. To restore communication, and hopefully mutual understanding, with those who have been influenced by this kind of view may already be easier because of the rude shock provided by our present economic crisis. It should at least dispel any illusion that 'social need' is an absolute and the scarcity concept a contrivance of mean-minded market economists.

'THE INTELLECTUAL OCCASIONS OF HESITANCY'

I now turn to the intellectual sales resistance. By this I do not mean the opposition to liberal political economy found among the socialist writers from Marx onwards, who share neither the liberal view about how the economy functions nor its definition of the tasks of the state. This is essentially an unending academic debate which, however fascinating, is only of vestigial interest in the present context. I am more directly concerned with how it has come about that intelligent, fair-minded and perceptive civil servants, members of senior management and some trade unionists have come to regard continuous state intervention on a large scale as at least a regrettable necessity given general recognition of the gap between British economic aspirations and our industrial performance. There may be no positive urge to solve our economic problems, if that were possible, solely by government action, but there seems to be something akin to a general belief that 'liberal political economy must know when to abdicate' in the teeth of the stern realities of an illiberal world. There is a coherent defensible position of some intellectual respectability, which requires serious consideration once one accepts the constraints on the operation of the market system its supporters regard as binding. Nor is this position a simple over-reaction to the immediate problems associated with the present economic crisis.

Ever More Selective Intervention?

The diagnosis of our economic condition (by the opposing groups, liberals and interventionists) is much the same, with the emphasis shifting very much more towards the inefficient use of factor inputs and away from the more simplistic views of the 1960s in which large-scale investment in physical and human capital was popularly considered both a necessary and sufficient condition for growth. In particular, the diagnosis points towards improving competitiveness in internationally traded goods and particularly in manufacturing.

Then we reach the dividing line between liberals and interventionists. The sceptical pragmatist will argue that there is little that the free market can do to improve performance. Internally we have to accept the monopoly power of the trade unions as a datum; and therefore we must also accept a whole range of restrictive practices in the labour market, and political support for collectivist social policies which preempt a large share of the annual output flow and generate pressure for further nationalisation.

Externally the development of export markets on the scale necessary to pay off our foreign debts (even allowing for North Sea oil) will bring manufacturers and exporters of services increasingly face to face not with private buyers but rather with public officials acting on behalf of governments in oil-producing countries and industrialised socialist countries. 'Common Property resources' in the sea and in the air are liable, so it is held, to be 'over-exploited' by private enterprise since they cannot be priced. Efficiency in their use will call for inter-governmental agreement, and at a minimum individual governmental regulation.

Reluctantly, so the pragmatic argument continues, the only solution will be to extend selective intervention by government. Indeed, in an international economy riddled with externalities this will be the only prudent way to ensure that private enterprise will be able to function efficiently at all. Paradoxically, therefore, selectivity will be the principal means of preserving rather than destroying the market economy.

A 'Jaw-Boning' Exercise

From this familiar line of argument to the understanding of the logic of specific proposals is a big jump. The *rationale* of those parts of the new industrial strategy which are *not* governed by political shibboleths is principally grounded in the belief that consensus can be reached in respect of both diagnosis and cure of our economic ills, and action to promote the cure lies in labour–management cooperation at the industry level. The government is not there simply to organise a 'jaw-boning' exercise but to assess the value of specific proposals for improving efficiency, and to use its fiscal and financial controls, if they can so be used, to alter the structure of industry in line with efficiency criteria.[15] At this early stage of such an ambitious, elaborate and fascinating exercise, one can predict with some confidence that all parties will continue to agree that they are against sin and can discern the common path of virtue, provided it is not too clearly delineated. The crunch will come when there is (as there clearly must eventually be) a plain statement, a brutal indication of who is to bear the costs of change. At that stage the full implications of the rigidities produced by trade union and industrial restrictive practices will have to be faced.

Easier to appreciate is the gist of the argument supporting government action on the international front. The organisation of effective bargaining with foreign governments to sell our goods and to negotiate over the distribution of property rights in the sea and in the air clearly makes something of a case for a stronger diplomatic capability; the support of large industrial consortia, if only on a temporary basis, to face the risks of dealing with rich overseas governments; and the use of selective methods of export promotion, if only as bargaining counters in the game of minimising international discrimination in traded goods and services.

Are the Rigidities Permanent?

The crux of the argument of the intelligent sceptics is that rigidities in both the national and international economy produced by the power of strong vested interest-groups cannot be removed. At best they can only be neutralised and by methods which will often go counter to the workings of the free market. As an erstwhile civil servant I have come to respect their views and their integrity; but I believe they offer us a counsel of despair, notably in relation to our domestic economy. Moreover, I contend that selective state intervention will proliferate across the whole of government, producing precisely the result that many of them are anxious to avoid – an administered centralised so-called planned economy, and an inefficient one at that.

Alan Peacock

Alan Peacock 97

RETAINING AND EXPANDING CREDIBILITY

I have advanced two main propositions. First, the skill and courage required to perceive and proclaim how liberal ideas apply to the operation of the economy have a high opportunity cost to professional economists. Secondly, the emotional sales resistance to liberal ideas is particularly virulent among those who play a crucial role in promoting government services which directly impinge on the everyday lives of citizens (the social services), while intellectual scepticism towards liberal policies is both marked and influential among those who run our industrial affairs inside and outside the public sector.

However, in trying to retain and expand the credibility of liberal political economy, it may not be the right course of action to concentrate only on persuading the patricians in our society. The main thrust of any campaign to remove the threat to individual freedom which is bound to result from the growth of collectivist policies must concentrate on improving the individual's chances of influencing governments, and on persuading voters in all sorts of elections that their interests are best served by voting in representatives who are not beholden to powerful minority interest-groups intent on fragmenting and ultimately destroying the market economy.

The Costs of Change

There is one particularly important dilemma encountered in trying to move towards a more liberal society. Individuals may accept the need for the restoration of incentives and the promotion of individual freedom as ultimate goals, but may not be prepared to suffer the costs of change in moving towards them. Thus it is quite possible that support could be enlisted for legislative changes which would eradicate coercion by simple majorities, for example through the safeguards proposed by Professor Hayek.[16] However, the process by which such changes would have to be instituted, and the uncertainty attached to the distribution of the burdens and benefits of change, make it reasonable for many individuals to refuse to face the risks. Moreover, as the present vacillations over the form and extent of devolution make patently clear, it is only when there is determined, persistent and extensive pressure that governments will consider constitutional changes which may in the long run circumscribe their own powers.

Despite what I have said earlier, there is perhaps a glimmer of hope for liberals in the growing discontent with the conduct of government, as reflected in the unpopularity of the long-term income prospects (including index-linked pensions) with security of tenure of civil servants, and of the disincentive effects of the present social security and income-tax systems. Is this perhaps a hint that voters believe that those who work for, or benefit from, government services should be paid something akin to their marginal productivity? It may not be evidence that voters wish to see major changes in the tasks of government, but it may show that as taxpayers they have a growing interest in seeing that these tasks are carried out more efficiently. A potentially dangerous situation arises when alienation among voters takes the form of avoiding or evading tax obligations on a large scale (including recourse to emigration) or making them feel impelled to organise in Poujadiste-type movements which defy the rule of law, instead of channelling their efforts through the normal political procedures.

Pressure for Electoral Reform . . .

We may have reached the stage in Britain at which voter pressure to change the whole electoral system can be mustered much more easily than at any time I can remember. My colleague, Charles Rowley, has come to much the same conclusion.[17] I agree with him that even the relatively simple (but not minor) constitutional change to the Single Transferable Vote offers the prospect of removing the power of the extremists in our two main parties to coerce their colleagues into immoderate action; for then there would be a strong probability that coalitions would become the conventional make-up of any government rather than government by a party with an absolute majority of seats.

Many of us would want to go much further than that in order to avoid the continuance of a system by which governments buy voters' support through lavish spending programmes. I have argued elsewhere the case for a form of political devolution which reduces voter alienation by greater participation in the political process and thereby offers an incentive to understand both the workings of government and, one hopes, recognition of its limitations.[18] However, this and other constitutional reforms, such as a review of the representation and functions of the House of Lords, rest on the creation of a political atmosphere in which the big issues raised can be properly discussed and, therefore, are not introduced under the pressure of immediate political events. The reflection of moderate, rational opinion in Parliament through electoral reform offers the best chance that this will occur.

... and Worker Participation

In order to tie in the interests of the working community with the need for removal of distortions caused by large-scale public intervention (which inhibit our economic advance and impair individual freedom), advocates of liberal political economy need to look closely at the genuine fears of workpeople that removal of imperfections in the labour market may work to their disadvantage. The traditional liberal view on this has been to point to the advantages to the consumer of more efficient allocation of resources produced by wider competition and new deployment of labour. If the price of winning acceptance for dismantling restrictive practices by labour unions, while retaining collective bargaining arrangements, is more worker participation in running industry, encouragement of labour-managed firms (as Peter Jay argued in the Sixth Wincott Lecture),[19] and the promotion of what Sam Brittan has called 'property rights in jobs',[20] then I am all for experimentation in such directions. There is no categorical imperative for liberals which requires us to accept that the organisation of productive activities along traditional hierarchical lines must be sanctified in our company legislation.

The real problem is how to devise systems of worker participation and control which are compatible with the survival and growth of the firm under competitive conditions, as John Stuart Mill realised over a century ago. He wrote, as I do, more in the hope than in the confident expectation that this problem could be solved; but surely his broad conclusion is correct:

> what is now required is not to bolster up old customs whereby limited classes of labouring people obtain partial gains which interest them in keeping up the present organisation of society, but to introduce new practices beneficial to all.[21]

'New practices' of genuine appeal and capable of implementation again require time for discussion and debate – and in a saner political atmosphere than we are currently experiencing.

Commitment and Credibility

Clearly the tentative agenda I have put forward needs filling out. It certainly calls for considerable adjustment in the attitudes and range of expertise of professional economists who have a genuine interest in the great issues of our day. There are dangers in directing one's intellectual energies towards support of one's philosophical position. In the heat of debate one can make analytical mistakes – but there are plenty of good economists about to point these out. There surely cannot be anything reprehensible in directing our skills towards the study of issues which those most affected by them consider important, and in trying to persuade them that a liberal solution should claim their support. The commitment offers at least as much excitement as withdrawal into more purely intellectual and professionally fashionable pursuits ... but remember the warning of the master about those who try to avoid the general contagion of faction:

> All such people are held in contempt and derision, frequently in detestation, by the furious zealots of both parties.... The ... impartial spectator, therefore, is upon no occasion, at a greater distance than amidst the violence and rage of contending parties.... Of all the corrupters of moral sentiments, therefore, faction and fanaticism have always been by far the greatest.[22]

Trying to expand the credibility of liberalism is certainly not an occupation for the faint-hearted or the pessimistic.

NOTES

* A number of colleagues read and commented on an earlier draft of this lecture, notably James Buchanan, Douglas Dosser, Ralph Harris, Keith Hartley, Graham Hutton, Michael Jones-Lee, Alan Maynard, Charles Rowley and Arthur Seldon. I am most grateful to them.

1. James Mill, *Selected Economic Writings* (introduced and edited by Donald Winch), published for the Scottish Economic Society by Oliver and Boyd, Edinburgh and London, 1966, p. 382.
2. Lord Robbins, Foreword to Harold Wincott, *The Business of Capitalism* Institute of Economic Affairs, 1968.
3. *The Later Letters of John Stuart Mill 1849–1873* (edited by Francis Mineka and Dwight Lindley), University of Toronto Press, Toronto, 1972, Letter 1,730.
4. Curiously enough the same Minister was heard by me to remark that 'so far as small firms are concerned, I believe implicitly in the wisdom of Adam Smith'.
5. Thomas H. Keir, *Faith and Response*, 1947, Introduction.
6. It says a good deal for the Department of Industry that it allowed the publication of the excellent study by Mr Nick Gardner, 'Economics of

Launching Aid', in *The Economics of Industrial Subsidies* (edited by Alan Whiting), HMSO, London, 1976, from which these figures are derived. It was Mr Edmund Dell, when Secretary of State for Trade, who remarked (before he became a minister) that 'Doubtful as governments might be of their ability to promote economic development in general, in aerospace and nuclear energy they seemed to have no doubt. Though the costs far exceeded the costs of empire, they have gone on. They have spent magnificently . . . the pressures of national prestige and of the thousands of persons employed in these industries are likely to determine the nation's future course rather than any more scientific calculations regarding investment and return.' (*Political Responsibility and Industry*, George Allen & Unwin, London, 1973, pp. 30–31.)

7. Here I simply echo Adam Smith's remarks about the officials of the East India Company: 'It is the system of government, the situation in which they are placed, that I mean to censure; not the character of those who have acted in it. They acted as their situation naturally directed, and they who have clamoured the loudest against them would, probably, have not acted better themselves.' (*The Wealth of Nations* (edited by R. H. Campbell and A. J. Skinner), Vol. II, p. 641.)

8. The contemporary relevance of Adam Smith's attack on mercantilism to the economic analysis of government is perceptively analysed in Martin Ricketts's 'The Relevance of Adam Smith for 1976', a prize-winning essay in the IEA Adam Smith bi-centennial essay competition.

9. For further analysis of modern welfare economics and its deficiencies, Charles Rowley and Alan Peacock, *Welfare Economics: A Liberal Restatement*, Martin Robertson, London, 1975.

10. In his *Political Economy Past and Present*, Macmillan, London, 1976, p. 3.

11. In this section I have concentrated on the emotional resistance to liberal political economy by social reformers in the narrow sense, i.e. those concerned with the development of social services on a collective basis. I have avoided the temptation of reviewing another and very potent source of resistance, namely the twentieth-century counterparts to William Blake and John Ruskin who so despised the liberal political economy of their own day. A splendid essay on this theme by a well-known English scholar is George Watson's 'The Myth of Catastrophe', *Yale Review*, Spring 1976; he reviews the attitudes of Orwell, Connolly, Eliot, Auden and others to capitalism.

12. Lewis Mumford, *The Culture of Cities*, Secker and Warburg, London, 1944, p. 464.

13. David Hume, 'Of the Origin of Government', in *Essays Moral, Political and Literary*, ed. Frederick Watson, Nelson, London 1951, pp. 84–5.

14. After the French Utopian socialist Ludwig von Mises, *The Free and Prosperous Commonwealth*, D. Van Nostrand, Princeton, NJ, 1962, Introduction. The 'complex', to von Mises, amounts to a neurotic hatred of those who question Utopian schemes on the grounds that they ignore the principle of scarcity.

15. For a skilful exposition of the 'new' industrial strategy, Alan Lord (Second Secretary, HM Treasury), *An Approach to Industrial Strategy*, Sir

Ellis Hunter Memorial Lecture, No. 7, University of York, 1977.

16. See Chapter 3 above.

17. In a provocative and stimulating paper, 'The British Disease: A Public Choice and a Property Rights Perspective' (mimeo). See also the conclusion of Jo Grimond, *The Bureaucratic Blight*, Unservile State Papers No. 22, 1976.

18. Alan T. Peacock, 'The Political Economy of the Dispersive Revolution', *Scottish Journal of Political Economy*, November 1976.

19. *A General Hypothesis of Employment, Inflation and Politics*, Occasional Paper 46. *IEA*, 1976.

20. 'The Political Economy of Labour Monopoly', *Three Banks Review*, September 1976.

21. J. S. Mill, *Principles of Political Economy*, Toronto, Toronto University Press, 1965, Book IV, Chapter 7, para. 7.

22. Adam Smith, *The Theory of Moral Sentiments* (edited by D. D. Raphael and A. L. Macfie), Oxford University Press, Oxford, 1976, pp. 156–7.

6 Economists and the British Economy

Alan Walters

A REMINISCENCE

In the late 1950s and early 1960s only a handful of British economists – for the most part associated with the IEA – began to swim against the mainstream of conventional wisdom of Cambridge, National Institute (NIESR), Treasury and Bank of England establishment. At first, the establishment ignored them – expecting, I suppose, that they would become weary once more and rejoin the mainstream. But the IEA went on its way. And the obloquy was poured in full measure: jejune, Neanderthal, antediluvian – ultimately becoming Selsdon man.[1]

Of course, all this robust criticism did have a point, for we were attempting to refloat many of the fundamental ideas of economics, which, it seemed to us, had long been regarded as sunk without trace.[2] We expected a long battle against the tide – and many of us were naive enough to believe that ultimately accepted doctrine and even policy would change dramatically. But our wise and very experienced pilot, Harold Wincott, harboured no such illusions. He had a shrewd idea where the mainstream was leading, of the shoals and swamps of state control, and the inflationary spiral ahead. Reading again *The Business of Capitalism*,[3] one is struck by the fact that he not only had a firm grasp of fundamental principles but periodically produced penetrating insights into the behaviour of men and markets. I do not think that financial journalism had shown such wisdom since the golden days of Walter Bagehot.

'A Sorry Scramble'

In the last seven years, since the First Wincott Memorial Lecture was delivered by Professor Milton Friedman,[4] we have witnessed events which in Harold Wincott's days would have been regarded by the clerisy as unworkable, unthinkable, 'politically impossible', and inconsistent

with social order. Britain has simultaneously suffered a massive inflation and rates of unemployment more than double what was thought
unacceptable only a few years ago. The pound floats along with many
other currencies. The grand 1963–65 crusade for growth has turned
into a sorry scramble to prevent the decline and de-industrialisation of
Britain. The search for scapegoats has introduced bitterness, divisive-
ness and recrimination. Now that the masses are under the delusion
that they have the keys to the national treasury, even the most thoughtful
observers are wondering whether democracy will survive.

LESSONS OF MACRO-ECONOMIC MANAGEMENT

My main purpose, however, is not to provide yet another review of
this sorry tale. But the experience of Britain over the 1970s has fur-
nished us with the most valuable tests of the conventional theories of
macro-economics; and you will not be surprised to learn that the theory
failed the tests. Thus, I shall reflect upon the curious process by which
certain doctrines of macro-economics – and, one must add, particularly
of Cambridge economics – manage to survive the most damning evidence that has been adduced to discredit them. It is surely worthy of
note that notions of economics continue to be widely disseminated
and accepted in spite of their inherent defects and of their lack of
correspondence to reality of common observation. It would be interesting to explain *why* these false notions persist, but, although I shall
speculate on the reasons, I am convinced I have not got an adequate
or even a plausible explanation.

Acerbity on British Economic Policy

These false theories – mostly but not entirely associated with Keynesian
economics – have been the bases of British economic policy for many
years. Although I too cannot resist the temptation to comment with
acerbity on the economic policy of successive British governments,
such criticism must be at best incomplete and at worst misleading.
Policy is determined by many considerations, only one of which is
economics.

Yet it is still vitally important to examine critically the ideas, principles and theories of economics on which policy is based. And in
British economic thinking, one can easily detect a recurring theme –
that free markets will perform in an unsatisfactory way and give rise

to unemployment and exploitation, externalities and social costs, inefficiency and excess. Massive government intervention is needed in order to ensure full employment, fair rewards, and the efficient allocation of resources.

On the other hand, the free-market system did in practice exhibit impressive stability and efficiency. Government intervention – as well as the new monopolistic exploiters, the trade unions – had largely contributed to the mess of declining output and high unemployment as well as rapid inflation.[5]

In this lecture, I shall review the plausibility of the main propositions on which the managers of the economy (Treasury and Bank) have leaned so heavily for so many years. You will all recall that one of those propositions, the 'Phillips curve', with its nice trade-off between unemployment and inflation, was convincingly discredited by experience in the late 1960s and early 1970s when both unemployment and inflation rose perversely together to new highs. Yet wage-rate rigidity or 'inflexibility' is still cherished as the heart of latter-day legitimate Keynesianism, and deserves at least a brief review.

The other two fundamental propositions of the theory of economic management – the consumption–income relationship and the investment function – remained more or less intact in 1970. I shall suggest that our experience during the mid-1970s has discredited the consumption (or savings) function as a basis for predicting economic events. This seems to be the most important lesson derived from the brute facts of the slump. A second lesson – perhaps somewhat less dramatic – is that we simply cannot account for that complex set of factors which determines the level of private investment. The behaviour of businessmen, just like the behaviour of households, was remarkably perverse during 1975–77 and no one knows why.[6] That is the lesson of the 'recovery'.

Expectations – 'A Fundamental Misconception'

Many monetary economists conjecture that one of the main reasons for the difficulty in tracking the economy and the consequential inefficiency of the management of demand is a fundamental misconception about people's and businessmen's expectations and confidence. Recent reflections on this conundrum suggest that if anticipations of future events are formed in a sophisticated rather than a Pavlovian fashion, the prospects for accurately forecasting events and the management of demand are indeed bleak.

Finally, I shall review some of the fashionable explanations for the behaviour of the economy in the 1970s and I shall attempt an assessment of current thinking about the management of the economy. So it is convenient to begin in 1970 with the monetarist counter-revolution.

MONETARISM 1970

In the First Wincott Lecture in 1970, Milton Friedman discussed what he regarded as a notion free entirely from ideological commitment – the quantity theory of money. In 1970, he demonstrated that the quantity theory had not merely emerged from the closet in the United States (oddly enough, with the assistance of massive federal spending programmes financed largely by increased growth of the money supply!) where it had been preserved from extinction by a few eccentrics, but it had also developed a vigorous research programme that showed itself rather more capable than any other theory of explaining much of the history of boom and slump, inflation and deflation. The essence is simple: if the quantity of money is increased by a substantial amount, the 'price' of money (in terms of goods exchanged per unit of money) is likely eventually to fall. In other words, the general level of prices will rise.

It is, of course, merely an illustration, but a very famous one, of the laws of supply and demand. But it produced powerful and, to modern ears, surprising predictions. For example, if government spending were increased and the authorities acquired the money, not by 'creating' new cash, but by selling long-dated gilts to non-bank domestic residents, there would be no expansionary (or inflationary or reflationary) effect on the economy. Now anyone trained in the high Keynesian tradition would dismiss such notions as absurd; of course an expansion of government expenditure would have an effect.[7] Whether the increased spending was financed by selling gilts or creating money was a secondary concern and had very little or no consequence on the outcome. But, Friedman argued, in order to predict its effects, the nature of the financing of such expenditure mattered very much. Whether the spending was financed by creating money or by 'crowding out' private expenditure through the bond market determined whether the policy was or was not expansionary (inflationary, etc.).

Money Does Matter

To the clerisy of demand managers and their academic supporters, this
was heresy. For many years – at least since the 1940s in Britain – it
had been widely accepted that 'money did not matter', or at least that
money mattered only for the purpose of preserving orderly financial
markets. (Here I paraphrase Lord Kaldor.)[8] The monetarist counter-
revolution showed not merely that 'money did too matter' but that it
mattered a lot.

Yet I do not think that this particular conclusion was the main result
of the counter-revolution. The primal point was that no model, whether
monetary or Keynesian, could foretell accurately the performance of
the economy over the next two years. The extensive empirical studies
and the critical evaluation of existing 'models' of the world's economies showed how very *little* we knew about the determinants of the
national economy. This was against the grain of contemporary wisdom. The belief was that, with Keynesian theory developed quantita-
tively, either formally in a model or through some more informal
accounting framework, one could predict with a high degree of confidence where the economy was going over the next year or so. True, it
was widely admitted that it was difficult to make good predictions
about the behaviour of foreigners.[9] But with few disclaimers, it was
commonly accepted that any body of Keynesian economists, suitably
equipped and financed, could foretell, under the assumption of unchanged government taxes and spending, what would happen to the
economy in the year or so ahead.

Confidence was no doubt nurtured by the unremarkable fact that all
models tended to tell the same tale. Thus the government was advised
on the adjustments in tax rates, government spending and controls on
hire purchase so that any forecast shortcomings in the performance of
the economy could be made good. Sailing analogies came readily to
mind. Windblown Chancellors could find a receptive and appreciative
audience when they talked of 'a touch on the tiller', 'leaning against
the breeze', 'steady as she goes', and so on. The steering instruments
were always taxes, government spending, hire purchase controls, bank
rate, but never the money supply.[10]

No Reliable Controls in Short Run

A common but understandable misinterpretation of the teaching of the
monetarist counter-revolution is that the quantity of money should be

used to control the economy – rather than taxes and government spending. This is almost the opposite of the intent. The primal conclusion is that *no* instruments of policy, whether money or taxes or spending, have well-defined and precise, predictable consequences in the short run, that is to say, over a period of up to two years. True, Friedman and many others (such as the economists at the Federal Reserve Bank of St Louis) have pointed out that the monetary model performs rather better than the Keynesian paradigm for a two-year horizon; but both predict very poorly.

In part, this performance is poor because extraneous, unforeseen and often unforeseeable events play a large role in determining economic conditions: famine and flood, trade unions and terrorists, political manoeuvring and foreign conspiracies – all influence economic conditions. There *is* a large element of chance. However, such chance elements may be tractable or at least tolerable if one could rely on certain constants of economic theory. Alas, our experience over the 1970s has shown that those 'constants' upon which the massive edifice of macroeconomics is built are given to disobliging shifts which occur unfortunately when the forecaster most needs them to stand still.

CONSUMPTION AND SAVINGS IN THE 1970s

One quite remarkable example of this occurred in the slump of 1974–76. Keynesian theory hinges on the stability of the consumption function – that is to say, on a stable and predictable relationship between the disposable income of persons and their spending on real goods and services. For many years this relationship has exhibited a long-run stability: in the United States, people spent about 90 per cent of their income; in Britain, the rate was somewhat higher at 92 per cent. In the short run, there was some variation about this value; but the variation was reliable and therefore predictable. Friedman himself contributed to this body of knowledge with what is, I believe, still his finest work, by demonstrating that a very wide variety of evidence was consistent with this so-called 'permanent income theory of consumption'.[11] It seemed that, if there were a dependable constant in economics, this was it.

Economic Theory Confounded, 1974–75

Yet, during 1974–75 in Britain, everything seemed to go wrong. Consumer spending fell far more than anyone had predicted – to less than

87 per cent of income. And the ratio of personal savings to disposable income rose from its normal 8 per cent to over 12 per cent. Nor was this confined to Britain; virtually all Western countries (and Japan) experienced the same surge in savings in the slump.[12] And savings ratios have remained far higher than normal and show no sure signs of falling to what was regarded as their historically normal levels.

No economist correctly predicted such events. Indeed, as the Americans would say, no one was even in the 'right ballpark'; so it is worth reflecting at length on this remarkable story of savings. It was the first important test of the stability of saving and consumption functions since the Second World War. The changes in incomes in 1974–76 were very large indeed and so provided a powerful test of the theory. Now the accepted principles of the consumption function allowed that there would be deviations from these constant overall marginal rates of saving. Cambridge economists (Lord Kaldor and Joan Robinson in particular) had long argued that the savings rate of workers was much lower than that of rentiers. (So important was this principle to them that the whole edifice of the Cambridge theory of the distribution of income was built upon it!)[13] Thus, a redistribution of income from workers to capitalists *would* give rise to a higher overall savings rate. In 1974–76, however, the massive redistribution was indeed unprecedented – but in *the opposite direction, from the rentiers to workers*. The Cambridge theory was not just wrong; it was perverse – *savings went up instead of down*.[14]

Lest anyone should harbour an inkling of a suspicion that I have a bias against Cambridge, let me immediately admit that the versions of the consumption function proposed by monetarists, such as the permanent income hypothesis of Friedman, gave rise to predictions which were belied by events. As real incomes fall temporarily below the long-term trend, as they did in the slump of 1974–76, Friedman's theory forecasts that real consumption would fall only slightly and so the savings ratio would fall quite steeply. *Perversely, it rose.*

And I must confess *mea culpa*. Readers of the 1974 *Sebag Giltedged Review* will see that I too thought that savings would fall. The combination of a persistent negative real rate of return, a government openly hostile to the saver and determined to make the pips squeak, and the likelihood of expropriation – all seemed to point to transfer from private provision for the future to more reliance on government hand-outs. I too was quite wrong.

Popperian Falsification Principle Ignored

To the informed non-economist, the experience of the 1970s would be regarded as sufficient to discredit this bed-rock of Keynesian economics. If the Karl Popper principle of falsification is applied in the social sciences, this surely is a case to which it is germane. Yet we may observe that this refutation of the consumption function has made little impact. Everywhere, teachers and textbooks continue to assert the fundamental stability of the relationship. The tendency is to regard the 1970s as an anomaly, or perhaps as a once-and-for-all change to higher savings. Advisers make *ad hoc* adjustments to their forecasts.

In any case, there were many *ex post facto* rationalisations of this extraordinary event. It was argued, for example, that the expropriated households were trying to restore the value of their assets, and that the slump had enormously increased the demand for precautionary liquid assets. Alternatively, it was suggested that the redistribution of income and wealth from middle class to miners and other wage earners gave rise to high transitory savings (but these would presumably disappear as the miners bought their Volvos). Any or all of these may be true – but excuses of hindsight do not eradicate the errors of prediction.

THE DISCREDITING OF 'NEW CAMBRIDGE'

The high savings of 1974–75 discredited the theory of the New Cambridge School just when it was being weaned from infancy in the pages of *The Times* to its presentation to the Public Expenditure Committee of the House of Commons in the summer of 1974. The New Cambridge Theory regarded the financial surplus of the private sector as being approximately constant at about £800 million per annum. Then, as a matter of accounting, it follows that a financial deficit of the public sector would be reflected in an overseas financial deficit of the same amount, less the £800 million which the private sector would reliably contribute year in, year out. (Hence, the ease with which the New Cambridge School forecast the 1973–74 financial deficit on the balance of payments.)

'Unforeseen and Unprecedented' Rise in Savings

In 1974–75, however, the rise in the savings rate of the personal sector, together with the rapid accumulation of liquid assets of the corporate sector, saw the financial surplus of the private sector leap to over £6000 million. This was an *eightfold* increase in the surplus – quite unforeseen and unprecedented. Thus the financial deficit of the public sector was in large part financed by the private sector buying financial assets issued by the public sector – and the financial deficit overseas shrank remarkably.

It is difficult not to feel a touch of sympathy for New Cambridge. It was widely believed – and by many competing forecasters perhaps widely feared – that they had discovered the keys to the Keynesian kingdom. It is rare that a theory is so quickly discredited by contemporary history. We might also suppose that, after this experience, it would no longer be necessary to preach the virtues of humility to those economists who were prominent in New Cambridge in promoting the virtues of 'steering the economy'. But not so! Policies of protection, import quotas, expansionary government spending, etc., are still being assiduously propagated.

What Happened to Investment?

The savings-income relationship is only one of the props of conventional macro-economics. Another is investment. If the lesson of slump was to show that we could not predict savings, then the discovery of the recovery is that we cannot forecast domestic fixed investment. In virtually every Western country, governments have been told that there would be a rapid increase in investment in 1976–77. But there was no confident surge, only a tremulous trickle. As with savings, there was a rash of *ex post facto* explanations for the shortfall. But even the rationalisation that appeals to most people, the loss of confidence (in profitability) by the business community, merely substitutes one unknown for another; it simply provides another label for our ignorance. All 'explanations' are empty, untested propositions.

The investment experience is not such a dramatic reversal for conventional macro-economics as the story of savings. Private fixed investment has not actually fallen during the 1976–77 recovery – it has shown some increase, but far, far less than anyone had anticipated.[15] Yet it is accepted that, for appropriate macro-demand management, it is crucially important to be able to forecast investment by the private sector. It is one of the key elements of aggregate autonomous expenditure – the main determinant, *via* the multiplier, of the level of income and employment. If we cannot accurately forecast investment then no confidence can be placed in the prediction of income and employment.

Rigidities – The New Vintage

Thus, I conclude that not only the stability of the consumption function but also the tractability of the investment relationship are now discredited. I am tempted to continue to what many consider to be the third prop of Keynesian economics – the downward rigidity of money wages.[16] Of course, with money wage-rates rising by anything between 10 and 35 per cent per annum over the 1970s, whatever may have been the use of such a postulate during the slump of 1929–33, one may be forgiven for regarding any such downwards rigidity as now rather otiose. But some sort of inflexibility is needed by modern macroeconomists, and two varieties are discernible.

First, it is said that the *rate of growth of money wages* cannot be deflected downward from its previous path; there is a floor to the rate of inflation of money wages.[17]

Secondly, that most distinguished Nobel Laureate, Sir John Hicks, has argued that there is now a rigidity in the level of *real* wages.[18] Fortunately there is no problem of choosing between them; both propositions have been convincingly discredited by events. The rate of growth of money wages fell remarkably over the years 1975–77, and the level of real wages, after showing a record rise of 12 per cent (April 1974 to April 1975), fell – again at record rates – for two years. What remains, therefore, of this proposition of inflexibility I leave you to judge.

THE COUNTER-REVOLUTION IN EXPECTATIONS

By this point, you will have realised that I have considerable sympathy with what I take to be the real thrust of the counter-revolution – that is to say, that we know little about the forces that determine detailed economic conditions, such as prices and employment, exports and imports, output and productivity, savings and investment. True, the monetarists' results showed that the rate of inflation was ultimately determined by the excess of the rate of growth of the money stock over the rate of growth of real national income. True, also, the variations in the growth of the money supply had some transitory effects on employment and output; but all were highly uncertain both in timing and in magnitude. A government could do no good and, on the average, would probably inflict much harm by trying to fine-tune the economy – and this holds true whatever the instrument used, whether monetary or Keynesian. I have great sympathy for this view. Thus the best that can be done is to pursue a moderate and stable growth rate of the money stock – Friedman's famous rule.

The Problem of Expectations

Since Friedman's lecture in 1970 there has been much additional reflection on the fundamental dilemma of discretionary policy (as distinct from a simple rule), much of which has centred on the problem of expectations.[19] The treatment of expectations is one of the most uncomfortable aspects of economics. For many years economists normally treated both business men and housewives as though they were idiots who simply extrapolate their past experience into the future. Current events, however momentous, were supposed not to affect their views of the future. Now this was a wild and wilful travesty, as any housewife or businessman knows. People *do* take account of current events in forming and reforming their anticipations of the future. I am persuaded not only that businessmen and housewives *are knowledge-able* about predicting the future; I am prepared to believe that they are as successful, or unsuccessful, as the economists.

'A Game of Attrition'

Suppose, therefore, that people expect what the economic theory predicts. (In my writings, I have called these *consistent* expectations, but they are usually known by the more presumptive title of *rational expectations*.)[20] But if people are as clever as economists, and if government policy operates according to economic models, then people will quite nicely offset the government's behaviour. For example, if people know that an increase in the rate of growth of the money supply will increase the rate of inflation, then they will adjust their behaviour (such as switch to gold or commodities) – and then the government must take this reaction into account in formulating their policies – but people will know this, and so it goes on. The normal concept of discretionary fiscal or monetary policy has now disappeared; it is a game – and a very serious game – of attrition.[21]

Examples of these games appear daily in the financial press. (And, in his perceptive way, Harold Wincott observed them many years ago.) In the textbooks, an increase in the rate of growth of the money supply is still said to reduce interest rates. In his Wincott Lecture, Friedman himself said that an increased rate of money growth will tend at first to reduce interest rates.[22] But now we know it does nothing of the kind; on the contrary, it *raises* them. Any market operator seeing an extraordinary increase in the money supply will know that the authorities are likely to tighten credit in the near future; consequently he will sell gilts and bonds in anticipation of the authorities' reaction. Then interest rates will rise.[23] Then the authorities are induced to play a double-bluff – but, of course, the clever market operators are quickly on to that.

A Return to Rules

One of the generalisations on which, I suspect, there may be virtual unanimity is that the private operator is much more adept at the market game and more fleet of foot than the bumbling bureaucrat. The authorities must expect to find their policy anticipated, frustrated, and offset. Games of this kind may be condemned as destructive. Certainly, at a very minimum they result in a diversion of activity into destructive stratagems – City trying to outguess the authorities and the Bank and Treasury duly bluffing and counter-bluffing.

One way in which the game-playing can be avoided is by the authorities eschewing discretionary policy and pursuing a fixed rule – by increasing the money supply at a fixed percentage rate or by aiming at a suitably 'standardised' public sector financial deficit.[24] The authorities should follow rules (of law?) rather than attempt to manage the system. Then government's behaviour would become virtually entirely predictable and the power of politicians to reward one group at the expense of another (to buy votes with other people's money) would be reduced. This reflects a great and abiding principle of constitutional government which was so eloquently and persuasively put by Professor F. A. Hayek in the Fourth Wincott Lecture.[25]

The Effects of the Counter-Revolution

But, if I am correct in reinterpreting Friedman's 1970 message as really a return to rules, whatever became of his counter-revolution? Was it really successful in capturing the minds of the mandarins? Economic policy in Britain provides the most dramatic evidence of its immediate failure to convince anyone in the corridors of power. The rise in unemployment in the years 1970 and 1971 apparently induced the Conservative Government to embark on a massive expansion of deficit spending. Notwithstanding the mountain of evidence that Friedman and others had adduced to show that money does matter, from September

1971 the government began to expand the money supply (M_3) at a rate which, for two years, never fell below 20 per cent per annum and often hovered at 30 per cent. Could one find a more convincing case that the counter-revolution had been repulsed – indeed, was held in contempt – by the clerisy of Britain?[26]

In 1970–73, this disdain was reflected in the various macro-econometric models – those of the London Business School, the NIESR, and, so far as one can see through the veil of secrecy, of the Treasury. All these models have their focus on the short-term conditions of the economy. Their basic objective is to give guidance on fiscal policy – to provide advice for the Chancellor in the frequent budgets (and other adjustments to the 'tiller'). Thus, the models purport to show where the economy would be in the months ahead without any change in tax rates or government spending, etc. Then, in order to restore full employment and promote economic growth, the amount of money to be injected into the system is calculated, and suitable adjustments are suggested for the Chancellor's budget.

The Treasury model, even as late as 1974, did not contain the money supply at all. And in the London Business School model (1972), the money supply entered only into the determination of the cost of capital. Clearly the counter-revolution had received short shrift in the macro-econometric models. Moreover, these models followed Keynesian (perhaps one should say Kahn–Kaldor–Harrodian) methodology in another, perhaps more fundamental, sense: the price level was regarded as largely given.[27] For many years the current rate of inflation was thought to be determined by the current rate of unemployment – the higher the rate of unemployment, the lower the rate of inflation. But the experience of simultaneous high unemployment and inflation has left the Phillips curve friendless.[28] In one sense, this result has had an important consequence. If one cannot contain an inflation by increasing unemployment, then there is no excuse for 'tolerating' a large volume of unemployment.

COST-PUSH AND EXPANSIONISM

But, in any case, the fall of Phillips left the rate of inflation just hanging there. It remained to be explained. And it is clear that most of the clerisy regarded (and, I believe, still regard) the rate of inflation as being determined by cost-push – in particular, by the monopolistic behaviour of trade unions and also by the largely independent behaviour of foreigners such as sheiks who demand high prices for their oil.

This 'cost-push' explanation of price change, particularly that due to monopolistic unions, comes in many forms. Some of the most sophisticated, such as that of Mr Peter Jay in the Sixth Wincott Lecture,[29] argue that the unions raise wages, cause unemployment and so induce the government to expand the money supply, etc., in order to reduce unemployment to levels consistent with electoral requirements. And this generates accelerating inflation. Thus the cost 'push' is through the *political* process rather than direct. And I would agree that this political cost-push was undoubtedly responsible for much of the inflation in Britain in the 1960s and early 1970s.

Simplistic 'Cost-Push' Versions

But I suspect that the vast majority of economists, politicians and informed people hold somewhat more simplistic versions of cost-push; they regard monetary conditions as either self-accommodating or largely outside the control of the authorities. Yet the evidence of the past few years (end-1973 to November 1977) has shown that, as in 1968–69, where there is a will there is a way. Monetary expansion has been contained. And in November 1977, much against the passionate advocacy of its erstwhile advisers, the Government allowed sterling to appreciate rather than loosen the monetary strings.[30] The crude cost-push theory regards such monetary discipline as largely irrelevant.

Another remarkable characteristic of economic thinking of the 1970–73 period was that it was still asserted that under conditions of quite modest levels of unemployment an increase of public expenditure would give rise to an increase in real output. There was little 'crowding out' and no large expansion of imports (and reduction of exports). Thus, by expanding public spending, the economy got something for nothing. Employment and output would grow with little or no effect on the rate of inflation.[31]

Barber's Boom and Rationalisation

Of course, with mature reflection on these 'something for nothing' convictions we should not be astonished by the reaction of the Conservative Government.[32] The same protestations of outrage that we hear today with more than one and a half million unemployed were even louder in 1971 with less than one million on the dole. Received and respected opinion, buttressed by the predictions of the models, showed that expansionary public spending and money supply from September 1971 onwards would not bring about significant increases in inflation. On the contrary, they would merely mop up the pool of unemployed. The siren's song of 'something for nothing' was too strong to resist. And the arguments of monetarism sounded negative, anti-social and even anti-Conservative: conventional expansionism prevailed.

You all know what happened in 1973–75. The inflation which was predicted by monetarists duly occurred on schedule. Prices and incomes controls were duly introduced. The balance-of-payments deficit turned out to be far worse than even monetarists had predicted – and this result was partly due to the increased price of imports.

How the Discredited Conventional Wisdom was Restored

One would have thought that such a massive discrediting of the conventional wisdom would have had a considerable effect on the profession and the Treasury. But such investment of time and effort had gone into the development of these demand management ideas that they were not to be lightly discarded. Nor should they be. Even the most successful and progressive theories have small anomalies and odd discrepancies. One swallow, however gigantic, does not make a summer. Indeed, attempts to explain away the 1974 inflation have normally taken two courses.

First, it is argued that the increase in the rate of inflation was entirely due to the extraordinary rise in the price of imports – something over which Britain is said to have no control.[33] Nor can one expect to predict such extraordinary events as the oil cartel, etc.

It is easy to show, however, that Britain's extraordinary inflation got under way with a current overseas deficit that more than offset the higher price of imports.[34] In 1973–74, we were *exporting* inflation, not importing it. Furthermore, it is clear that other countries such as Germany and Japan suffered similar rises in world prices of their imports, yet their inflation rates were about one-quarter and one-third of those in Britain. The point is, that although the import price rise entailed a loss of real income, the governments of the day pursued expansionary policies and paid for them with overseas borrowings. Reality was postponed for a year or two. No doubt, the aims were noble – to keep down the level of unemployment, to maintain incomes and to provide the world with an expanding British demand to offset the restricted demand of other countries – and were not calculated to win elections. But the results were sad.

The Slump and the Slowing Inflation

Since the world price of imports did not continue its rise relative to the price of Britain's exports in 1975–76, it was hardly possible to ascribe the continuing inflation to import prices. So the *second* and most important rationalisation for inflation was brought into play – the union-cost-push. And since the unions are an independent force, the only way to control them is by a body of legislation (or administrative extra-legal controls) which somehow limits their ability to generate inflation. Great ingenuity has been lavished on this problem – and, in Chapter 2 Professor James Meade provides what seems to me to be the best proposal so far that is consistent with the widest possible measure of freedom. I believe that most British economists accept that some sort of wage control is now a necessary, though not a sufficient, condition for the control of inflation. Indeed the experience of the 1970s – particularly the massive wage explosion in 1974–75 – lends plausibility to the view that wage control is the *only* way.[35]

The majority of men of affairs regard the £6 a week pay policy which was imposed in mid-1975, after the fiasco of the 'social contract', as an important or perhaps the main cause of the slowing-down of inflation from 1975.[36] Yet the sharp and prolonged slump of 1974–76 and the consequent slowing-down in the rate of inflation from 1975 was uncompromisingly predicted by monetarists in early 1974.[37] And this period provides an interesting test case for monetary predictions.

From the end of 1973 monetary growth declined sharply from an annual rate of approximately 25 per cent for the period September 1971–September 1973 to about 10 per cent. This *fall* in the growth rate of the money stock was associated, however, with highly *expansionary* public spending and budgets.[38] Here, then, was an acid test – monetarists predicted a sharp slump, whereas Keynesians would look to expansion. The outcome was a virtually unequivocal win for monetarism. Indeed the slump of 1974–76 was sharp and prolonged. The monetarist prediction that the inflation rate of prices would begin to moderate some two years after the end of 1973 was also borne out as the inflation rate declined to 13 per cent (year to July 1976).[37] The consequences of the prolonged monetary squeeze which began at the end of 1973 have not yet run their course, although even at this stage the provisional conclusions are clear, and it seems impossible to deny that monetary contraction played a major role in causing the slump and the arrest of inflation.

EXPANSIONISM AND THE ROLE OF MONEY

Yet the role of money in today's thinking on economic policy remains curious. Some economists regard the money supply as potentially dangerous if there are sharp and sustained changes in its rate of growth. Others, and a very influential group, such as Lord Kaldor, regard a constant growth rate of money as doing no great harm – after all, if money matters only for 'orderly financial markets' and does not affect anything that really matters (such as real growth and inflation), then the monetarists are welcome to their little rules provided they do not interfere with the running of the real economy.[40]

The essence is that, although monetary control is accepted as of some importance, there is a broad consensus that the government still must regulate the economy by means of varying public spending and tax rates. As evidence, witness the widespread calls for a stimulation of activity – for Germany and Japan to 'expand their economies' – and for Britain to reduce her unemployment and launch the economy once more onto a growth path. There has been little loss of faith in the ability of economists to plan and to manage the economy and 'to get the economy moving'. True, no-one pretends that government should 'fine-tune' but that does not mean that the government should not strike the right note. Although there has been a welcome admission that economic management is not, even approximately(!), an exact science, there has been little or no erosion of the belief that governments can much improve growth and employment by an active policy of stimulation. Active governments beget growth.

Money Control a Limited Check to 'Spending Sprees'

But, you may object, controlling the money growth will surely prevent any excesses. Alas, I believe it will help avoid only some of the most wild swings (such as the Heath–Barber expansion).

Britain can still go on a spending spree, financed by the import of foreign capital and by manipulating the exchange rate (as in 1974), with only a modest increase in the money supply. And the adoption of monetary rules such as DCE (domestic credit expansion)[41] that include foreign borrowing seems to me to generate more trouble than enough.[42] Ponder the present temptation when there is a substantial surplus on the overseas accounts and the domestic economy is slack. The seasonal call for a massive expansionary budget is to be heard in the land.

These calls for expansion have also cleverly employed the tools of monetarism to advance their case. One interesting example is the 'full-employment' budget. This calculates what the public sector's financial deficit would be if there were 'full employment'. It was designed to remove that part of the public sector deficit which was due to the fact that employment was lower than 'normal'; and 'normal' for this purpose was considered to be an arbitrary definition of full employment. Now the Cambridge Economic Policy Group shows that the 'full-employment' budget is in massive surplus rather than the observed deficit – and hence establishes the case for balancing the full-employment budget by expanding public spending.[43] And the rationalisation of it all is still the 'something for nothing'.

CONCLUSION

I conclude, then, that, since 1970 when these lectures first began, despite the accumulation of new evidence and experience, there has been virtually no fundamental change in the principles that have guided policy discussion in Britain. The most obvious and apparently far-reaching development – the adoption of monetary targets – is largely cosmetic and probably for foreign consumption only. When it proves more than a little inconvenient, as in 1970, it will be shed like an old coat and the mantle of the 'growth merchants' will be worn with pride once more.[44]

Persistence of False Theories and Policies

Finally, I must touch upon the conundrum which I mentioned at the outset. Why do these false theories persist and why are they still accepted as the basis for the most far-reaching economic policies? As Robin Pringle has recently suggested,[45] the explanation may be simple inertia which has been institutionalised and fossilised. There has been a considerable investment of effort and money and persuasion in the management techniques of the British economy. There is a natural reluctance to write it off. But more than that. There is a strong incentive to argue that the guidance system has been a success. True, it failed in 1972–74, etc., but that period was extraordinary and probably unique. Such anomalies, it has been argued, can be incorporated easily into a theoretical approach that is fundamentally correct.[46]

The assessment of evidence in economics is rarely, if ever, without equivocation. We cannot appeal, as the physicist may, to stunning experimental evidence. Furthermore, the macro-economic models fitted by econometricians are constantly shifting and virtually impossible for anyone who has not worked on them to pin down and to understand their complexities. But there is a rationale in persisting with trying to discover the detailed management models, for there is always the possibility that research *may* eventually enable us to forecast accurately. Meanwhile, however, economists should not claim more than they can deliver.

Of course, it is difficult to admit ignorance. After all, we are a highly paid profession – surely we *should* know better than the layman where the economy is going and how to put it right. There is a powerful temptation to respond to this understandable demand.

Democratic Process Encourages Expansionism

As Peter Jay showed in his sixth Wincott Lecture,[47] the democratic process itself is responsible for the demand for expansionism. And so the conventional models rationalise the expansionary role of government spending to eliminate unemployment and promote growth. Are economists then guilty of meretricious behaviour – rationalising what the customer wants, telling the political populist what he wants to hear? I do not know. Motives are impossible to observe and difficult to guess. I do suspect that most economists have virtuous motives: we really do want to do good. But we must beware of La Rochefoucauld's maxim 'Virtue would not go nearly so far if vainglory did not keep it company'.

But change is in the air. Just as the classical system of economic management was thought to have failed in 1929–33, so, I believe, the sustained view will be that the theory of the nicely managed growth economy died in the 1970s.

The world is demanding some new economic messiah (such as some latter-day Keynes) who will persuade us all that he has the key to understanding much that is now shrouded in mystery. And where there is demand, supply will not be far behind. But, ultimately, it is the poor suffering public who will pay the penalties or reap the rewards; and they will call us to judgement.

NOTES

1. I thought that the ultimate accolade was awarded when one economist referred to the 'marketeers' as 'Seldon men'.

2. The reader will notice that I have slipped into the first person plural – I believe I became involved with the IEA from 1959.
3. Institute of Economic Affairs, 1968.
4. See Chapter 1 above.
5. No doubt, it will be held that adherents of the 'free market' should not be taken too seriously. Although this view may be tenable with respect to proposals for policy, it is completely irrelevant for judging the veracity of substantive propositions. Both theories and facts are amoral, and are independent of the motives of the proponent. We ought to judge propositions by their correspondence to the truth and not by the intentions of those who advance them.
6. Oddly enough, this will be a source of great satisfaction to many left-leaning Keynesians (such as Joan Robinson, who attributes investment to businessmen's 'animal spirits'). It provides a rationalisation for the control of investment by the state through the National Enterprise Board (NEB), etc.
7. For example, if there were high unemployment, government spending would increase output and employment to higher levels both in the short and the long run. Government spending gave 'something for nothing'.
8. 'The New Monetarism', *Lloyds Bank Review*, July 1970.
9. Oddly enough, however, the New Cambridge School claimed that it was much easier to forecast the balance of payments than other elements. The New Cambridge economists have rather a Lady Bracknell view of the foreign balance; it is simply the residual after the government has determined its financial deficit.
10. On returning from the United States in 1959 just after publication of the Radcliffe Report, I was surprised to learn that there was no statistical series on the money supply in the United Kingdom. But since the vast body of evidence to Radcliffe had asserted that the money supply was of little or no importance, it was understandable that no one thought it worthwhile to measure it. I believe that the first comprehensive series on the stock of money was produced at the University of Birmingham in 1960–63.
11. *A Theory of the Consumption Function*, Princeton University Press, Princeton, N.J., 1957.
12. For Japan, for example, the savings ratio in 1960–73 was around 19 per cent; for 1974–76 it was more than 25 per cent – an increase of over 30 per cent.
13. The proportion of income going to rentiers had to be just high enough to ensure that savings equalled the predetermined level of investment.
14. From April 1974 to April 1975, real wages increased by 12.7 per cent.
15. For example, the CBI survey of investment intentions showed first a 15 per cent increase in 1977 on (October) 1976. But in October 1977 there was a doubt whether there would be *any* increase.
16. The failure of wage rates to adjust and clear the markets is, according to Joan Robinson, the true Keynesian theory; those who argue that the liquidity preference postulate is the essential element of Keynesianism are, according to her taxonomy, 'bastard Keynesians'. Most Americans are bastards, but not all bastards are American!
17. I must confess that I can find no precise statement of what distinguished

macro-economists mean by inflexibility or downward rigidity of money wages and indeed prices. Much is ascribed to these concepts by, for example:

'. . . the Monetarists were relatively optimistic about the possibility of deflecting money wages downward *from their previous path*, . . .' – Miller (Italics added.)

'. . . there have been major shifts in the United Kingdom in *relative* prices since the war [the Second World War], but one would be hard put to substantiate that there have been widespread falls in *absolute* prices . . .' – Ball and Burns (Italics in original.)

M. H. Miller, 'Can a Rise in Import Prices be Inflationary and Deflationary?', *American Economic Review*, September 1976, pp. 501–19; R. J. Ball and T. Burns, 'The Inflationary Mechanism in the United Kingdom Economy', *American Economic Review*, September 1976, pp. 467–84.

18. 'What is Wrong with Monetarism', *Lloyds Bank Review*, No. 118, October 1975, pp. 1–13. Sir John used the term 'real wage resistance' to describe this downward rigidity.

19. For example, Milton Friedman, *Unemployment versus Inflation?*, Occasional Paper 44, with a British Commentary by David Laidler, IEA, 1975 (3rd Impression 1977).

20. A. A. Walters, 'Consistent Expectations, Distributed Lags and the Quantity Theory', *Economic Journal*, June 1971.

21. Incidentally, it is often alleged that the authorities really *know* the system they are managing – after all, they have unrivalled access to data and resources. So they would always win. I doubt this. The private operators have much incentive to win, whereas the bureaucrats have different aims.

22. Chapter 1, p. 19.

23. But, you may object, this is merely the impact effect – surely, after a while, the additional money would flood into financial markets and so drive interest rates down. But not so. It would increase expectations of inflation and this would induce people to invest in assets denominated in real rather than monetary terms. Thus the demand for financial assets would diminish, depressing their price and increasing the yields.

24. Of course, not all games will be rendered otiose by the fixed rules; but they will be much smaller and well-contained in a narrow framework.

25. See Chapter 3 above.

26. A witty and clever response by a most distinguished member of the clerisy to the mounting evidence of monetarism was Lord Kaldor's lecture, 'The New Monetarism', at University College, London, on 12 March, 1970, published in *Lloyds Bank Review*, July 1970. I believe that this speech was most influential in confirming the clerisy in the comforting conclusion that monetarists were cranks. The important persons could get on with the really important business of running the economy.

27. Indeed, in this sense the modellers were perfectly consistent; the effects of the money supply on prices are in the longer term (i.e. over two to five years), while their concern was normally more in the shorter term than in the longer run.

28. There is no evidence of the modellers embracing the more sophisticated

'expectations-augmented' Phillips curve of Professors Friedman and E. S. Phelps.

29. *A General Hypothesis of Employment, Inflation and Politics*, Occasional Paper 46, IEA for the Wincott Foundation, 1976 (2nd Impression 1977).

30. See the letter dated 29 October by Lord Kaldor in *The Times*, 1 November, 1977. Lord Kaldor would allow the appreciation of sterling only if there were a general *ad valorem* duty of 20 per cent on all manufactures and an additional 10 per cent on 'sensitive items'. This programme would 'stop inflation', create an investment boom and recreate full employment. He then goes on to argue that such a policy would also generate a high growth rate.

31. I have discussed the characteristics of macro-economic models in 'Macroeconomic Models and Policy in Britain', in Michael Intrilligator (ed.), *Frontiers of Econometrics*, North Holland, 1977. Since I wrote that article in 1975, the models have been through many metamorphoses. In particular, the London Business School (LBS) model has incorporated many lessons from experience in the 1970s. And in the discussion of policy implications by Messrs T. Burns and A. Budd there has been a considerable movement towards the monetarist approach.

32. I must confess, however, that at the time, the Heath–Barber policy *did* greatly surprise me.

33. Of course, we do. The government has willingly entered into various restrictive agreements to maintain the price of many of Britain's imports. Coffee, wheat, sugar, shoes and shirts are examples.

34. A. A. Walters 'Importing and Exporting Inflation', *International Currency Review*, November–December 1973, pp. 7–10.

35. So ubiquitous is this view that sterling waxes and wanes according to the state of the unions. It would be painful to record yet again the massive evidence that has been accumulated on the inefficacy of wage and price controls. The fact that they are now widely regarded as the linch-pin, the *sine qua non*, of received opinion on macro-economic policy, gives one pause for reflection on the state of macro-economics.

36. M. H. Miller, op. cit., p. 516, where he argues that incomes policy was a significant factor in the inflation in 1974–75 and also an important ingredient in the containment of inflation from the end of 1975 onwards.

37. For example, David Laidler's evidence to the Expenditure Committee of the House of Commons, *Ninth Report*, Session 1974–75, HC-328, HMSO, 1974.

38. The Public Sector Borrowing Requirements (PSBRs) were: 1972–73 £1024 million; 1973–74 £4479 million; 1974–75 £7623 million.

39. The path of price inflation was much influenced by the third effect of monetary stringency – the gradual contraction of the deficit on current account of the balance of payments. Britain had to cease exporting inflation (as in 1973–74), and prices rose to reflect the smaller supply of goods on domestic markets.

40. There is a group of economists who may or may not regard monetarism as bizarre, but who argue that foreigners – and particularly conservative Swiss bankers – accept the principles of monetarism, and so one must put on a show for them or suffer currency crises. There is, finally, a

fringe of economists, such as Lord Balogh, who regard monetarism as absurd. But they regard all the laws of demand and supply as readily repealed for political purposes.

41. [Defined simply as the change in the money supply (M_3) plus the deficit on the balance of payments. – [ED.]

42. I argued that the DCE rule would be massively destabilising in the Second (1970) and Third (1971) Editions of *Money in Boom and Slump* (Hobart Paper 44, IEA, 1969). Five years later, there was an interesting illustration of the mordancy of a constant DCE rule. A normal DCE rule, if applied in 1974, would have called for a massive reduction in the money supply – and a considerable exacerbation of the slump.

43. Of course, one would get quite different prescriptions if the norm of full employment were regarded as, say, one million unemployed.

44. For a number of reasons why, see Robin Pringle, *The Growth Merchants*, Centre for Policy Studies, London, 1977. As I wrote, in October 1977, the new wave of expansion began to surge. We shall have to wait and see whether it again overwhelms us, as in 1972–73, and what the consequences are.

45. Ibid.

46. Mr David Worswick has argued this case in some of his recent publications, e.g. 'The End of Demand Management?', *Lloyds Bank Review*, January 1977.

47. Op. cit.

7 The Pleasures and Pains of Modern Capitalism

George J. Stigler

In my title I use the language of Bentham, and perhaps I should have asked Lord Harris to use his good offices to borrow Mr Bentham from University College, London, for this occasion. I am far from confident, however, that Bentham would approve of my preferences; and if he were to begin frowning as I spoke, I should be quite unnerved. Nevertheless, Bentham – who was an instinctive social planner – might well approve of some of the pleasures of capitalism which I shall emphasise.

Capitalism is a complete economic system: a method of production, of recruiting labour, of mobilising savings, of directing enterprise in old and new tasks. We know that in a literal sense the labour force is the largest part of capital in a capitalistic economy; the skills of workers are more expensive to produce, and more productive to use, than all the dazzling machinery of factory and office. Nevertheless, the fundamental organisational unit of capitalism is the business firm, and it is the fortunes of the business sector in a modern capitalistic system that I propose to discuss.

THE PLEASURES

I shall start with the pleasures of modern capitalists. My thesis is that the business community is the beneficiary of more governmental favours than it ever received in the past, and that it continues to play a major role in the economic and political life of our times.

There is no more notorious fact than the modern proliferation of governmental policies designed to control and direct economic activity. The Center for the Study of American Business at Washington University periodically issues a *Directory of Federal Regulatory Agencies*. For the United States – where the praises of Adam Smith are sung more often and more loudly than in Glasgow – the *Directory* reports 88 000 employees of 57 federal agencies busily directing our economy, triple the number so engaged 10 years earlier. But the extent of regulation can scarely be measured by this tip of an iceberg, which excludes such powerful and pervasive agencies as the Internal Revenue Service, and the panoply of state and local governmental regulators, let alone the thousands of lawyers and other experts employed by the industries that are regulated. I recently estimated that one small, self-effacing clan, the economists, receive about $45 million a year – chiefly from private parties – as a result of American anti-trust policies.

What is the source of this biggest of all growth industries, the regulating sector? I shall approach the answer indirectly.[1] I shall illustrate my arguments from the American economy, but I am reasonably confident that Great Britain, Canada, Germany, France or a dozen other Western countries would provide comparable examples.

Two Propositions

1. All Consumers Benefit from an Efficient Economy

My first proposition is that consumers have a primary interest in the efficiency of the operation of the economy. If I am a wealthy person I wish to have my mansions and psychiatric treatment and racks of lamb produced and sold at the lowest prices compatible with the maintenance of their quality. If I am a middle–class person I will have the same desire about my suburban home, college instruction for my children, and my golf club membership. That is obvious enough.

What may be less obvious is that, if I am a recipient of welfare benefits, I should have an even stronger desire for economic efficiency. Not only will a dollar go further in an efficient economy, but there will also be more dollars to give to, or be taken by, those on welfare. Whatever the political power of the welfare classes, or the benevolence of the taxpayers who provide the funds, the absolute amount which goes to welfare will rise with the national income. It is no paradox that he who milks a cow prays for good pasturage.

Two Kinds of Exceptions   There are two kinds of exceptions to the rule that consumers are, and in their own interest ought to be, the supporters of a highly efficient economy, which I will identify with an unregulated private economy. The first is illustrated by rent control, where a particular group of tenants – those in possession of the premises on the day rent control is imposed – succeed in bringing the determination of rents under political supervision.

The second exception is the correction of market failures, the familiar textbook example of which is pollution controls. Both kinds of consumer-oriented regulation have grown substantially in recent times. I shall return to the first one at a later stage (pp. 14–15), but shall pass over the far fewer policies required to correct market failures.

These not unimportant exceptions aside, most economic regulations do not benefit even an important sub-class of consumers. Consumers do not gain from the regulation of public utilities, financial institutions, labour markets, imports and exports – and literally thousands of other regulatory policies of almost inconceivable variety. There is in the United States a compensation scheme for the owners of bees whose death may have been hastened by pollutants. The introduction of this policy a few years ago, one Department of Agriculture employee has observed, has led to the complete disappearance of bees who die a natural death. The consumers of honey did not get this programme adopted. Nor did consumers support state licensing laws requiring a barber to have more hours of training (as many as 1200) than an airline pilot. (It would appear less difficult to navigate about the earth than about the human skull.) If consumers had their way, modern economies would be relatively free, productive and progressive, populated with individuals buying vast quantities at low prices, and taxing the rich the maximum amount permitted by their political power or suggested by a prudent regard for the health of the golden-egg-laying geese.

My first proposition, therefore, is that consumers, especially poor consumers, have no interest in efficiency-destroying regulation of the economy. Maximum output is truly their goal; *laissez-faire* is their creed.

Professor Walton Hamilton, once a member of the Yale Law School, maintained that our language lags behind the times. The common greeting, 'Good Day', is appropriate to an agricultural society, he claimed, where it represents its desire for good weather for the crops. He predicted that, eventually, the greeting of urban dwellers would be 'Low Prices'.

2. Entrepreneurs and Managers are the Elite-class

My second proposition is that entrepreneurs and managers are the elite class in a modern society. They are the people with energy and ideas, and they ultimately control the resources of the society. This is true whether they are high-born aristocrats, the army of functionaries of a communist state, or the public bureaucrats and business executives of a modern 'mixed' society. The proposition is also true, I believe, whether the society is democratic or dictatorial, whether the energies of its entrepreneurs are directed to pleasing consumers or voters or currying favour with the central party committee.

The entrepreneurs and managers, almost by definition, are the movers and shakers of society. But the economic organisations within which they operate produce considerable differences in their behaviour. In a socialistic system their explicit salaries will be smaller than under private enterprise, but their perquisites will be larger. In a socialised system the rivalry for power will eliminate the weak from control, but a different set of winners will probably emerge than under private enterprise. It is hard to believe that a present-day Henry Ford would get a chance to control large resources in modern England or Sweden. He would find it utterly impossible in the Soviet Union – and much, much more difficult in the United States today than in 1910.

So powerful is this class of entrepreneurs and managers – and so powerful was it in the United States in the closing decades of the nineteenth century – that it is quite impossible to believe such widespread political interference in the economic system could have taken place without the permission of the industries so regulated. Let us try to imagine the railroad industry under the unwilling control of the Interstate Commerce Commission in 1890. The industry had 700 000 employees, $10 billion of capital (when $10 billion was the approximate value of the national income of the USA), and dozens upon dozens of powerful, able entrepreneurs. The ICC had five commissioners, a staff of 61, and a budget of $15 000. It also had infinite respect for the members of Congress, who in turn were not lacking in respect for the great industry of railroading. If he had been told that the ICC controlled the railroads, the Duke of Wellington would have repeated himself: any one who believed that would believe anything.

Businessmen Initiated Governmental Controls on Business

So the major part the regulations to which businessmen are subjected must be of their own contriving and accepted by them. It is they who persuaded the federal and state governments to initiate the controls over financial institutions, transport and communication systems, extractive industries, and so on. The railroad industry is a graphic example; scarcely born before it started asking for loans from local governments and grants of land from the federal government, it has now advanced to such eleemosynary forms as Amtrak[2] and Conrail.[3] Even the burial of business enterprises has become a public activity,

and the savings and loan institutions of America are currently providing a large number of corpses.

If the late Joseph Schumpeter – that profoundly wise and infinitely
clever economist – were here, he would tell you that I am quite wrong
in my explanation of the luxuriant growth of public regulation. He
would say that, despite the immense contributions of the private enterprise system to the economic prosperity of the Western world – or
indeed of the whole world – it is being undermined by a body of
critics. Some are intellectuals; some are 'activists' (meaning usually
that their mouths, not their minds, are active); and some are simply
people who will gain power by increasing governmental controls. All
view the unregulated private enterprise system as their primary enemy.

I do not deny that there are more than enough of such critics of
private enterprise and that they have attracted a lot of public attention
for many years. What I do deny is that they would be remotely a
match for a nation's business community if that community were united
in its opposition to public intervention in economic life. The American business community in particular possesses vast numbers of very
able people – steadily being augmented by an élite class of recent
college graduates who are passing through the leading business schools.
It has ample financial resources, even in these days of onerous taxation. What it lacks is the will to eliminate most business regulation.

Intellectuals Have Been the Unintentional Friends of Business

That the intellectuals have been the chief pleaders for regulation, while
the business community has verbally opposed regulation in general,
may well have fostered the illusion that it is the intellectuals who
have been responsible for the regulatory policies adopted. If, my reading of history is correct, however, the intellectuals – miserable souls –
were basically serving the business community they profess to dislike
by creating a façade of public interest for the regulatory regime.

It is instructive to observe the behaviour of the Reagan Administration – avowedly dedicated to deregulation – towards the desires of the
business community. The financial sector did not wish to see a serious
curtailment of the powers of the Securities and Exchange Commission,
and an informed and responsible figure from the financial industry was
appointed to be its new chairman. The Administration's initial position that the Federal Trade Commission should withdraw from antitrust enforcement was hastily modified in response to pressure from
small businesses. The Interstate Commerce Commission retreated from

an anti- to a pro-regulatory stance. The picture was not, however, unmixed: the deregulation of the oil industry was a major reform, and antitrust policy became much more sensible. But the persistence of the vast array of regulations was evident – and was inevitable.

I must hasten to add that it is not only the business community, as that phrase is commonly understood, which has lobbied for and obtained those bountiful regulatory favours. The agricultural industries have secured many regulatory boons, especially in the last 50 years. The labour unions, and particularly those representing employees in the railroad and coal-mining industries, have done very well in Washington. It would be more precise to say that most regulatory policies have been sought by producer groups, of whom the business community is the most important. The *academic* community is by no means the least demanding.

A Golden Age of Business?

Thus I emerge with two propositions: consumers are opposed to most regulations; businessmen are selectively in favour of most regulations. If I add the commonplace that regulations are both pervasive and increasing, should I conclude that business is enjoying its golden age? Should people who write of the twilight of capitalism be told that they awakened rather early – that today is really the high noon of capitalism?

At this point some of you will be tempted to say that I have misread the regulatory scene with my perverse arguments; that business wishes to be freed from its regulations. I hope you will re-examine my arguments at leisure and ponder whether the ocean of regulations could possibly have been introduced under high capitalism except with the consent of the capitalists. Business likes what it is getting and complains publicly only because so many intellectuals take affront at the sight of a happy businessman.

Economic Prosperity Not Dependent on Political Favours

Although my focus is on the political scene, it would be grossly misleading to infer from this orientation that the fortunes of a capitalistic system are inherently dependent upon the favours of a political sector. Indeed, a more accurate title for this lecture would have been 'The Modern Pleasures and Pains of Capitalism'.

The two principal sources of economic prosperity in the nineteenth century were not political. They were:

(i) An economic system which placed command over resources in the hands of anyone who could demonstrate his skill and integrity in employing them; and

(ii) A structure of economic rewards which allowed and encouraged innovation in

    (a) the discovery of resources,

    (b) the development of new technologies, and

    (c) the organisation and financing of economic activities.

There is no evidence that these springs of action, as Bentham would have called them, have begun to run dry. They still serve, within the differing constraints imposed on their freedom in different areas of economic life, as the main sources of the wealth of nations. I believe that the automobile industry, *or* the chemical industry, *or* the computer industry, has done more for American civilisation than the US Congress, with the Presidency and the courts thrown in for good measure. Together with other industries not yet born, they are capable of doing as much in the future. But will they be allowed to? Let us seek a partial answer in the *pains* of modern capitalism.

THE PAINS

The pains of modern capitalism have the same source as the pleasures. The state has become open-handed in bestowing regulatory favours on various producer groups – such as subsidies and protection against new rivals. It has also become much more accommodating to other groups and interests which are distinctly less well-disposed towards business prosperity. In short, the state is no longer a mistress but a harlot.

The growth of consumer groups seeking to appropriate resources through prices set by government was noted above. The illustration I used was the control of residential rents, a policy which continues to expand – albeit not very rapidly – in the United States but is more fully developed in Europe.

Rent-Control: Losers Lose More Than Winners Gain

A particular group of tenants – those in possession of premises on the day rent control is imposed – early gain at the cost of a set of landlords who lack either of two defences: *(i)* as many votes as the tenants; or *(ii)* the flexibility to be able to withdraw their investments from the regulated area and employ them elsewhere.

In the long run almost everyone other than the favoured tenants loses from this kind of regulation. New tenants must pay more in one way or another for access to the regulated properties; landlords are despoiled; and since rental properties are not maintained nor new units built except with public funds, the tax base and the supply of housing are impaired. There may be other winners besides the original tenants; owners of single-family dwellings, for example, may find the prices of their properties rising. On balance, however, the losers lose much more than the winners gain; national income is reduced by rent controls.

So long as such policies were local (in the United States they have been municipal) there were not many opportunities for a group of consumers to play this type of game. At the local level the game requires an immobile victim, like a landowner. But immobile victims are rare except for the owners of land. Such consumer-oriented regulatory programmes have therefore become increasingly national in scope. In recent years, for example, the regulation of energy prices has transferred large amounts of income to selected groups of consumers. The telephone rate structure in the USA displays some of the same consumer influence.

It is still exceptional, however, for a consumer group to win out over a producer group in the competition for political power. If that were the only opposition the business community had to combat in Washington, London, Paris and other capitals, the pains of capitalism would be small compared with the pleasures.

A Self-Defeating Outcome

But if many industries and occupations obtain access to the political system, the outcome is self-defeating. This is a second, self-inflicted pain of modern capitalism. If steel is protected, steel-users must pay higher prices and are handicapped in competition with other metals and other nations. If the transportation industries are burdened with restrictive licences, economic activity is driven to less efficient locations of production. If an inappropriate agricultural system is protected against international competition, the costs must be borne in substantial part by industries processing agricultural products. The various producer claimants for political favours become so numerous as to tread on each other's toes. Indeed, at times they tread on each other's throats. In the aggregate, the self-inflicted costs far exceed those imposed by consumer groups.

That a subsidy to sugar producers is a tax on fruit growers, or that an understanding with Hong Kong or Tokyo to limit their exports of some textile or electronic product is costly to our own export industries, is implicit in the arithmetic of economic life. The custodians of that arithmetic, the economists, have done little, however, to estimate the costs to business enterprises of the network of business-oriented public policies. We have a propensity to assume that the deadweight losses of economic policies fall on the owners of resources or on final consumers, on the ground that businesses can escape exploitation in the long run by moving out of unremunerative activities. So they can. But the cost of moving out may be high – and even higher if suitable destinations become fewer and more remote.

State Welfare – 'Myopic Robin Hood'

There is, finally, a third set of policies whose consequences for the business community have been grave: the welfare programmes of the modern state. In the USA the biggest is an extraordinarily burdensome social security system which, together with direct welfare payments, public health outlays and a host of other programmes, now accounts for the largest part of public expenditure. The modern state is a myopic Robin Hood: stealing from almost everyone but giving to many people, not only the poor, the fraction of the booty which survives the substantial administrative costs.

I argued above that even Robin Hood should interfere as little as possible with the productive efficiency of the economy he exploits in order to maximise his potential revenue base. If economists were asked how to conduct such affairs – their opinions on which are offered rather than solicited – they would propose a system of redistribution which interfered as little as possible with production. They would recommend – and, indeed, have done so – that no taxes at all be levied on business and that most public revenues be raised from personal income taxation.

The modern state has not followed a policy of minimising the adverse effects of taxation on production – for a simple reason, I believe. In modern states it would involve tax rates approaching 40 to 50 per cent on the lowest incomes, with very modest exemptions. John Stuart Mill observed[4] that

> An income tax, fairly assessed on these principles, would be, in point of justice, the least objectionable of all taxes. The objection to it, in the present low state of public morality, is the impossibility of ascertaining the real incomes of the contributors. . . . The tax, therefore, on whatever principles of equality it may be imposed, is in

practice unequal in one of the worst ways, falling heaviest on the most conscientious.

Whatever Mill, who was rather a snob, thought of public morality in 1848, he never dreamed of asking the exorbitant price that is set on virtue when direct taxes of 50 per cent are levied on nearly everyone.

Taxation, Redistribution and Productivity

So the modern state employs a host of excise and corporate taxes, as well as high-speed printing presses, to finance its vast programmes of income redistribution. Indeed, it is finding that even to allow adequate provision for the replacement of business capital would reduce its revenues more than seems tolerable. Similarly, the workforce has lost some of its discipline and energy – or, alternatively put, has found other ways, financed by government, of making a living.

The Puritan ethic in us tells us that, in the long run, the beneficiaries of such redistributive programmes must suffer for their neglect of the importance of economic productivity. Of course that is true. But, with a 10 per cent interest rate, it is correct – and rational – to say that 40 pence in the hand is worth one pound in a bush that will not be reached for a decade. Patience and self-restraint have higher costs in political life than in the market-place.

In fact the choice is simpler than that. Any group receiving the state treasury's largesse which tempers its demands for favours has no way of preventing other beneficiaries from simply scaling up their requests. A pound saved on public housing is a pound available for eyeglasses.

THE BALANCE OF PLEASURES AND PAINS

So modern capitalism has its pains as well as its pleasures. How has it fared, taking both of Bentham's sovereign masters into account? Fortunately we have a balance sheet of remarkable accuracy.

That balance sheet is of course the value of the stockholdings in private corporations. The most comprehensive measure for the United States is in a study by Lawrence Fisher and James H. Lorie.[5] They trace the experience of someone who buys the same percentage of all securities listed on the New York Stock Exchange at various dates and re-invests all dividends promptly in the appropriate shares. They show a sharp fall in the nominal rates of return by 1976 (Table 7.1).

Table 7.1   Nominal Returns on Initial Investment of $100 in New York
Stock Exchange, 1925–70
(Dividends reinvested; initial weighting of portfolio by value)

Date of initial investment	Value of investment ($)		10-year rate of return (%)
	10 years later	In 1976	
1925	162	8479	4.9
1930	126	6421	2.3
1935	233	5483	8.8
1940	355	5203	13.5
1945	421	2311	15.5
1950	405	1455	15.0
1955	297	553	11.5
1960	219	344	8.2
1965	147	186	3.9
1970	–	148	–

Loss of Real Wealth

Their account can be brought up to date with the Standard and Poor Index of 500 common stocks (Table 7.2). The story is grim. The average price of shares (corrected for stock splits) has been rising slightly since 1965 – by about 1 per cent a year. Meanwhile the price level had been rising at an average rate of nearly 8 per cent a year. Thus the net return to stockholders, even allowing for dividends, has been a substantial negative sum, perhaps minus 5 per cent a year during the last decade. Over a decade the owners of corporations have suffered a loss of about 55 per cent in their real wealth.

Two decades of steadily declining performance do not spell the end of an economic system. In the United States the 1970s were no worse than the 1930s, which were succeeded, after the Second World War, by a period of reasonably high prosperity. Even so, it takes a sanguine prophet to extrapolate the recent history of the fortunes of investors in the private sector into a rosy future. Of late the pains have much exceeded the pleasures.

This result is almost necessarily implicit in the nature of the pleasures, which generally confer a once-for-all benefit upon the recipients. A subsidy or tariff, for example, changes the profit picture of an industry and leads to rises in the capital values of that industry. Unless the subsidy or tariff is increased, the mere continuance of the first programme will bring no further rises in capital values. That famous

Table 7.2 Standard and Poor's Index of Common Stocks, 1950–82

Year	S. & P. Index[a] (1941–43 = 10)	Price Level (Consumer Price Index) (1967 = 100)	Deflated S. & P. Index
1950	19.1	72.1	26.5
1955	42.0	80.2	52.4
1960	58.0	88.7	65.4
1965	91.6	94.5	96.9
1970	86.9	116.3	74.7
1971	102.1	121.3	84.2
1972	113.4	125.3	90.5
1973	111.5	133.1	83.8
1974	85.7	147.7	58.0
1975	90.6	161.2	56.2
1976	105.9	170.5	62.1
1977	102.0	181.5	56.2
1978	99.8	195.4	51.1
1979	107.9	217.4	49.6
1980	118.7	246.8	48.1
1981	128.0	272.4	47.0
1982 June	109.7	290.6	37.7
1982 20 Aug.	113.0	n.a.	n.a.

Sources: 20 August 1982 and June 1982: *New York Times*, 22 August 1982; 1979–81: *Federal Reserve Bulletin*, average of daily prices; Previous years: *Statistical Abstract* and *Historical Statistics*, changes in annual averages of monthly figures, linked to 1979 *FRB* series.

query, 'What have you done for me lately?', simply expresses the ability of a capital market to forecast and discount the future effects of present acts. Thus one measure of the balance of pleasures and pains, the stock market, tells us that things will go badly in the years immediately ahead.

THE OUTLOOK FOR CAPITALISM

A bleak or disastrous outlook is the stock-in-trade of every reformer; it is apparently difficult to attract support for a proposed reform simply with extravagant promises for it. Perhaps that is one reason for Adam Smith's remark that there is a great deal of ruin in a nation.

The extent to which modern capitalistic systems have been altered by pervasive political controls and heavy taxation is difficult to assess. Controls which look onerous and exhaustive, and attract much attention, may have very little influence on the course of events. The extensive legislation in favour of minorities in the labour market is perhaps a good illustration of this possibility. The competition thrown against old industries by new ones – the kind of competition dramatised by Schumpeter – may still be extremely powerful. The computer industry, which is immense, reaches into a thousand areas, and is virtually free of public controls, is a dramatic example of this Schumpeterian force. Among other things, the computer is driving the International Typographical Union, once the most powerful of unions, into limbo.

Similarly, the escapes from taxation devised by clever men acting under irresistible incentives have made the tax burdens somewhat lighter – and their final location somewhat different – than a literal reading of the tax laws would suggest.

I do not wish to imply that the controls and taxes are simply minor annoyances. Ludwig von Mises spoke with scathing contempt of 'loophole capitalism'. But I do wish to suggest that, so far as economic considerations go, modern capitalism is a viable institution. It could be more efficient and progressive, but it is not in a parlous state. The economic competition of other social systems is not going to push capitalism out of the running. The *military* competition of other social systems is an entirely different matter on which I have nothing to say.

Towards an Open, Competitive Economy?

At this point, the customary message of Chicago-trained economists is to call for a return to an open, competitive economy in which the government plays an inconspicuous though essential role as the guardian of civil order and monetary responsibility. The businessman, in particular, is asked to forgo campaigning for a protective tariff which would increase the value of his company's stock by 10 per cent.

The advice to take the long view has great appeal to economists because we are utterly convinced of the efficiency and progressiveness of an open competitive economy. It is rather self-serving advice, however. We cannot assure every industry and company that it would be better off in an unregulated regime, or that any benefit of self-denial by one industry would not quickly be swallowed up by some other claimant. To re-state the advice of economists: if you know anyone who represents a company which is successfully opposing a grant of governmental favours, I promise to write a sincere, warmly admiring letter to its chief executive. I shall also buy the stock of the company since it seems clearly destined for a take-over bid.

And so we face an embarrassing problem if we wish to return to a freer, more traditionally liberal society: the business community does not wish to be released from the public interventions to which it is subject. The merchant marine does not want unregulated, unsubsidised cargo ships; the steel industry does not want free imports; the construction industry does not want competitive interest rates. Each industry will agree on the desirability of making *other* industries freer and more competitive, but will assert that its own industry would become disorganised and perhaps even non-viable if the state withdrew. There are mavericks in many industries – entrepreneurs and firms that are eager to take their chances in the freer winds of competition – but they are seldom in a majority.

Business Must be its Own Saviour, with Some Help from Economists

Unless and until the business community is persuaded that on balance it will gain from a freer regime, it is unreasonable to expect the rest of society to join the movement towards deregulation. The defenders of a market economy usually view liberal (in the modern, not the nineteenth-century sense) intellectuals and confused humanitarians as their chief opponents, and address their arguments primarily to them. If my reading of the situation is correct, these intellectuals and humanitarians are not the important supporters of modern interventionism by the state. It will be necessary to show the business community in convincing detail that it is playing a losing game.

I do not know whether it will be possible to persuade the business community that its general interests outweigh the sum of its sectional interests. If it can be done, it will require more than warm, admiring letters from economists. Indeed, it will require cold, unflattering scientific studies. But we have more to contribute.

This is the age of quantification. On the Social Science building at the University of Chicago there is carved the statement by Lord Kelvin:[6] 'If we cannot measure a thing, our knowledge of it is meagre and unsatisfactory.'[7] An inconvenient *a priori* argument can always be eroded or blunted by challenging its exclusion or inclusion of some assumption, but economists find it difficult to resist well-established *empirical* findings.[8]

The quantitative study of the effects of public policy on the efficiency of the economy, and the identification of the beneficiaries and victims of particular policies, has grown prodigiously in the United States in the past 20 years. This kind of study is substantially changing the attitude of economists towards public policy. For a long, long time a criticism of business was alone sufficient to warrant a new piece of state intervention in the economy. The resulting mixture of costly inefficiencies and perverse income redistributions is changing that response. Economists are developing the knowledge which will eventually permit the limits of the competence of the state to be defined in a way that can be usefully applied. If we pursue this programme with sufficient skill and zeal, the long-run prospects of capitalism will surely improve.

With or without the help of economists, however, it is surely businessmen who must bear the main burden of defending and extending the system of private enterprise. I have argued that, if they will undertake this task, they can achieve much even single-handedly. But will they undertake it? The answer will determine the future balance of the pleasures and pains of capitalism.

NOTES

1. The section that follows borrows heavily from my *American Capitalism at High Noon*, published by the Graduate School of Business, University of Chicago, 1982.
2. National Railroad Passenger Corporation.
3. Consolidated Rail Corporation.
4. *Principles of Political Economy*, Ashley ed., pp. 529–30.
5. *A Half-Century of Returns on Stocks and Bonds*, University of Chicago Press, 1977.
6. Lord Kelvin (William Thomson, 1824–1907), British physicist and inventor.
7. Though Jacob Viner rejoined that our knowledge after measurement would still be meagre and unsatisfactory!
8. The demonstration by my Chicago colleague, Professor Sam Peltzman, that the National Highway Safety Act did not reduce the total number of highway deaths, but substituted more deaths of pedestrians for fewer of vehicle drivers, allows of no easy dismissal.

8 The Limits of International Cooperation

Deepak Lal

INTRODUCTION

When Milton Friedman delivered the first Wincott Lecture in 1970 on *The Counter Revolution in Monetary Theory*,[1] he could hardly have imagined how quickly the ideas of economic liberalism would be accepted and, however imperfectly, begin to be adopted in the conduct of the internal affairs of most countries. So much so that my former colleague, David Henderson, viewing the world from the vantage point of the OECD, has called the second part of this decade an 'emergent new Age of Reform'.[2]

For economic liberals, however, the contemporary scene provides a strange paradox. On the one hand, in the internal policies of most countries in the First, Second and Third Worlds, from Ghana to Russia to the Antipodes, economic liberalism seems to be winning its battle against the dead-hand of *dirigisme*. Yet in many aspects of thought and action in international economic relationships, there seems to be a reincarnation of the Dirigiste Dogma[3] among those very groups of politicians and 'opinion formers' (as the American admen have it) who were in the forefront of the recent destruction of the domestic *dirigiste* consensus. Its two most notable manifestations are, *first*, the conversions during the last few years of both the seemingly economic liberal governments of the UK and USA to international economic co-ordination of macro-economic and exchange rate policies, and, *second*, their acceptance of the desirability of establishing (what I may call) an International Green Economic Order.

INTERNATIONAL COOPERATION TO MAINTAIN FREE TRADING AND PAYMENTS SYSTEMS

At the outset, I must make some important qualifications to my argument. As the title of this chapter makes clear, I and most economic liberals are not against *all* economic cooperation. There are at least two areas in the existing anarchic world society of nation-states[4] where some international cooperation is essential for the establishment and maintenance of a liberal international economic order. These concern the maintenance of an international system providing for freedom of trade and payments, including the free convertibility of national monies. Despite repeated attempts by *dirigistes* to undermine the classical case based on the logic of comparative advantage, the case for free trade in commodities and assets as serving both the national and cosmopolitan weal remains secure.[5] Moreover, this case underlines the desirability of unilateral free trade for each country – even if the rest of the world is protectionist – except for one important theoretical exception. This occurs (as has been known since J. S. Mill) if a country has some monopoly or monopsony power in its foreign trade (in either commodity or asset markets). Then (in the absence of foreign retaliation) it can garner for itself more of the potential cosmopolitan gains from trade by levying the so-called optimum tariff to turn the commodity terms of trade in its favour. If its trading partners retaliate, the final outcome in terms of the welfare gains and losses for our country is indeterminate, as the cosmopolitan gains from trade shrink in the ensuing trade war.[6] Marshall emphasised that the long-run elasticities of demand and supply for traded goods were likely to be high and hence that there was not likely to be any sustainable gain from this type of protection. But in the short run these elasticities would be lower and hence the possibilities of gains or losses greater. This meant, as Lord Robbins, noted, particularly when the removal of existing protective structures is at issue, that:

> The politician would be courageous indeed who would risk a short-run loss by the unilateral lowering of tariffs. And if we take this into account and all the special pleading which can be mustered in support of special interest, it is not difficult to see where power to restrict exists, where it is often likely to be employed, and that a condition in which, without deliberate supra-national contrivance, there prevails a general absence of restrictions is not likely before the Greek Kalends.[7]

This 'supra-national contrivance' was provided after the Second World War by the General Agreement on Tariffs and Trade (GATT). Having overseen a number of trade rounds which have progressively liberalised foreign trade regimes around the world, and despite some backsliding, this form of international cooperation, though by no means perfect, and constantly under threat,[8] has proved its worth. Moreover, despite the repeated fears expressed about its imminent demise, its future is not as bleak as many commentators claim.

THE THEORETICAL CASE FOR INTERNATIONAL *DIRIGISME*

Whereas the international cooperation required to promote liberal foreign trade regimes entails a *reduction* in government intervention, that being advocated for implementing international coordination of macro-economic and exchange rate policies by the major OECD countries, and increasingly for creating an International Green Economic Order, implies an *increase* in the role of governments.[9] The underlying econ-omic argument for this international *dirigisme* is based on the pre-sumed existence of what economists call externalities. These refer to the uncompensated side-effects of a producers' or consumers' activity on other economic agents.

But externalities are a very slippery concept. Two theoretical points need to be kept in mind in their identification. The first is a distinction made by James Buchanan and Craig Stubblebine between Pareto-rel-evant and Pareto-irrelevant externalities.[10] Pareto-relevant externalities are said to be present when, in a competitive equilibrium, the mar-ginal conditions of optimal resource allocation and hence for Pareto-efficiency (i.e. a definition of an efficient economic state where one person cannot be made better off without making someone else worse off) are violated. Then government intervention may be required. But not all the side-effects on consumers and producers in a highly inter-dependent market economy will result in Pareto-relevant externalities (as we shall see).

The second distinction, due to Jacob Viner,[11] is between pecuniary and technological externalities. Pecuniary externalities are those in which one individual's activity level affects the financial circumstances of another. But this does not imply any resulting misallocation of re-sources. Consider, for example, a perfectly competitive economy in which there are continuous shifts in tastes and technology. Suppose that some group increases its consumption of whisky, the price rises, and that this affects the welfare of other consumers of whisky. This has no significance for the efficiency of the economy, which *ex hy-pothesi* is perfectly competitive and hence (in the jargon) Pareto-efficient. Or suppose there is a cost-saving invention by one producer. He in-creases his output and reduces his price. Through market interdependence other producers lose rents and are hurt, and consumers gain (consumer's surplus). It is readily shown that the consumer gains and those of the cost-reducing producer are always greater than the losses of the inefficient producers. What is more, the cost-reducing producer must *not* take account of the losses of the inefficient producers, for if he did, he would restrict output and would therefore be behaving as a quasi-monopolist; thus the industry's output level would be sub-optimal.

Pecuniary externalities are therefore synonymous with market inter-dependence and the price system. They must be Pareto-irrelevant. By contrast, technological externalities are interdependencies between economic agents which are *not* mediated through the market, and hence *not* reflected in relative prices. A well-known example is the smoke emitted by a factory which raises the costs of a nearby laundry.

It is recognised that the existence of so-called technological externalities in a competitive economy requires government intervention in the form of Pigovian taxes or regulation for efficiency.[12] Such domestic measures for dealing with externalities which are internal to a particular domestic national economy are well known and in principle uncontroversial. A clear statement of these measures for the obvious externalities associated with local, national and some forms of trans-national environmental pollution is provided in Nicholas Ridley's excellent pamphlet for the Centre for Policy Studies (CPS)[13] and were set out in a Hobart Paper many years ago by my former colleague, Wilfred Beckerman.[14]

But the proponents of international policy coordination argue that there are international spillovers or externalities flowing from national macro-economic policies and nationally generated pollutants that require corrective action at a global level. As there is no world government, the world economy is pictured as consisting of a set of self-interested nations who, if they follow their own national interests, are likely to be faced by that sturdy work-horse of the game theorists, the so-called non-cooperative non-zero-sum game, the Prisoners' Dilemma. In that game, if you remember, there are two suspects. They are questioned separately by the police and each is told that he will be offered a better deal if he confesses than if he remains silent while the other confesses. If neither confesses then both are acquitted. The prisoners, who are not allowed to communicate with each other, do not know this, so fearing that the other will confess, both of them confess. If they could have coordinated their responses neither would have confessed and both would have been better off.

Let us see how the theory of externalities and the strategic aspects of the Prisoners' Dilemma relate to questions of international cooperation.

Types of International Cooperation

Some years ago Henry Wallich distinguished three types of international cooperation (in macro-economic policy).[15] The *first* was the sharing of information between governments about their current and future policies. This form of cooperation has been carried on for a number of decades mainly under the auspices of the OECD and to some extent in the IMF, and we need say no more than that there can be no objection to such inter-governmental exchange of information. The *second* is consultation about decisions. The *third* is an actual coordination of policies which Wallich noted 'implies a significant modification of national policies in recognition of international economic interdependence'. It is this last form of cooperation, namely, policy coordination, that I wish to consider in two areas of contemporary concern – macro-economic and exchange rate management, and the environment.

INTERNATIONAL MACRO-ECONOMIC AND EXCHANGE RATE COORDINATION

It is alleged that there are two transmission mechanisms, one through the terms of trade and the other through interest rates, whereby the macro-economic policies of one country impinge on others.[16] The first channel of transmission is well known and I do not want to discuss it at any length here, nor to outline the various spillovers it is supposed to entail.[17]

The second channel of transmission is through the capital account. This supports the effects from the terms-of-trade channel in a monetary expansion, but offsets them in a fiscal expansion. Thus with a monetary expansion in the USA, the US interest rate falls, capital flows out to the UK and the dollar depreciates even further, while in the UK there is an inflow of capital and an appreciation of the pound allowing a further expansion in UK output.

If, however, there is a fiscal expansion in the USA, its terms of trade and exchange rate will depreciate. This will improve other countries' terms of trade. But the capital market effect will be to raise US interest rates (to attract foreign capital to finance the fiscal deficit), leading to an appreciation of the dollar which will improve the US's and worsen the rest of the world's terms of trade.

It is argued that these various spillover effects, say, between two countries will, by altering relative prices, change the relative fortunes of export, import-competing and non-traded goods industries in the two countries.[18] Policy co-ordination, it is argued, could lead to a better outcome for all countries by avoiding adverse spillovers and strengthening benign ones.

Be that as it may, what I wish to note and emphasise is that these spillovers are pecuniary externalities and hence (as Roland Vaubel noted in a 1983 paper[19]) not Pareto-relevant. This can be seen as follows. The post-1973 international monetary system in the period when governments were not seeking to co-ordinate policy – roughly the early 1980s before the 'Plaza accord' of 1985 – can best be described (as Max Corden has labelled it) as an international *'laissez-faire'* or 'non-system'.[20]

At its most general level, the world economy can be looked upon as an international general equilibrium system (in the language of technocratic economics), where governments, central banks, households and firms are all economic agents. Each agent is acting in its own perceived 'self interest' and its own objectives (thus governments can have different objectives regarding, say, desirable inflation rates). The international markets for goods and assets will coordinate these myriad decisions into changing relative prices of goods and assets, which at the 'national' level imply changes in national interest rates and real exchange rates. With both public and private agents maximising their own interests, this decentralised international system is exactly like a market system. The changes in prices and outputs that arise as a result of the different actions of these agents are exactly like the increase in the demand for shoes, say, within a national economy, which *ceteris paribus* raises the price of leather and hence affects the financial circumstances of the purchaser of handbags. The macro-economic international spillovers are exactly like those affecting the handbag buyer which are, clearly, pecuniary externalities, and hence Pareto-irrelevant. As at the national level, there is no need for any further harmonisation or coordination at the international level than is provided by the market.

Assertions to the contrary will be recognised by development economists as old friends. They were used to justify central planning by Rosenstein-Rodan[21] and in a muted way by Scitovsky[22] in favour of so-called 'balanced growth', while Hirschman[23] used them in the form of so-called backward and forward linkages to justify 'unbalanced growth'.

If pecuniary external economies were Pareto-relevant then, as Scitovsky noted, 'the complete integration of all industries would be necessary to eliminate all divergences between private profit and public benefit' (p. 249), or, as Rosenstein-Rodan advocated, 'the whole of industry to be created is to be treated and planned like one huge firm or trust' (p. 204). But it is now generally accepted[24] that pecuniary external effects are not relevant in identifying market failure and the need for government intervention. Hence the case for international macro-economic coordination which is implicitly based on these considerations is logically flawed.

What of the case based on the strategic interactions of a small number of official actors, as represented by the Prisoners' Dilemma? This is puzzling for a number of reasons. What is being asserted is a purported analogy with the supposed inefficiencies of resource allocation in a market economy when there are monopolies and oligopolies. As Corden has recently put it:

> If all nations were small actors in the system the policies of any one would not affect the others. We would have the equivalent of perfect competition. But when there are several larger actors, or groups of actors acting in concert, the policy of one group (or country) is likely to affect the welfare of the others.[25]

Thus, it is the oligopolistic nature of the public agents in the otherwise competitive international environment which is taken to lie behind the so-called 'strategic' argument for policy intervention.

Theory of 'Contestable Markets'

But this ignores the insights from the modern developments in the theory of industrial organisation which go under the name of 'contestable markets'. The essential point is fairly straight forward. The number of firms in an industry does not provide a good indicator of whether or not the competitive outcome will in fact be established. The 'contestable markets' theory[26] argues that even a single (monopoly) or few (oligopoly) firm(s) will be unable to exploit any potential market power when the market is *contestable*. By this is meant that potential competitors can enter and exit rapidly from the market, and that the existing firm has no inherent cost advantage over potential competitors. As applied to international trade in commodities, it has been shown that the existence of seemingly oligopolistic or monopolistic industries in particular countries does not destroy the classical gains from trade as long as the market for the goods they produce is contestable.[27] In practice, the opening up of trade increases the contestability of what might have been relatively uncontestable national markets under autarky.

We would expect that the same argument could be extended to the case of the international 'market' in the macro-economic policies of different large economic agents – the governments and central banks of the Group of Seven (G7), say. To understand this point, consider a simple example.[28] The United States and Germany have very different levels of tolerance for inflation, say, with the US willing to tolerate higher rates of inflation than the Germans. Suppose there is an expansion of the money supply in the US. The consequent increase in demand leads to imports from Germany being sucked in to the US. These are paid for by an increased supply of dollars, which flow into the accounts of German exporters. If the dollar–DM exchange rate *is fixed* the German government would have to buy the dollars flowing into Germany with marks to prevent the flood of dollars from depressing the dollar and revaluing the mark.[29] This increase in the supply of marks would transfer the inflation to Germany.

But this effect arises because of the price-fixing entailed in the fixed DM–dollar exchange rate. If this price were not fixed, the US central bank's policy of exporting its inflation (and hence its implicit inflation tax) would be contestable. How? Very simply, with the increased supply of dollars, and with the Bundesbank maintaining a constant supply of marks, the DM would appreciate and German exports to the US would decline, with little net outflow of dollars from the US. The US would get most of the inflation it deserved, with little effect on Germany. But, and this is the central point of this example, for this market contestability of macro-economic policies (i.e. to prevent the US from using its potential oligopolistic power to levy the inflation tax on foreigners), *the exchange rate must not be fixed.* A fixed exchange rate in this context is rather like the government-imposed barriers to entry into otherwise contestable national markets which are a major source of effective monopolistic or oligopolistic behaviour by firms in domestic economies.

Moreover, for the sake of argument assume that there was a logical case for international policy coordination based on the argument of the Prisoners' Dilemma. What would be the gains from such coordination? The first problem is that there is no agreement about the true macro-economic model for any country or the world economy. Frankel and Rocket[30] have examined the consequences of governments having different views of the world. They use ten of the leading international macro-economic models to examine coordination of macro-economic policies between the USA and the rest of the world. They assumed that the two sets of governments could subscribe to any of the models, while the true state of the world could in turn correspond to any of the ten models. They examined all of the 1000 combinations that are possible, and found that coordination can make matters worse for at least one of the countries in about 40 per cent of these cases! Estimates by Sachs and Oudiz of the likely gains from cooperation between the USA, Japan and Germany in the years 1984–86 show them to be trivial – less than 0.2 per cent of GNP per year in the US and 0.7 per cent of GNP per year for Japan.[31] So at best, even if we disregard the fundamental economic illogicality of the case for international macro-economic coordination, there may not be any 'gains', and indeed there could be 'losses' for some participants, while for others the 'gains' themselves would be extremely modest.

Non-Cooperative Solution Preferred

The final ambiguity in using arguments based on the Prisoners' Dilemma is apparent if instead of the interests of the prisoners we consider those of the policeman representing the law. While collusion or collaboration by the prisoners is in their own interest it is clearly not in the interest of the law! The non-cooperative solution is in fact the more moral one from the viewpoint of the general weal. The same point applies from a public-choice perspective of the motivation of public actors. Unlike technocratic economists who assume that a government's interests are coterminous with those of its citizens – the benevolent, public-interest view of government – the more realistic public-choice viewpoint ascribes predatory motives to most governments. In that case it is by no means apparent that policy collusion by governments (the cooperative solution) is to be preferred to their policy competition (the non-cooperative solution) from the viewpoint of the citizens of the world.[32]

This can be most clearly seen by briefly examining the reasons for the explicit instances of international macro-economic coordination since 1973. The first occurred at the Bonn Summit of 1978[33] when the United States, worried about the slide of the dollar, persuaded the Germans to act as the locomotive of the world economy by increasing their domestic demand. The result was a higher German rate of inflation than they had bargained for; which, as Professor Harberler comments on this episode, 'gave policy coordination a bitter taste for German policy makers'.[34] The dollar remained weak until after Paul Volcker took the necessary corrective domestic action. The following period of 'benign neglect' of the dollar was followed in 1985 by the Plaza accord, again at American instigation, but this time to bring *down* a soaring dollar. The main industrial countries agreed to concerned intervention to bring down the dollar to 'equilibrium' levels – which of course are unknowable. But, as another Wincott lecturer, Sir Alan Walters, noted of this episode:

> As usual, the joint interventions only got under way some eight or nine months *after* the dollar had started to fall rapidly. Indeed, looking at the path of the dollar over the period of the Plaza interventions, it is quite impossible to detect any effect whatsoever. The pace of the fall was the same both before and after Plaza. But this in no way inhibited the participants from admiring their own perspicacity; Plaza was reckoned a success.[35]

The subsequent Louvre accord and all the other G7 interventions (including the latest at the last (1989) IMF meeting) have fared no better, and we need not concern ourselves with their tortuous history.

One consequence of all these interventions to keep the dollar up or down ought, however, to be noted. It has led to a large unintended expansion in world liquidity. Figure 8.1 shows expansions in the world dollar base[36] (the major component of international liquidity) lagged 29 months and the US rate of inflation, estimated by John Mueller (a former economic adviser to the House Republican conference). Two features are remarkable. One is the link, as monetarists have maintained, between money and prices. The second are the global monetary and price consequences of the international economic coordination in 1978 after the Bonn summit, which show up in the increase in world liquidity and, two years later, in increases in the price level. Also clear is the stability in these two variables as a result of the benign neglect of the dollar in the early Reagan years, as well as the subsequent explosion in world money after the Plaza and subsequent accords, whose inflationary effects on the international price level have now begun to emerge and will continue into the foreseeable future.

Figure 8.1 thus shows that international exchange rate coordination has not served the world too well.[37]

Clearly it is not the high-minded cosmopolitan gains from the cooperative solution to the non-zero sum Prisoners' Dilemma game that our politicians have been seeking to achieve in their periodic attempts at international policy coordination. It was the US which instigated international policy coordination, egged on by the IMF, which since the ending of the Bretton Woods system has been searching for a role – as in Pirandello's *Six Characters in Search of an Author*. America

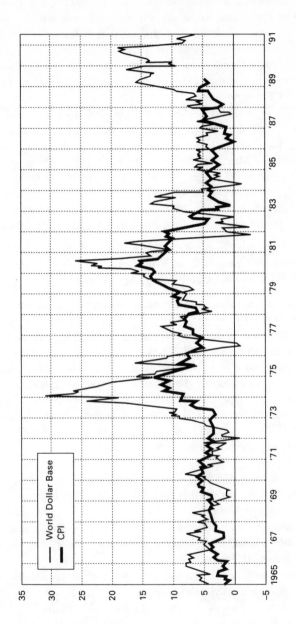

Figure 8.1 World dollar base *vs* US Consumer prices: annualised rate of change from six months earlier; dollar base lagged 29 months.

Source: Wall Street Journal, 24 February 1989.

has sought to externalise its internal problems of a domestic policy logjam created by the interaction of the shifting sectional interests and distributive coalitions, which its past domestic policies have engendered.[38] This is not a new phenomenon for students of developing countries. Third World Countries with internal problems have periodically sought to externalise them, most recently in their demands for a new International Economic Order.

What is surprising is that Thatcherite Britain should have joined in this charade. As Tim Congdon has cogently argued,[39] Britain had been well served by the four interdependent elements in the successful monetarist policies of Mrs Thatcher's tenure until 1985. These were: monetary targeting of broad money, domestic coordination of monetary and fiscal policy, an active funding policy, and a floating exchange rate. Congdon traces the shift to the self-destructive policies of managing the exchange rate to 1985 and the Plaza accord, when Mr Lawson

> had begun to take part in regular meetings with finance ministers from other industrial countries, with the ambitious aim of stabilising exchange rates and managing the global economy.[40]

This participation in US-inspired international *dirigisme* 'compromised the domestic orientation of monetary policy'. Why did Mr Lawson, an architect of the Medium-Term Financial Strategy (MTFS), fall for the false blandishments of international policy coordination? Could it have been that universal desire of politicians to eat at the top table, which of course is very easy to exploit by those with a top table? Mephistopheles has many guiles and comes in many guises. It would be better to end this farce and revert to the international 'non-system', where countries manage their domestic economies according to their own lights and let nominal exchange rates find their own levels.[41]

INTERNATIONAL ENVIRONMENTAL EXTERNALITIES

The economic case for international coordination or cooperation to deal with spillovers of national environmental pollution is more cogent, if its logical and empirical basis can be shown to be sound.

The externalities involved in environmental pollution are the prime examples of those non-market interdependencies called technological externalities. The principles of dealing with such externalities, as we have seen, are well known and relatively uncontroversial. I shall not therefore discuss the problems of, and solutions to, local pollution confined to national boundaries. I am more concerned with transnational pollution which supposedly results from technological externalities. Clearly, in the absence of a world government, some international cooperative agreement is required here to deal with the externality. The economic logic is clear.

The 'Greenhouse' Effect

Recently there has been much concern about the so-called 'greenhouse effect' and depletion of the ozone layer. If the claims being made about the nature and effects of this externality are correct, it could from the viewpoint of economic liberals be the externality to end all externalities. If as a result of *laissez-faire* and the decentralised production of the so-called greenhouse gases the very human race is likely to be extinguished, then internalising this externality could require a world central plan imposed by a world government.[42]

But before we jump to any such gloomy conclusions we must look at the facts, and ask what the rational response to them should be.

The Prisoners' Dilemma Again

It may be useful to note first that the general problem posed by the greenhouse effect is claimed to be yet another example of the Prisoners' Dilemma. In the environmental context this is called the 'Tragedy of the Commons'. Hardin (and others) have argued that the cooperative solution in the Prisoners' Dilemma 'game' must be instituted with

> whatever force may be required to make the change stick ... [for] if ruin is to be avoided in a crowded world, people must, be responsive to a coercive force outside their individual psyches, a 'Leviathan' to use Hobbes's term.[43]

What are we to make of all this?

The first point to note is that we have been here before.[44] In the 1960s and 1970s there was general hysteria about a world food shortage and discussions of various models of triage – where, in a boat too small to hold all the shipwrecked, those who are the weakest from hunger and hence cannot be saved are simply pushed overboard. The Green Revolution put an end to that.

Then there was the scare about the possibility of a nuclear winter, with the world entering a new ice age as a result of a war in which tactical nuclear weapons were used. When Mount St Helens erupted and dumped just such dust clouds into the air and we did not get a new ice age, the nuclear winterwallahs retired into their warrens.

THE GREENHOUSE EFFECT

Next, in 1975 *Science* magazine reported that 'meteorologists were "almost unanimous" that a [cooling] trend was taking place and that its consequences, especially for agriculture, were potentially disastrous'.[45] Now we have the greenhouse effect on the climate which it is claimed will lead to a global warming of between 0.6°C and 3.7°C by the year 2030, with a best guess of 1°C to 2.1°C warmer than today.[46] This prediction is based on current trends of the emission of the greenhouse gases – carbon dioxide (CO_2), methane (CH_4), nitrous oxide (N_2O) and chlorofluorocarbons (CFCs).

Of these gases, CO_2 is supposed to be the predominant contributor to the greenhouse effect. The major culprits identified in the past and future increase in CO_2, are the burning of fossil fuels and (by some) of tropical forests. Ecological activists are arguing for an international carbon tax on fossil fuels, and for legislation to impose eco-morality on the Brazilians, who are being bludgeoned to stop the economic exploitation of their Amazonian rain forests. Chris Patten, who became Minister for the Environment in July 1989, to resounding cheers at the recent Tory Party conference, has committed the UK government to 'negotiate an international convention on climate change which eventually would include binding agreements on subjects like energy and forestry'[47] – in short, the legislation of an International Green Economic Order.

What do the available facts suggest? The first fact, acknowledged by all sides, is that there has been some increase in greenhouse gases over the last 100 years and that this is likely to accelerate. But beyond that everything becomes uncertain. For as Figure 8.2 shows, the effects of these emissions on the climate are not straightforward, because of the complexity and numerous positive and negative feedback loops which determine the climate. But there is also agreement that the projected changes in greenhouse gases are within their past variation in the earth's geophysical history. In fact, it was the much higher concentration of CO_2 in the earth's atmosphere in the past than that currently projected for the future which is held to have allowed life to evolve. It is because of the *past* greenhouse effect that our planet is live while others are not.[48]

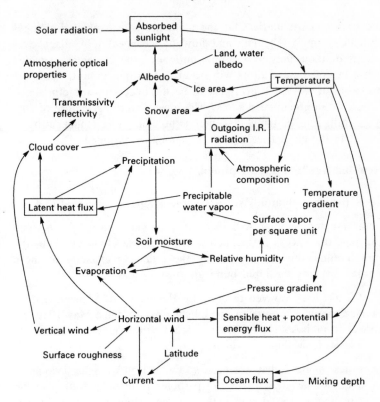

Figure 8.2 Causes and feedback linkages of climate

Source: H. E. Lansberg, 'Global Climatic Trends,' in Julian L. Simon, Herman Kahn (eds.), *The Resourceful Earth*, Oxford: Blackwell, 1984, p. 276.

Moreover, in the past one billion years, when most biological evolution took place, the earth's climate has been between 10 and 15°C warmer and not more than 5°C cooler than our present climate. Hence the projected increase in temperature is well within this range. Schneider also notes that:

> from the perspective of the overall existence of life on earth, even a 15°C (27°F) temperature change is not threatening. For example, 100 million years ago dinosaurs roamed a planet some 15°C warmer than today, and tropical plant and animal forests have been found in high-latitude locations such as Alaska.[49]

But it is also agreed that, whereas these changes in greenhouse gas concentration (particularly CO_2 and methane) and associated changes in climate (namely, the ebb and flow of ice ages) took place over hundreds of thousands of years or millennia, the currently expected increase in greenhouse gases will occur over a much shorter period.

But what of it? What are likely to be the effects on the climate of this increase in greenhouse gases? The most disturbing feature of current scientific knowledge is that there is no conclusive evidence that it will lead to the earth frizzling, as is commonly assumed.

A New Ice Age?: A 1938 Opinion

In 1938 British meteorologist Sir George Simpson suggested that

> increasing temperature will increase evaporation from the oceans, transport the excess to the poles, and increase cloud cover in the high latitudes, thereby increasing the reflective capacity of these regions, causing the rapid build up of snow and ice'.[50]

This idea has been revived recently by Hamaker and Weaver.[51] More recently, Schneider reports an unpublished paper (dated May 1989) by scientists from NASA's Goddard Space Centre (Y. Kaufman, R. S. Frace and R. L. Mahoney) which

> quantifies an issue that has been speculated on by Sean Twomey[52] for over two decades; that extra particles from air pollution in the atmosphere could seed clouds, thereby increasing their reflective capacity and in turn cooling the earth. . . . Based on many links and admittedly speculative assumption, they concluded that 'cooling would dominate heating' from coal burning.[53]

So, on the view of some respectable scientists, we are as likely to freeze as to frizzle as a result of the greenhouse effect!

Finally, there is the so-called 'Gaia hypothesis' of the British scientist, James Lovelock, which states that life on earth serves as an active feedback mechanism so that there will by and large be climatic stability. 'Lovelock and Margulis[54] argue that life has mechanisms to cool the planet before it overheats or to warm it up if it is cooling down too much.'[55] They emphasise the importance of tiny photosynthesising aquatic creatures (phytoplankton) in achieving this balance.

It is important to note that these alternative views of the likely greenhouse effect on climatic changes *are still current*: that is, we could frizzle or freeze or there may be no change.[56] Moreover, as even the climatologist, S. Schneider, one of the leading proponents of the green-house effect and of Draconian measures to deal with it, notes:

> there does not seem to be much chance that Earth is vulnerable to a runaway greenhouse effect as on Venus in which oceans would boil away or to a cold catastrophe as on Mars, no matter what we do in the next century.[57]

This seems to suggest that we do not have to face a Prisoners' Dilemma of non-cooperative extinction. Fearing this end-result, Schneider, however, adds: 'Still, climatic changes as great as an ice age would almost certainly be disastrous for *humanity*, if they occurred rapidly.' Let us see if this is true.

Climate Forecasting Models – 'Thin Reeds'

As climatologists are the first to admit, their forecasting models are very thin reeds on which to base any firm conclusions.[58] As with macro-economic models, there is also great uncertainty about the 'true' model – as we have seen. The more suggestive evidence therefore comes from historical evidence of past variations in climate. During the current interglacial period, temperatures at their warmest (some 5000–9000 years ago) were about 2°C warmer in summer than today. This is also the best estimate of the warming trend over the next 50 years from these highly uncertain climatic models.

Schneider reports the estimated change in the world's climate by region on the basis of a reconstruction of the past climate when the world was 2°C warmer, by climatologist Wilson Kellogg,[59] and anthropologist K. W. Butzer.[60] This climatic change is represented in Figure 8.3. Lo and behold, instead of the global warming being disastrous for humanity, it actually turns out on this historical reconstruction to be quite beneficial for India and Africa – where some of the deserts and drylands bloom.[61] The US grain belt suffers. It is not necessary for my purpose to accept this or the other regional effects derived from climatological forecasting models.

What Figure 8.3 illustrates is that even on the basis of the dubious and uncertain models on which the ecologists are asking us to frame global environmental and economic policy, what we have is *not* the negative sum Prisoners' Dilemma game – where everyone suffers if we do not cooperate to reduce the greenhouse effect. We now have a purely distributive, possibly zero-sum game. Unless we define 'humanity' to be identical with the interests of US farmers, it is difficult

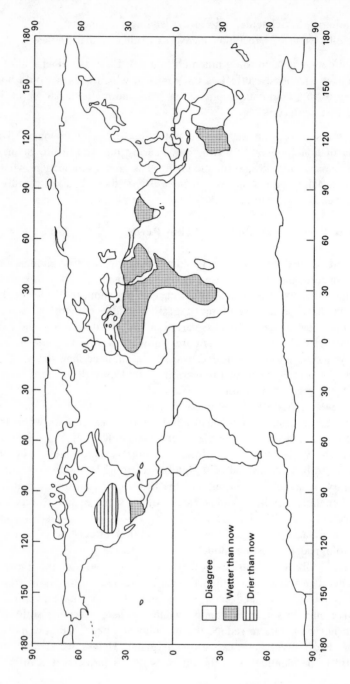

Figure 8.3   Effects of historical climate changes

In the absence of direct evidence of how CO_2-induced climatic warming might affect regional distribution of aridity or increased wetness, William Kellogg looked to the middle of the present interglacial, some 5000 to 9000 years ago, when (according to inferences made from a number of climatic proxies) summer temperatures were apparently a few degrees warmer than at present. While probably not caused by CO_2, the results he mapped could provide warm-earth analogies. Anthropologist Karl Butzer also produced such a map, and Kellogg combined on to another map (seen here) the areas of agreement and disagreement between these two paleoclimate interpretations. Note that although the authors' reconstructions disagree over most of the land area, they do agree that there was increased dryness in central North America and increased wetness in parts of tropical and subtropical Africa, Asia, and Australia. Agreement between Kellogg and Butzer does not, of course, necessarily imply correctness, as there is a possibility that these maps could agree or disagree by chance. (*Source:* Kellogg, William W., and Schware, R., *Climate Change and Society: Consequences of Increasing Atmospheric Carbon Dioxide* (Boulder: Westview Press, 1981), Figure C.3.)

Source: Stephen H. Schneider, *Global Warming*, San Francisco: Sierra Club Books, 1989.

to see how humanity as a whole will be hurt if the outcomes depicted in Figure 8.3 come to pass.

But, once the greenhouse effect is seen as leading to a zero-sum distributive game, all the moral authority of the cooperative solution to the Prisoners' Dilemma game disappears. What is more, when the economic effects of the positive distributional changes in world climate for some countries are taken into account, the externality involved in the greenhouse effect looks surprisingly like a Pareto-irrelevant pecuniary externality.

For the changes depicted in Figure 8.3 are equivalent to an international land redistribution – away from the North to some of the poorest regions in the South. Or equivalently, it is akin to the development of various synthetic substitutes for primary commodities which led to world-wide shifts in the pattern of production and consumption. But neither a change in the distribution of world economic resources nor in technical 'progress', which affects different countries differentially, and both of which can be expected to be mediated through the international price mechanism, yield technological externalities. Similarly, with the climatic consequences of the greenhouse effect shown by Figure 8.3, we have, at best, Pareto-irrelevant pecuniary externalities. Hence, there is no logical basis or need for any *international* cooperation on the issue of the greenhouse effect.

THE OZONE LAYER

But what, you may ask, about AOH? AOH is of course the acronym for the Antarctic Ozone Hole which is almost a British national treasure having been discovered by a British scientific team, whose financial salvation was authorised by the Prime Minister herself.

The Antarctic Ozone Hole is the latest in a series of scares about the ozone layer. Currently, if the media 'hype' is to be believed, unless we stop the use of CFCs, the ozone hole will expand and lead to us all dying of skin cancer. Clearly, if this were the case, then the externalities connected with ozone depletion would undoubtedly be technological ones, and Draconian measures to phase out the emissions of gases leading to ozone depletion would be justified.

For anyone who believes this, I recommend an excellent recent article by S. Fred Singer,[62] an atmospheric physicist who was involved in the earliest rocket experiments on the ozone layer and who invented the instrument that later became the ozone meter for satellites.

The first scare concerning the ozone layer, Singer notes, began when the USA was planning to build supersonic transports (SSTs) like the Concorde. It was argued by opponents that an SST fleet would destroy some 70 per cent of the ozone layer, leading to lethal ultraviolet radiation and an epidemic of skin cancer. That killed the SST. Later research, however, showed that

> the SST effect was only 10 per cent, and by 1978, the SST effect on the ozone layer had become positive: SSTs would add to the ozone. It became slightly negative again after 1980.[63]

'Wild Gyrations in Predictions' – CFCs In, Cows Out

These wild gyrations in theoretical predictions have been common in the scientific literature on the ozone layer.

By 1974 CFCs were implicated in ozone depletion, and public concern switched to banning them even though it was becoming clear by then that an important component of ozone-depleting actions was methane gas emissions from animal flatus! But as Singer notes:

> No one felt excited about it: stopping cows from belching and emitting other gaseous exhalations didn't ignite the environmental community. Cows are all so natural and low tech. Not a great cause. And besides, controlling their emissions could be messy.[64]

So the ecologists moved to a war on CFCs, and the gradual phasing out of these supposedly noxious gases. Mrs Thatcher's London Conference (March 1989) sought to extend the previously agreed ban on aerosols to other industrial uses of CFCs (like refrigeration and air conditioning).[65] But some developing countries – India and China in particular – demurred. As well they might. For as Singer reports:

> A National Academy of Sciences study in 1980 predicted an 18 per cent ozone decrease, based on a certain standard CFC scenario. During 1982 the effect had decreased to 7 per cent, and by 1984 to between 2 and 4 per cent. Ironically, much of the reduction was due to the discovery of the counteracting effects of those other pollutants . . . [which] hasten the arrival of global warming by the greenhouse effect while reducing the destruction of ozone.[66]

The Antarctic Ozone Hole

Then came the AOH. Singer states that there is some scientific doubt whether the ozone hole is linked to CFCs. It could be ephemeral, and linked to variations in the solar-cycle. Moreover, 'there could have been substantial changes in average ozone levels in the past, approximating those feared to result from the CFCs'.[67]

But what if the worst comes to pass? First, take the more pessimistic assumption that there will be a 5 per cent decrease in the ozone layer, if the world does not change its ways. Singer notes:

> This would increase ultra violet ray exposure to the same extent as moving about sixty miles south, [in the US] the distance from Palm Beach to Miami, or from Seattle to Tacoma. An increase in altitude of one thousand feet would produce the same result.

Second, 'melanomas have not been related directly to increased UV exposure'. The link is at best between benign non-melanoma skin tumours and UV.[68]

Third, melanoma rates have increased by 800 per cent since statistics began in 1935, without any corresponding change in the ozone layer or the amount of UV reaching sea level.

> To the contrary, measurements of UV-B (the biologically active component) have shown a pronounced and steady *decline* at every location.[69]

On the basis of this flimsy and contradictory data, with speculative and, at worst, seemingly not very serious effects of ozone depletion, the British Government is launching an international crusade to save the ozone layer! One consequence of this crusade will be that the cost of replacing CFC-using equipment, and any substitute that may emerge, will again damage the growth prospects of developing countries – particularly countries like India – where the spread of cheap refrigeration and air conditioning promises large increases in human productivity. This is *eco-imperialism* of the worst sort. As Singer notes:

> Third World countries are already heard accusing the West of protecting its pocketbooks [as the reduced supply of CFCs under the various current agreements will raise their price and the profits of the few Western producers making them] as well as its fair skins. Keeping in mind that olive-skinned and dark-skinned people are not very susceptible to skin tumours caused by solar ultra-violet rays.[69]

Thus it would appear that the externality associated with ozone depletion is likely to be trivial. As Matthew Parris noted jokingly:

> A little hole above Antarctica is perhaps the equivalent of a holiday in Lanzarote, a day skiing, or the 1956 Clean Air Act. It is absurd to apply your ozone-friendly deodorant stick then rush into the solarium for a quick tan. In our globally warmed planetary greenhouse you will tan faster *if you want to*. Otherwise wear a hat.[70]

Finally, as with macro-economic policy, it would clearly be open to any country to choose to mitigate the effects on itself of possible future warming. But there would be no basis for an agreement with those developing countries which stand to gain not only from their current burning of fossil fuels but also from the resulting global warming.[71]

This also implies that the various uses of aid to foster the green tastes of the politicians, and the public in the West, are likely to be misguided. To the extent that this slows down Third World growth in the interests of Western tastes (and the non-existent global technological externality that is assumed), it will hurt the drive against poverty in the Third World (which in turn will delay the decline in birth rates induced by rising living standards – also a concern of the eco-imperialists).

Much of the current 'hype' about 'sustainable growth' is terribly confused. As a researcher at the World Bank has shown, the concept can have at least 24 meanings.[72] No wonder so many people find it easy to subscribe to such a slippery concept which can mean whatever one wants it to. What cannot be gainsaid is that, as applied to the Third World, promoting what Western eco-imperialists call sustainable development will imply lower economic growth. The impact on living standards cannot be mitigated by any new fancy set of environmental accounts appended to the material national income accounts which show that growth, though slower, is greener.

Hands Off the Brazilian Rain Forests!

Nor is there a case for using aid money to save the Brazilian rain forests. As *The Resourceful Earth*, the counter report to *Global 2000* by Julian Simon and Herbert Kahn showed, it is not true that tropical rain forests are declining in the world. Though there are some reasons for Brazilians in their own national economic interest to change the current fiscal distortions which lead to an uneconomic exploitation of the Amazon,[73] there are none to bully them through tied aid and economic pressure into converting the Amazon into an internationally controlled 'wilderness reserve'. The economic exploitation of the Amazon (without taking into account the speculative and certainly Pareto-irrelevant pecuniary externalities connected with the greenhouse effect),[74] offers the prospect of raising the living standards of many poor people.

If there is any rationale left for foreign aid it must be on the moral grounds that (if effective) it redresses poverty in the world. It is doubly immoral, therefore, to transfer aid funds to save plants rather than people, and to reduce further the future income growth prospects of the poor by promoting the growth-reducing programme of 'sustainable development'. Moreover, by giving material and intellectual support to the existing *dirigiste* impulses in the Third World, this policy would, as we now know, do great damage to the prospects of their poor.

Why then has the West and the UK in particular launched this eco-imperialism of an International Green Economic Order? There are the obvious self-interested gains from what economists now call rent-seeking on the part of the scientists, bureaucrats and diplomats involved. But I do not think this is all. There is also a natural failing of politicians at work, which has been accentuated by the growth of a professional politician class which has no other career apart from climbing up the greasy pole. This natural failing was clearly identified by Trollope who wrote (in *Phineas Finn*, Ch. 13): 'It has been the great fault of our politicians that they have all wanted to do something.' Having supposedly slain the dragon of socialism, what else is there left to do but save the environment? But to the extent that successful democratic politicians are in part entrepreneurs, mediating the changing public mood, we also need to explain the shift of fickle public opinion towards greenery. The fear of 'Apocalypse Now' has been an enduring superstition of mankind. When there are more immediate dangers (recession, war, natural disasters) these fears are suppressed, to arise again when times are better. It is therefore no accident that the two waves of eco-doom in the last two decades have both followed two of the longest economic expansions in the history of the world.

CONCLUSIONS

My conclusions can be brief. The arguments for international *dirigisme* supposedly flowing from the externalities associated with global interaction in the macro-economic and environmental spheres are deeply flawed. They are ultimately based on the purported existence of what in effect are the Pareto-irrelevant forms of pecuniary external effects, which are part of the working of the price mechanism. If accepted as Pareto-relevant, the implication (as advocates in the early planning literature on developing countries clearly saw) is a global command economy. It is particularly sad, therefore, to see economic liberals not being clear-sighted enough to see these flawed arguments for what they are. The burden of my case is that, to echo Doctor Johnson,'externalities are the last refuge of the *dirigiste*'.

NOTES

1. See Chapter 2 above.
2. P. D. Henderson, 'A New Age of Reform', 1989 Annual Lecture to the Institute of Fiscal Studies, London.
3. For an exposition of this dogma, D. Lal, *The Poverty of 'Development Economics'*, Hobart Paperback No. 16, London: Institute of Economic Affairs, 1983.
4. This is how the late Hedley Bull described the existing world order in his book *The Anarchical Society*, Macmillan, London, 1977.
5. For a discussion and refutation of the most recent attempts to subvert this case – so-called strategic trade theory – see J. Bhagwati, *Protectionism*, MIT Press, Cambridge, Mass., 1988.
6. Harry Johnson, 'Optimum Tariffs and Retaliation', in his *International Trade and Economic Growth*, Allen & Unwin, London, 1958.
7. Lord Robbins, 'Liberalism and the Economic Problem', originally published in his *Politics and Economics*, London 1961 and reprinted as Ch. XI in his *Money, Trade and International Relations*, Macmillan, 1971, London, p. 262.
8. Most recently as a result of the bilateralism inherent in the USA's so-called 'Super 301' trade legislation.
9. This contrast has been noted explicitly by Martin Feldstein (see his Introduction in M. Feldstein (ed.), *International Economic Co-operation*, University of Chicago Press, Chicago, 1988), a trenchant critic of this new international *dirigisme*.
10. J. M. Buchanan and C. Stubblebine, 'Externality', *Economica*, Vol. 29, 1962; reprinted in K. J. Arrow and T. Scitovsky (eds), *Readings in Welfare Economics*, Allen and Unwin, London, 1969.
11. J. Viner, 'Cost Curves and Supply Curves', *Zeitschrift für Nationalokonomie*, Vol. III, 1931, reprinted in G. J. Stigler and K. E. Boulding (eds), *Readings in Price Theory*, Allen and Unwin, London, 1953.
12. A good modern discussion of the theory of externalities is in W. J. Baumol and W. E. Oates, *The Theory of Environmental Policy*, Prentice-Hall, New York 1975. The case for such corrective taxes goes back to A. C. Pigou, *The Economics of Welfare*, Macmillan, London, 1920.

13. N. Ridley, *Policies Against Pollution*, Policy Study No. 107, CPS, London, June 1989.

14. W. Beckerman, *Pricing for Pollution*, Hobart Paper No. 66, IEA, 1975. Also see the recent restatement of these principles in D. Pearce *et al.*, *Blueprint for a Green Economy*, Earthscan, London, 1989.

15. H. Wallich, 'Institutional Co-operation in the World Economy', in J. A. Frenkel and M. L. Mussa (eds), *The World Economic System: Performance and Prospects*, University of Chicago Press, Chicago, 1984.

16. A vast literature has grown up on international macro-economic coordination. A survey is provided in R. N. Cooper, 'Economic Interdependence and Coordination of Economic Policies', in R. W. Jones and P. B. Kenen, *Handbook of International Economics*, Amsterdam, North Holland, 1985. Three collections of essays in addition to Feldstein (ed.), op. cit., may also be noted; W. Buiter and R. C. Marston (eds), *International Economic Policy Co-ordination* (Cambridge, 1985); Paul Volcker *et al.*, *International Monetary Co-operation: Essays in Honour of Henry C. Wallich*, Princeton Essays in International Finance No. 169, December 1987, and R. N. Cooper *et al.*, *Can Nations Agree?*, Washington, DC, Brookings Institutions, 1989. An accessible summary of the arguments is in W. M. Corden, *Inflation, Exchange Rates & the World Economy*, 3rd edn, University of Chicago Press, Chicago, 1986.

17. The terms of trade effect is ultimately based on some form of Keynesianism. It is assumed that a nominal demand expansion in one country can affect its level of real output and employment. For example, say, the USA expands aggregate demand through a monetary expansion but with an unchanged fiscal policy. This will raise US income and output, but as part of the rise in US income will be spent on the goods of the rest of the world, its terms of trade will worsen and those of the rest of the world improve to absorb the excess of US domestic output not absorbed by US residents. The improvement in the UK's terms of trade and the appreciation of its currency allow a non-inflationary expansion in output and employment in the UK. Without this positive transmission from the USA, it is argued, the UK could not have expanded, as this would have led to a deterioration of its terms of trade and a devaluation which could have been inflationary. A coordinated expansion by both the UK and the USA would thus allow the terms of trade and exchange rates to remain unchanged.

18. Thus, for instance, the capital markets effects in the UK of a US fiscal expansion, which leads to a fall in the UK terms of trade and hence a reduction in UK spending, hurts its non-traded goods producers. But the devaluation which accompanies the outflow of capital from the UK by raising the relative domestic price of tradeables benefits producers in both export and import-competing markets.

19. R. Vaubel, 'Co-ordination or Competition Among National Macro-Economic Policies?', in F. Machlup *et al.* (eds), *Reflections on A Troubled World Economy*, Macmillan, London, 1983.

20. W. M. Corden, 'The Logic of the International Monetary Non-System', in F. Machlup *et al.* (eds), ibid.

21. P. N. Rosenstein-Rodan, 'Problems of Industrialisation of Eastern and South-Eastern Europe', *Economic Journal*, Vol. LIII, 1943.

22. T. Scitovsky, 'Two Concepts of External Economies', *Journal of Political Economy*, Vol. 17, 1954.

23. A. O. Hirschman, *The Strategy of Economic Development*, Yale University Press, New Haven, 1958.

24. For a critical discussion of the literature on 'pecuniary externalities' and 'linkages' to developing countries, see I. M. D. Little, *Economic Development*, Basic Books, New York, 1982, pp. 38–47. A clear account of the modern theory of externalities which excludes pecuniary externalities as Pareto-irrelevant is in Baumol and Oates, op. cit.

25. W. M. Corden, 'Fiscal Policies, Current Accounts and Real Exchange Rates: In Search of a Logic of International Policy Co-ordination', *Weltwirtschaftliches Archiv*, Vol. 122, No. 3, 1986, p. 7.

26. W. J. Baumol, J. C. Panzar and R. D. Willig, *Contestable Markets and the Theory of Market Structure*, Harcourt Brace Jovanovich, New York, 1982. But the seminal article introducing the importance of contestability in establishing competitive conditions even in a natural monopoly is H. Demsetz, 'Why Regulate Utilities?', *Journal of Law and Economics*, April 1968.

27. See E. Helpman and P. Krugman, *Market Structure and International Trade*, MIT Press, Cambridge, Mass., 1985.

28. This is taken from another Wincott lecturer, Alan Walters: 'International Co-ordination of Economies', *The National Interest*, Winter 1988. He accepts the logical impeccability of the international *dirigiste* case '*on its own assumptions*', but does not point out the economic illogicality from the viewpoint of standard micro-economics of the Pareto-relevance of pecuniary external effects, and of the non-contestability of the 'markets' for macro-economic policies that is also the implicit assumption underlying this view.

29. This, as Walters notes, implies unsterilised intervention. Sterilised intervention would imply that the German government does not create new marks, but acquires the marks it needs by selling long-term mark bonds. But, as Walters notes: 'Experience has shown, however, that this so-called "sterilisation" of the exchange rate intervention is effective only in the short-term; ultimately the quantity of marks and the inflation rate must increase.'

30. Jeffrey Frankel, 'Obstacles to International Macroeconomic Policy Coordination', *Princeton Studies in International Finance*, No. 64, Princeton, December 1988, and J. Frankel and K. E. Rockett, 'International Macroeconomic Policy Co-ordination When Policy Makers Do Not Agree on the True Model', *American Economic Review*, Vol. 78, June 1988.

31. G. Oudiz and J. Sachs, 'Macroeconomic Policy Co-ordination Among the Industrial Countries', *Brookings Papers on Economic Activity*, No. 1, 1984.

32. This point has been made among others by Martin Feldstein, for instance in his introduction to M. Feldstein (ed.), *International Economic Cooperation*, University of Chicago Press, Chicago, 1988.

33. See R. D. Putnam and C. R. Henning, 'The Bonn Summit of 1978: How Does International Policy Co-ordination Actually Work?', *Brookings Discussion Papers in International Economics*, No. 53, 1986.

34. G. Haberler, 'Further Thoughts on International Policy Co-ordination', in P. Volcker *et al.*, op. cit., p. 26.

35. Walters, op. cit.

36. This is defined as the stock of high-powered money: currency (dollars) *plus* bank reserves in the USA *plus* the dollars held by foreign central banks. See John Mueller, 'CPI at 7 per cent? Bet Your Reserve Dollar', *Wall Street Journal*, 24 February 1989.

37. In practice, such coordination has introduced a further element of uncertainty into world financial markets, and the two stock market crashes of October 1987 and 1989 can in fact be traced to the perverse effects of this international *dirigisme*.

38. D. Lal and M. Wolf (eds), *Stagflation, Savings and the State*, Oxford University Press, Oxford 1986.

39. T. Congdon, *Monetarism Lost*, CPS, London, 1989, p. 16.

40. Congdon, ibid., p. 24.

41. I have dealt with various arguments against floating, many of which are still current, in Lal, 'A Liberal International Economic Order: The International Monetary System and Economic Development', *Princeton Essays in International Finance*, No. 139, October 1980. The major alternatives to floating are: McKinnon's 'New Gold Standard Proposals', and John Williamson's 'Target Zone Proposal'. For the most recent versions of their schemes, see R. McKinnon, 'Monetary and Exchange Rate Policies for Financial Stability: A Proposal', *Journal of Economic Perspectives*, Vol. 2, No. 1, Winter 1988, and 'An International Gold Standard Without Gold', *Cato Journal*, Vol. 8, No. 2, Fall 1988; and J. Williamson, *The Exchange Rate System*, revised edn, Institute for International Economics, 1985. Trenchant critiques of McKinnon are contained in the comments by R. Dornbusch on the above articles. A balanced critique of target zones is in Jacob Frenkel, 'The International System: Should It Be Reformed?', *American Economic Review*, May 1989. The best critique of exchange rate targeting *à la* EMS remains Alan Walters, *Britain's Economic Renaissance*, Oxford, 1986, Ch. 7; also M. Fratianni, 'The European Monetary System: How Well Has It Worked?' *Cato Journal*, Vol. 8, No. 2, Fall 1988.

42. Two collections of essays are particularly useful in providing accessible summaries of the scientific evidence and controversies surrounding various environmental issues: Julian Simon and Herman Kahn (eds), *The Resourceful Earth*, Blackwell, Oxford, 1984, which presents a counterview to the *Global 2000* report sponsored by US President Carter. The others are The Darwin College Lectures edited by L. Friday and R. Laskey, *The Fragile Environment*, Cambridge, 1989.

43. G. Hardin, 'Political Requirements for Preserving our Common Heritage', in Howard P. Brokaw (ed.), *Wildlife and America*, Washington, DC, Council on Environmental Equality, 1978, p. 314. The article in which Hardin introduced the Prisoners' Dilemma game of the Commons was 'The Tragedy of the Commons', *Science*, Vol. 162, December 1968.

44. J. Simon and H. Kahn (eds), *The Resourceful Earth*, op. cit., for a detailed scientific critique of the environmental hysteria contained in the 'Global 2000' Report sponsored by President Carter.

45. P. Shaw, 'Apocalypse Again', *Commentary*, Vol. 51, April 1989, cites both these instances of post-1973 eco-hysteria.
46. 'The Green House Effect, Climatic Change and Sea Level: An Overview', Climatic Research Unit, University of East Anglia, April 1988, p. 17 (mimeo).
47, Report in *The Financial Times*, 11 October 1989.
48. The first part of S. H. Schneider, *Global Warning*, Sierra Club, San Francisco, 1989, provides a concise and fair account of the scientific history of the greenhouse effect, and the great scientific uncertainties that surround it. The following discussion is based in large part on this work by a reputable climatologist, who himself is an environmental activist, seeking international action to halt global warming. But, as he states, there is a distinction between the weight of the scientific evidence 'including all the uncertainties and caveats' and the scientists' desire 'as human beings [to] want to leave the world a better place than they found it' (p. xi). It is the scientific part of his book I cite and not its 'human' policy part!
49. Schneider, ibid., p. 37.
50. Sir George Simpson, 'Ice Ages', *Nature*, Vol. 141, 1938.
51. J. D. Hamaker and D. A. Weaver, *The Survival of Civilisations*, Hamaker-Weaver, Burlingham, California, 1982.
52. S. Twomey, *Inadvertent Climate Modification, Report* on the Study of Man's Impact on Climate, MIT Press, Cambridge, Mass., 1971.
53. Schneider, op. cit., p. 293.
54. J. Lovelock and L. Margulis, 'Atmospheric Homeostasis by and for the Biosphere: the Gaia Hypothesis', *Tellus*, Vol. 26, 1973.
55. Schneider, op. cit., p. 68.
56. For the scientific controversy surrounding one climatologist's (James Hansen) claim to the US Congress that 'with a high degree of confidence we could associate the warming with the greenhouse effect', see R. A. Kerr, 'Hansen *vs* the world on the Greenhouse Effect', Research News, *Science*, 2 June 1989, p. 1041, and the subsequent letters in *Science*, 4 August 1989. In one of these W. S. Broecker, a defender of Hansen, concludes: 'Hansen may prove to be incorrect in his prediction of the potential seriousness of the greenhouse gas buildup, but it should be understood that concerns such as his are born of a deep regard for the future of our planet and not by fame or funding'! How often have we heard similar statements about the altruistic motives of politicians and bureaucrats, seeking to clothe self-interest in public interest. A recent vivid example which briefly removed this veil was the in-fighting between the World Bank and the IMF on which body should have primary responsibility for drawing up macro-economic adjustment programmes for the highly indebted countries. The international bureaucrats were like vultures, fighting over the carrion of the 'debt crisis' countries. Their rent seeking became patent.
57. Schneider, op. cit., p. 77.
58. For estimates of the regional effects from these highly dubious climatological models, *Developing Policies for Responding to Climate Change*, World Meteorological Organisation, WMO/TD, No. 225, April 1988 (mimeo).
59. W. W. Kellogg and R. Schware, *Climatic Change and Society: Consequences of Increasing Atmospheric Carbon Dioxide*, Westview Press, Boulder, Colorado, 1981.

60. K. W. Butzer, 'Adaptation to Globe Environmental Change', *Professional Geography*, Vol. 32, No. 3, 1981.

61. The World Meteorological Organisation's survey op. cit., of the scenarios developed with mathematical climate models, provides an alternative set of regional effects. But as it emphasises: 'Essentially all scientific studies of the greenhouse effect agree that the resulting climate changes will differ among regions. Uncertainties in the forecasts of regional climatic responses are greater than those in the forecasts of a global climatic response' (p. 7).

62. S. Fred Singer, 'My Adventures in the Ozone Layer', *The National Review*, 30 June 1989.

63. Singer, ibid., p. 35.

64. Ibid., p. 35.

65. It is not too surprising that agreement was reached on banning CFCs in aerosols, as Scott Barrett notes that 'the marginal costs of abatement are fairly flat for some uses of CFCs . . . the costs of substituting for CFCs in aerosols is trivially small'. (F. Scott Barrett, 'Ozone Holes, Greenhouse Gases, and Economic Policy', London Business School, July 1989, published as an IEA Occasional Paper in 1990.) Also he notes that there are only a few producers of CFC – of which DuPont and ICI are the main producers, who are supporting a ban on production of CFCs by the year 2000. This announcement *preceded* the decision by the US and the EEC to ban hard CFCs. He suggests that the reason for this altruistic behaviour is strategic interaction between the firms, who are competing to persuade 'governments to modify the nature of demand by forcing customers to buy a different, perhaps even more expensive, product. . . . If Du Pont develops cheap and more environmentally friendly substitutes for CFCs and if regulatory policy concomitantly forces users to switch to the alternatives, then Du Pont will have a competitive edge over its rivals. Indeed, if the government forces all users to switch to the substitutes, Du Pont will have the market all to itself.' Seeing this, its competitors will also have an incentive to join in the CFC ban, and quickly develop the race for substitutes.

66. Singer, op. cit., p. 35.

67. But as Singer notes: The incidence of benign skin cancer 'increases as one approaches the equator where the sun and UV are both stronger. . . . But we should not assume that all the increase is due to higher UV intensities. Life-styles in warmer climates are conducive to longer exposures and therefore contribute at least as much to skin tumours as the UV values themselves.' (p. 36)

68. Ibid., p. 36.

69. Ibid., p. 38.

70. Matthew Parris, 'Flourishing in the Greenhouse', *The Times*, 20 May 1989.

71. For a game-theory-based analysis of why an international agreement on greenhouse gases apart from CFCs would be virtually impossible (even if the greenhouse effect was a technological externality), see F. Scott Barrett, op. cit.

72. J. Pezzey, 'Economic Analysis of Sustainable Growth and Sustainable Development', Dept of Environment Working Paper No. 15, World Bank, Washington, DC, 1989.

73. H. Binswanger, 'Brazilian Policies that Encourage Deforestation in the Amazon', Dept of Environment Working Paper No. 16, World Bank, April 1989; D. Mahar, *Government Policies and Deforestation in Brazil's Amazon Region*, World Bank, 1989.
74. See Simon and Kahn (eds), *The Resourceful Earth*, op. cit., for a rebuttal of the arguments concerning the so-called 'species loss' involved in burning the rain forest.

9 Do Currency Boards Have a Future?

Anna J. Schwartz

INTRODUCTION

I shall discuss a subject that has recently come to life after decades of dormancy. Sir Alan Walters in his entry on currency boards in *The New Palgrave Dictionary of Economics*, published in 1987, observed that 'it would be rash to imagine that currency boards are the wave of the future'.[1] Yet five years after that observation, Sir Alan has become an active proponent of currency boards as the wave of the future under certain conditions. The subject is topical, since a currency board is a way of providing a stable monetary system, an essential prerequisite for a well-functioning market system in economies such as the newly independent East European countries.

WHAT IS A CURRENCY BOARD?

Historically, a currency board consisted of a small number of commissioners appointed by a government head (generally of a colony but in a few instances of a non-colonial territory). The board issued local coin and notes at a fixed exchange rate with a foreign money. The foreign money was usually British sterling, although in some colonies it was the rupee, the US dollar or the Australian dollar.

One distinctive feature of British currency boards (and possibly of some others) was that they had a statutory obligation to exchange local currency on demand for the foreign money and the foreign money for local currency. The legislation establishing the boards stipulated the fixed exchange rate between the local currency and the foreign money. The boards were bound by this rule to supply local currency to anyone who offered the foreign money to the board and to supply the foreign money to anyone who offered the local currency to the board. Thus, currency boards passively supplied the demand for local currency. They had no discretion. Historically, no central bank operated where a currency board existed.

Fixed-Rate Convertibility of Local Currency Assured

Currency boards thus assured convertibility of local currency into the foreign money. They maintained a fixed exchange rate between the local currency and the foreign money without intervening in the exchange market. No foreign exchange risk vis-à-vis British sterling could arise for the local currency. The purchasing power of the local currency for tradeable goods was linked to that of British sterling. Productivity differences can explain divergence of prices of non-tradeable goods in a colony from the corresponding prices in Britain.

By investing their reserves in interest-bearing form, equal to at least 100 per cent of their currency liabilities, currency boards earned seigniorage[2] on the local currency they issued. The governments of the colonies were the recipients of the seigniorage. Had the foreign (i.e. mother country) currency been used directly, the foreign country would have received the seigniorage.

Banks operated as non-note-issuing loan and deposit institutions alongside currency boards. They held currency board notes and coins in their vaults to enable depositors to convert deposits into local currency. Analytically, currency boards provided the monetary base (the sum of currency held by the public and currency held by the banks as vault cash), whereas the banks determined the money multiplier (the ratio of the money supply, the sum of the public's currency and deposits, to the monetary base).

In usual practice, only the banks dealt with a currency board. Both individuals and governments deposited their funds in the banks. Since a bank's legal obligation was to redeem its deposits on demand in local legal tender, it had to hold easily convertible assets. The assets were marketable securities in London. A colonial bank that wanted additional currency transferred funds from its own London accounts to the board's headquarters in London or to the Crown Agents – the link between the colonial governments and the London money market – for the account of the board. As soon as the London payment was confirmed, local agents of the board supplied the currency to the bank. Smaller banks obtained currency from a branch in the colony of a bank with a London head office.

Although the colonial branches of London banks were not subject to capital and reserve requirements, the legal tender requirement governing their operations gave little leeway for independent credit policy. They could presumably economise on cash and vary somewhat the ratio of vault cash to deposits. In general, however, credit policies of local colonial branches of expatriate banks depended on head office decisions.

Dependence of Trade Financing on London Money Market

Colonial banks were dependent on the London money market not only because the local money was linked to sterling but also because colonial trade was predominantly centred on the UK and was financed through the London bill market. The London offices of the expatriate banks bought and sold bills covering shipments of manufactured goods to the colonies and raw materials to the UK. These trade arrangements persisted during the heyday of currency boards despite the change in the London money market, beginning in the 1930s, so that it increasingly accommodated UK Treasury financing.

The linkage of colonial monetary arrangements with London was formed when the Gold Standard ruled and sterling was a convertible currency. The linkage was not broken after sterling was devalued in 1931; thereafter political decisions determined at what rate or, indeed, if sterling was convertible into foreign currencies.

Nineteenth-Century Colonial Origins of Currency Boards

Currency boards were first established in a few British colonies in the second half of the nineteenth-century. The definitive form of the currency board, however, was not attained until the establishment in 1912 of the West African currency board for the four territories of Gambia, Gold Coast, Nigeria and Sierra Leone. It served as the model for many new currency boards formed during the next five decades. It was also a model for a currency ordinance developed by the Colonial Office in the 1930s, on the basis of which some pre-existing currency boards were altered to conform with the model.

The West African currency board was also the inspiration for the National Emission Caisse established, on the advice of J. M. Keynes, by the provisional government in Northern Russia in 1918–19 to issue roubles for sterling at a fixed rate of 40 roubles to the £1, backed by 75 per cent in sterling and 25 per cent in North Russian government bonds (which were denominated in roubles). With the end of Allied intervention in Northern Russia, the Caisse was shut down.[3]

Two other non-colonial currency boards included one which was bank-owned in the then city-state of Danzig in 1923–24, and one that operated in the Irish Free State from 1928 until 1943. In the case of each of these non-colonial currency boards, a central bank replaced the boards.

ABANDONMENT OF THE CURRENCY BOARD SYSTEM

Currency boards worked well in the 100-year period during which they operated, mainly in colonial countries. The boards limited monetary growth. Home-grown inflation was not a problem. A local lender of last resort was not needed. The head office of an expatriate bank had resources to support a troubled local branch. Effects on confidence of a local indigenous bank failure were contained by the cooperative actions of the bank community. The bank community acted in this way because indigenous banks were only a small part of the banking system. Currency boards did not extend loans to governments, banks or non-financial firms. If colonial governments borrowed, they did so in London where they were held to international standards of creditworthiness.

Yet, except for the currency boards that still exist principally in the remaining British colonies (Hong Kong, the Cayman Islands, Gibraltar, and the Falkland Islands) but also in several other places (Brunei and Singapore), the dozens of other locales where there once were currency boards abandoned them in the post-Second World War period. Why?

Collapse of the 'Mystique of Empire'

Two sets of factors may be cited. One set relates to the dramatic change in conventional intellectual beliefs invigorated by the Second World War. Foremost was erosion of the belief in the legitimacy of imperialism. Political leaders in the colonies, along with leaders of public opinion in the West, rejected the mystique of Empire. Ideas of democracy and nationalism defeated imperialist ideas. The British, the French and the Dutch had to relinquish colonial possessions in the postwar period.

Another belief that gained ground was that imperial economics served the selfish interest of the home country at the expense of the colonies, and that economic progress had been retarded by colonial status. Some economists argued that the absence of a central bank had precluded development. On this view, a central bank with discretion was bound to outperform a rule-bound currency board. Independence would enable former colonies, once freed from imperial control, to utilise their resources more productively and to achieve faster economic development.[4]

In addition to the change in general ideas, specific criticisms of currency board operations also account for the withdrawal of support for the institution. These criticisms included the charge that a secular rise in output under a currency board had deflationary consequences, that a 100 per cent reserve requirement imposed an excess burden on colonies, and that a fatal shortcoming of currency boards was that colonies could not pursue independent monetary, credit, or banking policy.

Currency Board Criticisms

Critics assumed that the colonies would have been better off had they not been tied to UK policies. Clearly, the colonies would have been better off had sterling been a more stable currency both before and after the Second World War, with fewer exchange rate restrictions. But the specific criticisms are refutable.

A secular rise in output could have been accommodated without deflation under a currency board, even if the current account were not in surplus, if banks expanded credit, leading to a fall in the currency-deposit and the currency-reserve ratios, and if there were capital inflows. A secular rise in output did not necessarily betoken a falling price level. The theoretical argument against a currency board is not supported by the evidence.

The 100 per cent reserve requirement was not an excess burden since the reserves were invested in interest-bearing securities, yielding a return not lower than alternative uses of the reserves. Investments were distributed along the yield curve. Part were in short-term maturities, representing the fraction of currency likely to be exchanged for foreign money, part in long-term maturities, representing the balance of currency outstanding.

The critics took for granted that a fatal institutional shortcoming of currency boards was that they could not engage in discretionary monetary policy. What the critics sought was the replacement of currency boards with central banks which in the immediate postwar period were regarded as the source both of stabilising countercyclical operations and of the wise use of discretion to improve economic performance.

Central Banks *vs* Currency Boards: the 1990s Standpoint

From the vantage point of the 1990s, the grounds for condemnation of currency boards and for the implicit esteem of central banking are not obvious. The central banks of the industrialised countries themselves no longer believe that they know how to produce monetary surprises that are stabilising and that they are masters of discretion. Did the central banks of the newly independent countries fare better?

For the critics, another advantage of central banks was their role as lender of last resort, and their provision of deficit financing to governments. As I have noted, during the currency board regime colonies did not need a lender of last resort, and it was hardly a shortcoming that currency boards could not monetise government deficits.

Nevertheless, the attack on currency boards succeeded. Most of them were replaced by central banks.

PRESENT-DAY CURRENCY BOARDS

The main surviving currency boards, by today attenuated versions of their classic form, are in Hong Kong and Singapore.

The Hong Kong version of a currency board dates from 1935, when Hong Kong nationalised all privately held silver. The government turned the silver over to an Exchange Fund as a reserve against bank and government notes. In exchange for their silver, three note-issuing banks – no other banks had the right to issue – received non-interest-bearing Certificates of Indebtedness. To issue more notes, the note-issuing banks had to buy more Certificates of Indebtedness. The fact that the banks, not the Exchange Fund (which is the equivalent of a currency board), issued notes is unique to the Hong Kong system.

The chairman of the Exchange Fund and his advisory committee were all appointees of the Governor of the colony. The Exchequer Fund kept its reserves mainly in sterling or sterling bank deposits in London, with an initial 100 per cent cover of its notes, later raised to 105 per cent. The note-issuing banks had to pay sterling for the Certificates of Indebtedness.

Hong Kong Currency Board's Changing Role

The performance of the Hong Kong currency board fell short of classic precepts. The Exchange Fund did not maintain a fixed exchange rate between the Hong Kong dollar and sterling during the period up to 1971 when it was linked to sterling; it then shifted to a link to the US dollar between 1971 and 1974, during which the exchange rate also varied; from 1974 the Hong Kong dollar floated until 1983. Since 1983 the Exchange Fund has again assumed responsibility for converting Hong Kong dollars into US dollars at a fixed exchange rate, but until 1988 only the note-issuing banks could acquire US dollars at the official parity rate. Since 1988, the Exchange Fund has had the power to conduct open-market operations, and since March 1990 to issue three-month Treasury bills. It has since proposed opening a discount window to provide liquidity to banks.

Limited as these central banking powers of the Exchange Fund may be currently, they strike me as a slippery slope that portends further erosion of rule-based behaviour. China's willingness to maintain it, once the island reverts to its control, adds to the uncertain future of a currency board in Hong Kong.

I say this despite the Sino-British Joint Declaration of 1985, in which China promised that Hong Kong would maintain its own capitalist system for 50 years after 1997, and despite the Basic Law approved by Beijing in 1990 which established Hong Kong's status as a Special Administrative Region of China. The Basic Law, which will become the constitutional document for Hong Kong after 1997, states that Hong Kong will retain its own currency and independent monetary policy, will have the right to designate banks to issue its currency, the Hong Kong dollar will remain freely convertible, and that no controls are to be applied to foreign exchange or capital movements. These declarations notwithstanding, confidence is generally lacking that China will live up to them.

The Monetary Authority of Singapore

Singapore, originally part of the Straits Settlements currency board, established its own board in 1967. Since June 1973 the Singapore dollar has floated with respect to the US dollar. It is currently backed by external assets, including gold, sterling and other foreign exchange.

In January 1971 Singapore created the Monetary Authority of Singapore. The Authority acts as banker to the government, holds the balances of commercial banks and finance companies, necessary to satisfy statutory reserve requirements, serves as lender of last resort to discount houses, and allows commercial banks to rediscount export bills at a subsidised rate of interest.

The currency board that has operated in Singapore since the float has the same board of directors as the Monetary Authority of Singapore, chaired by the Minister of Finance. Its business is confined to transactions with the Monetary Authority, which tries to adjust the value of the Singapore dollar to the value of a basket of currencies. The currency board obviously violates a basic condition that defined the institution in its classic form. It does not redeem Singapore dollars in foreign exchange on demand at a fixed rate of exchange. The monetary base includes not only currency issues but also the deposits of the Monetary Authority of Singapore.

A New Kind of Currency Board in Argentina?

One new development that possibly represents a currency board approach in another part of the world is a change in the way that Argentina issues its local currency, the peso. As of 1 April 1991, Argentina (by a law passed in March) established one-to-one convertibility of the peso and the US dollar. The issue of additional pesos requires the presentation of 100 per cent foreign exchange cover. Since Argentina has not appointed a currency board separate from its central bank, to determine currency issue and redemption, it has been suggested to me that it must be the Board of Governors of the Federal Reserve System which fills that role.

Although strategies to end inflation in Argentina in the 1980s repeatedly failed, linking the peso to the dollar has been successful thus far in anchoring inflationary expectations. Consumer price inflation fell from 84 per cent in 1991 to an estimated 14 per cent in 1992. Wholesale prices rose by only 3 per cent in 1992, indicating convergence with the US price level for tradeable goods. Financial markets find Argentina's commitment to stable prices credible enough to have induced a private capital inflow of $5 billion in 1991. The sustainability of the fixed exchange rate with the dollar, however, is still to be tested.

ARE CURRENCY BOARDS THE WAVE OF THE FUTURE?

Sir Alan Walters, who in 1987 doubted that currency boards were the wave of the future, has recently promoted a currency board solution for countries with intractable inflationary problems, especially the former Soviet republics. A small group of economists has taken up Sir Alan's prescription in numerous publications, either as co-authors with him or on their own.[5]

It is no doubt true that establishing a stable monetary system would be one key to the transformation of an inflation-plagued command economy into a viable market economy. The proposals for monetary reform outline two steps. The first is to abolish the central bank or a branch that exists in a former Soviet republic. The next is to replace the central bank with a currency board. The authors of the proposals offer these two recommendations to reform the Russian rouble, the Bulgarian lev, and the Estonian kroon.[6]

One problem I find with the proposals is that disestablishing a central bank and establishing a currency board would require political support. However compelling the economic case for a currency board, the authors of the proposal pay no attention to the task of mustering the required political support. They merely assure the reader that it is 'fairly simple to convert a central banking system into a currency board system'.[7]

I doubt that countries will forgo central banks, whether or not they introduce a currency board. If a currency board is introduced while a central bank continues to operate, central bank currency and currency board currency would compete, the currency with stable purchasing power presumably trading at par, the depreciating currency at a discount from par, with floating exchange rates between them. The market would determine which one currency holders preferred. I believe that currency boards could succeed as issuers of a currency parallel to depreciating central bank notes, but it is doubtful that governments would be willing to tolerate their existence, let alone establish them, to play that role.

Choosing the Right Foreign Reserve Currency

There is also a fundamental economic issue governments face if they decide to form currency boards. To which foreign currency should the local currency be linked? The issue is dramatised by the case of Estonia. In February 1992 the authors of the prescription for that country proposed linking the Estonian kroon one-to-one with the Swedish kronor. The Swedish kronor had a fixed exchange rate with the ECU. In mid-September 1992, in a desperate effort to defend the exchange rate, despite rising unemployment, recession, and severely troubled banks, Sweden raised the marginal rate on central bank loans from 15 to 24 to 50 to 500 per cent, and then back to 50 per cent. Market rates of interest rose to unprecedented levels – a 23 per cent yield on the benchmark six-month Treasury bill.

Suppose Estonia had adopted the plan the authors were promoting in early 1992. It would have been exposed to a severe deflationary shock in September 1992 and thus to the same economic problems with which the Swedish economy is wrestling. The currency board solution would have meant not improvement but a devastating setback for the Estonian economy. In fact, Estonia has not introduced a currency board but has linked the kroon to the Deutschemark.

The choice of the right foreign reserve money clearly is crucial to the success of a currency board, but the advocacy literature does not sufficiently emphasise the possible undesired effects of an unanticipated disturbance in the reserve money.

When the pre-First World War Gold Standard ruled, the relative stability of the foreign money chosen could be taken for granted, and was less important than choosing the country which dominated foreign trade with the currency board country. It was that country's money into which currency board local money was convertible. That is why some British colonies linked the local currency not to sterling but to the Indian rupee or the US dollar. Their main trading partners were India or the United States, not Britain. If, in the course of time, the colony's trading relations changed, the currency board changed the foreign money to match. Nowadays, the main trade partner need not coincide with the country with the preferred foreign currency.

The proponents of a currency board for the Bulgarian lev propose linking it to the US dollar, and for the Russian rouble, to the D-mark or Swiss franc. Each of these currencies is relatively stable, but they have all been subject to periodic appreciations and depreciations that would not necessarily affect prices and incomes in the currency board country in a benign way.

Competing Currency Boards?

Some currency board advocates have proposed not one currency board to replace a central bank but *competing* currency boards, each one presumably offering convertibility in a different foreign reserve money – for example, Swedish kronor, Swiss francs, or French francs. These advocates suggest that the competing boards they envision could be owned and operated by private firms as a financial mutual. The customers could force liquidation of a board that did not live up to its representations by redeeming domestic currency for the reserve currency.

If I find it hard to believe that governments will agree to forgo the discretion of a central bank, how much more difficult it is to believe that governments will readily cede to the private sector the right to form currency boards.

A Good Temporary Solution for Eastern Europe?

Despite these doubts, I do not dispute that a currency board may be a good temporary solution for the East European countries with undeveloped financial markets, rapidly depreciating central bank notes, and the urgent need to revitalise their economies. A law establishing a currency board would signal a commitment to limit currency issue to the available foreign exchange. Hoarders of foreign exchange would have an incentive to transfer their holdings, whether or not ill-gotten, to the board for local currency.

If East European countries opt for a currency board solution, the headquarters of the board, to depoliticise it, should be established in the country to whose money the local currency is linked. The board should have a main office and branches in the currency board country. Members of the board should include well-known reputable nationals of foreign countries as well as nationals of the currency board country.

The main function of the currency board should be to issue local currency to those who tender foreign exchange, and to provide foreign exchange to those who proffer local currency. The board should also be responsible for investing the foreign exchange in interest-bearing securities denominated in the currency of the reserve country. The maturities of the assets acquired should be distributed between short and long ones to match the expected proportions of notes and coin with a high and low probability of demand for conversion.

Sir Alan Walters has recommended a currency board solution not only to East European countries but also to Australia and Sweden which have faced stubborn inflationary tendencies that have not yielded to other solutions. I discuss the likelihood that these countries will adopt his recommendation in my conclusion.

CONCLUSION

Even if East European countries adopt currency boards as a temporary solution to their present monetary instability, I am sceptical that they will permanently abjure a role for discretionary monetary policy that a genuine currency board enjoins. Indeed, they would be abjuring simply their *own* discretion. Policy would still be discretionary, but the discretion would be that of some other country. My scepticism is even more profound that countries with advanced financial markets like Australia and Sweden will find a currency board acceptable, even as a temporary solution.

The problems of inflation in Eastern Europe and elsewhere have stimulated a nostalgia for currency boards by economists who accept the superiority of rules over discretion. If theirs were the only voices that influenced the rulers of these countries, their advice might prevail. In practice, however, the rulers hear other, more influential voices. The International Monetary Fund from its foundation has championed the role of a discretionary central bank as essential to sovereignty. That view is shared by the mainstream of economists.

Mainstream views are not the only reason for scepticism that currency boards are the wave of the future. The fundamental hurdle to a successful return to a currency board system is the resistance of political authorities and modern democracies to precommitment and to forswearing of discretion. Governments since the First World War have expanded their participation in economic activity and relied on deficit financing to support policies demanded by interest groups wielding political influence.

Where they existed, currency boards were swept away in the wake of the Second World War because rules were devalued. They were replaced by central banks that exercised discretion, made loans to governments and banks, and increased or decreased the monetary base at will.

The notion that currency boards can be revived to function as they did in the past idealises them and neglects the need for precommitment by governments and their constituencies to the discipline these institutions exact. The Hong Kong and Singapore currency boards in their present form seem to me to represent the progressive dilution of precommitment.

Currency boards worked well in the past for two reasons. First, the local currency was linked to some other currency which itself was regulated by a rule or else was subject to discretion only to a limited extent. Second, the local currency was always linked to the currency of the country with which foreign trade was conducted. There are now *no* currencies in the first category, and trade is more diversified, so few countries would choose a link which did not produce substantial relative price changes from time to time. Accordingly, neither *economic* condition for a well-functioning currency board is now in place.

To conclude on a more optimistic note, perhaps the climate of opinion is changing and rules rather than discretion are now thinkable by heads of government. After all, the hopes of great improvement under central bank management of the economies of former colonies by those who disparaged currency boards were clearly not realised. Another straw in the wind may be the example of Argentina, which apparently has enacted a rule that resembles a currency board arrangement. At this date, of course, no one knows how long the rule will be honoured. If East European countries also decide that a currency board suits their circumstances, a watershed will have been reached in the annals of political economy.

NOTES

1. Alan Walters, 'Currency Boards', in J. Eatwell, M. Milgate and P. Newman (eds), *The New Palgrave: A Dictionary of Economics*, Macmillan, London, Vol. 1, 1987, p. 740; a revised and updated version of this article, by Walters and Steve H. Hanke, has been included in *The New Palgrave Dictionary of Money & Finance*, Vol. 1, Macmillan, London, 1992, pp. 558–61.
2. Historically, seigniorage was the fee or royalty charged by the monarch to cover the cost of minting coins from bullion and to provide the ruler with revenue. Currently, seigniorage refers to the net revenue of a monetary authority from issuing money.
3. See Steve H. Hanke and Kurt Schuler, 'Keynes's Russian Currency Board', in Steve H. Hanke and Alan A. Walters (eds.), *Capital Markets and Development*, ICS Press, San Francisco, Ca., 1991, pp. 43–63.
4. Montagu Norman, then the Governor of the Bank of England, advised New Zealand in 1932 to form a central bank if it wanted to be in charge of its own affairs. (G. R. Hawke, *Between Governments and Banks: A History of the Reserve Bank of New Zealand*, A. R. Shearer, Government Printer, Wellington, New Zealand, 1973, p. 38.
5. Alan Walters, 'Currency Boards', in Eatwell, Milgate and Newman (eds.), *The New Palgrave: A Dictionary of Economics*, op. cit., pp. 740–42; Walters, 'A Hard Rouble for Boris', London: *Evening Standard*, 22 November 1991; Walters, 'Should Australia Have a Currency Board?', in Des Moore (ed.), *Can Monetary Policy Be Made to Work? Papers Presented at the IPA Monetary Policy Conference*, Jolimont, Australia, Institute of Public Affairs, Economic Policy Unit, 1992; Walters and Steve H. Hanke, 'Currency Boards', in *The New Palgrave Dictionary of Money & Finance*. Vol. 1, op. cit., pp. 558–61; Hanke and Walters, 'Reform Begins with a Currency Board', London: *Financial Times*, 21 February 1990, p. 17; and Hanke and Walters, 'East German Currency Board', *Financial Times*, 7 March 1990, p. 19.

6. S. H. Hanke and Kurt Schuler, 'Currency Boards for Eastern Europe', Heritage Lecture No. 355, Washington, DC: Heritage Foundation, 1991; and Hanke and Schuler, *Teeth for the Bulgarian Lev: A Currency Board Solution*, International Freedom Foundation, Washington, DC, 1991.
7. S. H. Hanke, Lars Jonung and Kurt Schuler, *Monetary Reform for a Free Estonia: A Currency Board Solution*, SNS Förlag, Stockholm, 1992, p. 109 (of manuscript).

10 Free Trade, 'Fairness' and the New Protectionism[1]

Jagdish Bhagwati

INTRODUCTION

The Multilateral Trade Negotiations (MTN) under the umbrella of the Uruguay Round were concluded in April 1994, after over seven years of tortuous history during which they came close to death by neglect or murder by hostile intent. The GATT was declared impotent or dead; the Uruguay Round was treated as a script with all talk and no action.

Arthur Dunkel, through years of pessimism, held the Round together doggedly when few gave him any odds; Peter Sutherland had the good fortune and the political agility to stand on Dunkel's broad shoulders and successfully reached out for the elusive prize.

The drama ended exotically in Marrakesh. It was hard then not to think of *Casablanca*, the film that none of us can forget and yet watch over and over again, and to let one's imagination run wild. What would the film *Marrakesh* look like? Evidently, the portly Peter Sutherland would be played by Peter Ustinov, the elegant and suave Sir Leon Brittan by Kenneth Branagh, and the feisty Mickey Kantor by Dustin Hoffman.

But one could also recall Humphrey Bogart's saying: 'Play it, Sam' and, drawing inspiration from our success, ask: 'How about the next Round?' Indeed, whether the format of a Round will ever characterise MTN again is a question to which the common answer today is in the negative. But then it was equally so when the Tokyo Round, itself often a cliffhanger, was concluded. Regardless, however, there is little doubt that MTN will continue in *some* form.[2]

Indeed, the Uruguay Round could not have been concluded, certainly in the United States, unless the many lobbies had the sense that it was not the end of the game and that there would be another innings to play. This applied not just to issues such as liberalisation of agriculture and services. It applied equally, perhaps even more forcefully, to a number of yet newer questions such as the interface between trade and the environment and labour standards.

186

In particular, it is now manifest that the World Trade Organisation (WTO), the successor to the GATT, will have a new agenda whose outlines are already clear. Among the principal issues will be:[3]

- trade and the environment;
- trade and labour standards; and
- competition policy.

These issues are 'universal', and cut across all nations. But the precise nature of the demands for change in the WTO they have generated and the solutions which the new leadership of the WTO (as yet undecided) must shape, cannot be understood without realising that the environmental and labour standards issues are being driven by concerns that create a *North–South*[4] divide. Competition policy, however, has emerged as an issue primarily because of *North–North* concerns.

These three issues, and the precise demands to deal with them at the WTO, undoubtedly reflect the growing interdependence of the world's economy, binding the world's trading nations today in enlarged and expanding *trade* and *investment* transactions and flows, even when adjusted for increased national incomes. These trends have produced opportunities and benefits, and yet have created fears and challenges that now shape the WTO's new agenda at its very creation.

Equally, the WTO must now confront the phenomenon of a proliferation of preferential trading arrangements, regional and non-regional Free Trade Areas, that characterise the world trading scene. It must seek a new equilibrium between the WTO and these arrangements, the former embodying non-discrimination among trading nations while the latter are inherently preferential and discriminatory. This is not an issue that member-nations are eager to put before the WTO at any time. Yet it speaks to the very core of a free, open, multilateral trading system, as envisaged at the end of the Second World War and as sought by many of us today. The new leadership of the WTO must address it on its own initiative.

THE WTO: THE MAIN AGENDA

I begin with the phenomenon of the increased trade and investment flows, the opportunities from it that characterise the world economy and the problems it is feared to pose to trading nations.

Economists are generally likely to see the increasingly interdependent world – with its growing exchange of goods and services and flows of funds to where the returns are expected to be higher – as one gaining in prosperity as it exploits the opportunities to trade and to invest provided by the postwar dismantling of trade barriers and obstacles to investment flows. This is the conventional 'mutual-gain' or 'non-zero-sum game' view of the situation. I would argue it is also the appropriate one.

An Ironic Reversal

Many developing countries that were sceptical about, even hostile to, this *benign-impact* view of the interaction between themselves and the world economy at the beginning of the postwar period, and indeed through much of it, have now embraced that view. But I must point to an irony: where the developing countries (the South) were sceptical of the benign-impact view and the developed countries (the North) were confident of it, today the situation is the other way around.

(i) The Earlier Situation

Thus, if you look back at the 1950s and 1960s, the contrast between the South and the North was striking and made the South strongly pessimistic about the effects of integration into the world economy while the North was, in contrast, firmly optimistic:

- The South generally subscribed to *malign-neglect* and even *malign-intent* views of trade and investment interactions with the world economy.[5] It was feared that 'integration into the world economy would lead to disintegration of the domestic economy'. While the malign-neglect view is manifest most clearly in the famous *dependencia* theory that President Cardoso of Brazil formulated in his radical youth as Latin America's foremost sociologist, the malign-intent view was most vividly embodied in the concept and theory of *neo-colonialism.*

  Trade thus had to be protected; investment inflows had to be drastically regulated and curtailed.[6] The inward-oriented, import-substituting strategy was the order of the day almost everywhere. Only the Far Eastern economies, starting mainly in the early 1960s, shifted dramatically to an outward-oriented policy posture. The results, attributable principally to this contrast in orientation to the world economy but partly also to initial advantages such as inherited land reforms and high literacy rates, were to produce the most remarkable growth experiences of this century. As I shall presently argue, in recent years they have also facilitated by example the reversal of inward-looking policies. But, at the time, the developing countries were certainly in an inward, cautious mode about embracing the world economy.

- By contrast, the developed countries – the North[7] – moved steadily forward with dismantling trade barriers through the GATT Rounds, with firm commitment to multilateralism as well. They subscribed to the principles of multilateral free trade and of freer investment flows as the central guiding principles for a liberal international economic order that would assure economic prosperity for all participating nations.[8]

(ii) Role Reversal – The Turnaround

Today however, the situation is almost reversed. The fears of integration into the world economy are being heard, not from the developing countries which see great good from it as they have extensively undertaken what the GATT calls 'autonomous' reductions in their trade barriers (unilateral reductions outside the GATT context of reciprocal reductions). Of course, not all these reductions, and increased openness to inward direct foreign investment (DFI) in developing countries, have resulted from changed convictions in favour of the liberal international economic order and its benefits to themselves. The failure of policies based on the old pro-inward-orientation views and the contrasting success of the Far Eastern countries following the pro-outward-orientation views have certainly played an important role, especially in Latin America and Asia. But some measure of the shift must also be ascribed to necessity, resulting from the conditionality imposed by the World Bank (and, at times, by the IMF) as several debt-crisis-afflicted countries flocked to these institutions for support in the 1980s. Equally, the shift arises from their own perceived need to restore their external viability by liberal domestic and international policies designed to reassure and attract DFI.

But as the South has moved to regard integration into the world economy as an opportunity rather than a peril, so the North is now fearful. In particular, it fears, after the decline in the real wages of the unskilled in the United States and the rise in unemployment in Europe in the 1970s and 1980s, that by trading with the South with its abundance of unskilled labour, the North will find its own unskilled at risk.[9] The demand for protection that follows is then not the old and defunct 'pauper-labour' argument which asserted falsely that trade between the South and the North could not be beneficial. Rather, it is the theoretically more defensible, income-distributional argument that trade with countries with paupers will produce paupers in our midst – that is, that trade with the poor countries will produce more poor at home.

Now, it is indeed true that the real wages of the unskilled have fallen significantly in the United States during the last two decades. In 1973, the

> real hourly earnings of non-supervisory workers measured in 1982 dollars . . . were \$8.55. By 1992 they had actually *declined* to \$7.43 – a level that had been achieved in the late 1960s. Had earnings increased at their earlier pace, they would have risen by 40 per cent to over \$12.[10]

The experience in Europe has generally been similar except that, because of more 'inflexible' labour markets, the adverse impact has been on jobs rather than on real wages.[11]

But the key question is whether the cause of this phenomenon is trade with the South, as unions and many politicians feel, or rapid information-based technical change that is increasingly substituting unskilled labour with computers that need skilled labour. As always, there is debate among economists about the evidence: but the preponderant view today among trade experts is that the evidence linking trade with the South to observed distress among the unskilled is extremely thin. The main study by labour experts that first suggested otherwise was methodologically unsound in not appreciating that if real wages were to fall for unskilled labour due to trade with the South, the prices of the unskilled-labour-intensive goods would have had to have fallen;[12] and subsequent examination of the US data on prices of goods shows that the opposite happened to be true.[13,14]

The consensus currently is that technical change, not trade with the South, has immiserised our proletariat. Nevertheless, the fear still persists that such trade is a threat to the unskilled. In Europe, there has thus been talk of the difficulty of competing with 'Asiatic ants', leading in turn to calls for protectionism.

Alongside such fears there is anxiety that multinationals will move out to take advantage of the cheaper labour in the poor countries, as trade becomes freer, thus adding to the pressure that trade alone, with each nation's capital at home, exerts on the real wages of the unskilled. This too is unsubstantiated fear. But it has even greater political salience since the loss of jobs to trade is less easily focused on specific competing countries and their characteristics than when a factory shuts down and opens up in a foreign country instead. As it happens, I suspect that, at least in the United States, the flow of capital is in the wrong direction from the viewpoint of those who are gripped by such fear. For, during the 1980s, the United States surely received more DFI than it sent out elsewhere, both absolutely and relatively to the 1950s and 1960s. Besides, if foreign savings are considered instead, the 1980s saw an influx, corresponding to the current-account deficit that has bedevilled US–Japan trade relations.

North–South Issues[15]

Because of such fears, demands have spread in the USA and in Europe for the inclusion of Environmental and Labour Standards in the WTO, requiring either that they be moved up in the developing countries or that developed countries should be allowed to countervail the 'implied subsidy' represented by these lower standards. Proposals for such legislation have been introduced in the US Congress, as in Congressman Gephardt's so-called 'blue' and 'green' bill which would authorise the administration to impose 'eco-dumping' duties against lower environmental (i.e. *green*) standards abroad and 'social dumping' duties against lower labour (i.e. *blue*-collar workers') standards abroad.

Several factors contribute to the emergence of these demands. But a principal one surely is the desire to raise the costs of production of rivals abroad: what is easier than to say they are deriving *unfair trade* advantage by having lower environmental and labour standards? It is surely easier to get the sympathetic ear of the politicians if the appeal to them for assistance, in the shape of protection or otherwise, is couched in terms not of an appeal that one cannot cope otherwise and requires relief, but the contention instead that one's distress is the result of rivals' perfidious, unfair ways.

(i) Environmental Standards

Why indeed should one object to differences in different nations' environmental standards in the same industry (that is, cross-country intra-industry (CCII) differences in standards), typically in the shape of pollution tax rates? It should be emphasised that the issue here is purely *domestic* environmental problems – for example, if a country is polluting its own lakes. We are not discussing environmental problems that arise when pollution creates *transborder* externalities, as with global warming, ozone layer depletion, and acid rain (which raise problems about the WTO of a different, and more compelling, nature).

(a) *Indefensible Demands for Eco-dumping*   In fact, for an economist, the basic presumption is that different countries, even if they accept the same 'polluter pays principle', will have *legitimate diversity of CCII environmental taxes/standards* for environmental problems which create purely domestic pollution.

This diversity will follow from differences in trade-offs between aggregate pollution and income at different levels of national income – as when richer Americans prefer to save dolphins from purse-seine nets whereas poorer Mexicans prefer to raise the productivity of fishing and hence accelerate the amelioration of Mexican poverty by using such nets. Again, countries will have natural differences in the priorities attached to which kind of pollution to attack, arising from differences of historical and other circumstance: Mexicans will worry more about clean water, as dysentery is a greater problem, than Americans who will attach higher priority to spending pollution dollars on clean air. Differences in technological know-how and in endowments can also lead to CCII diversity in pollution tax rates.

The notion therefore that the diversity of CCII pollution standards/taxes is illegitimate and constitutes 'unfair trade' or 'unfair competition', to be eliminated or countervailed by eco-dumping duties, is itself illegitimate. It is incorrect, indeed illogical, to assert that having to compete with foreign firms that do not bear equal pollution-tax burdens is unfair. I would add two more observations:

- If we lose competitive advantage because we put a larger negative value on a certain kind of pollution than others, that is simply the flip side of the differential valuations. To object to that implication of the differential valuation is to object to the differential valuation itself, and hence to our own larger negative valuation. To see this clearly, think of a closed economy without trade. If we were to tax pollution by an industry in such an economy, its implication would be precisely that this industry would shrink: it would lose competitive advantages *vis-à-vis* other industries in our country. To object to that shrinking is to object to the negative valuation being put on the pollution. There is, therefore, nothing 'unfair' from this perspective, if our industry shrinks because we impose higher standards (for example, pollution taxes) on it while others, who value that pollution less, choose lower standards.

- Besides, the attribution of competitive disadvantage to differential pollution tax burdens, in the fashion of CCII comparisons for individual industries, confuses absolute with comparative advantage. Thus, for instance, in a two-industry world, if both industries abroad have lower pollution tax rates than at home, both will not contract at home. Rather, the industry with the *comparatively* higher tax rate will contract. The noise each industry makes on the basis of CCII comparisons, aggregated to total noise by all industries, is likely to exaggerate seriously the effect of different environmental valuations and CCII differences on the competitiveness of industries in higher-standards nations.

A COMPETITIVE LOWERING OF STANDARDS?

One more worry needs to be laid to rest if the demands for upward harmonisation of standards (or eco-dumping duties in lieu thereof) are to be effectively dismissed. It is that free trade with countries with lower standards will force down one's higher standards. The most potent concern arises from the fear that 'capital and jobs' will move to countries with lower standards, triggering a *race to the bottom* (or more accurately a race *towards* the bottom), where countries lower their standards in an inter-jurisdictional contest, below what some or all would like, in order to attract capital and jobs.[16] Therefore, the solution would lie in coordinating standards-setting among the nations engaged in freer trade and investment. In turn, this *may* (but is most unlikely to) require harmonisation among countries to the higher standards (though, even then, not necessarily to those in place) or perhaps there might be improvement in welfare from simply setting minimum floors to the standards.

This is a theoretically valid argument. The key policy question, however, is whether the empirical evidence shows, as required by the argument, that:

(1) capital is in fact responsive to the differences in environmental standards; and
(2) different countries/jurisdictions then actually play the game of competitive lowering of standards to attract capital. Without both these phenomena holding in a significant fashion in reality, the 'race to the bottom' would be a theoretical curiosity.

As it happens, systematic evidence is available on the former proposition alone. But it is not supported by the studies to date: there is very weak evidence, at best, in favour of interjurisdictional mobility in response to CCII differences in environmental standards.[17] There are many ways to explain this lack of responsiveness:

- differences in standards may not be significant and are outweighed by other factors that affect locational decisions;
- exploiting differences in standards may not be a good strategy relative to not exploiting them; and
- lower standards may paradoxically even repel, instead of attract, DFI.[18]

We do not have similar evidence on the latter proposition. It is, however, hardly likely that, as a systematic tendency, countries would lower environmental standards in order to attract capital. Countries, and even state governments in federal countries (as when President Bill Clinton was Governor of Arkansas), typically play the game of attracting capital to their jurisdictions. But this game is almost universally played, not by inviting firms to pollute freely but instead through devices such as tax breaks and holidays and land grants at giveaway prices. The most likely result is a 'race to the bottom' on business tax rates which wind up below their optimal levels! It is therefore not surprising that there is little systematic evidence of governments' lowering environmental standards in order to attract scarce capital. Contrary to the fears of environmental groups, the race to the bottom on environmental standards therefore seems an unlikely phenomenon in the real world.

I would conclude that both the unfair trade and the 'race to the bottom' arguments for harmonising CCII standards, or else legalising eco-dumping duties at the WTO, lack rationale: the former is theoretically illogical and the latter is empirically unsupported. In addition, such GATT–WTO legalisation of eco-dumping would without doubt facilitate protectionism. Anti-dumping processes have become the favoured tool of protectionists today. Their extension to eco-dumping (and equally to social-dumping), where the 'implied subsidy' through lower standards must inevitably be 'constructed' by national agencies such as the US Environmental Protection Agency in the same jurisdiction as the complainant industry, will lead even more surely to the same results.

The 'fixing' of the WTO for environmental issues, therefore, should not proceed along the lines of legitimising eco-dumping.[19] However, the political salience of such demands remains a major problem. Are there 'second-best' approaches, short of the eco-dumping and CCII harmonisation proposals, which address some of the political concerns at least economic cost?

(b) *A Proposal to Extend Domestic Standards in High-Standards Countries to their Firms in Low-Standards Countries, Unilaterally or Preferably Through an OECD Code*   Demands for eco-dumping duties and CCII harmonisation are strongest when *plants are closed* by multinationals in one country and shifted to another. The shifting of location, and the associated loss of jobs in that plant, magnify greatly the fear of the 'race to the bottom' and of the 'impossibility' of competing against low-standard countries. Similarly, when investment by one country's firms is seen to go to specific countries which happen to have lower standards, resentment is focused readily against those countries and their standards. However, as explained earlier, when jobs are lost simply because of *trade* competition, it is much harder to focus resentment and fear on one specific foreign country and its policies as a source of unfair competition.[20] Hence, a second-best proposal could well be to address this particular fear, however unfounded and often illogical, of migration of plants and investment to low-standard countries.

One proposal would be to adapt the so-called 'Sullivan Principles' approach to the problem at hand. At the urging of Reverend Sullivan, US firms in South Africa were asked to adopt US practices, not the South African *apartheid* ways, in their operations. If this principle – that US firms in Mexico be subject to US environmental policies (choosing those desired from the many that obtain across different states in this federal country) – were adopted, that would automatically remove whatever incentive there was to move because of environmental burden differences.[21]

This proposal that a country's firms abroad behave as if they were at home – do in Rome as you do in New York, not as the Romans do – can be either legislated unilaterally by any high-standard country or by a multilateral binding Treaty among different high-standard countries. Or it could be reduced to an exhortation, just as the Sullivan Principles were, by single countries in isolation or by several as though it were a non-binding but ethos-defining and policy-encouraging OECD Code.

The disadvantage of this proposal, of course, is that it violates the diversity-is-legitimate rule. A country's investment flows, like its own investment, production and trade, should reflect this diversity. Adoption of the Sullivan principle would, therefore, reduce present efficiency gains from a freer flow of cross-country investments. But, if environmental tax burden differences are not all that different or do not figure prominently in firms' locational decisions, as the empirical literature just cited (above, note 17) suggests, the efficiency costs of this proposal could also be minimal. The gains – in allaying fears and therefore moderating the demand for bad proposals – could, however, be very considerable.

'HORIZONTAL INEQUITY'

Yet another objection may focus on intra-OECD differences in high standards. Since there are differences among the OECD countries in CCII environmental tax burdens in specific industries for specific pollution, this proposal would lead to 'horizontal inequity' among OECD firms in third countries. If the British burden is higher than the French, British firms would face a bigger burden in Mexico than French firms. But such differences already exist among firms abroad since tax practices among OECD countries on taxation of firms abroad are not harmonised in many respects. Interestingly, the problem of horizontal equity has arisen also in relation to demands of poor countries (which find it difficult to enforce import restrictions effectively) that domestic restrictions on hazardous products be automatically extended to exports by every country. That would put firms in the countries with greater restrictions at an economic disadvantage. But agreement has now been reached to disregard the problem.

Other problems may arise: (i) monitoring of one country's firms in a foreign country may be difficult; and (ii) the countries with lower standards may object on grounds of 'national sovereignty'. Neither argument seems compelling. It is unlikely that a developing country would object to foreign firms doing better by its citizens in regard to environmental standards (that it cannot afford to impose, given its own priorities, on its own firms). In fact, it is more likely to assist in monitoring the foreign firms.

(c) Transborder Externalities: Global Pollution and the WTO   The preceding analysis considered the trade issues which arise between countries even when environmental problems are purely domestic in their scope. More complex trade issues arise when there are transborder spillovers or externalities. I now consider the problems that arise when the issue is not simply *bilateral* (as with, say, acid rain, where the United States and Canada were involved) or regional, but truly *global*.

The chief questions for trade policy arising from global pollution problems (such as ozone layer depletion and global warming) concern multilateral treaties oriented towards a cooperative solution. In essence they boil down to non-compliance ('defection') by members and 'free riding' by non-members. Targeted actions by treaty members, such as reducing CFCs or CO_2 emissions, are intended to achieve perceived public goods: thus the benefits are non-excludable, so that if I incur the cost of doing something, I cannot exclude you from benefiting from it. The use of trade sanctions to secure and enforce compliance then inevitably winds up as a desired policy tool in global-environmental treaties.

At the same time, difficulties are compounded because any agreement has to be *legitimate* in the eyes of those accused of free riding. Before those pejorative epithets are applied, and punishment prescribed in the form of trade sanctions legitimised at the GATT/WTO, such nations have to be satisfied that the agreement being pressed on them is efficient and, especially, that it is equitable in burden-sharing. Otherwise, nothing prevents the politically powerful (the rich nations) from devising a treaty that puts an inequitable burden on the politically weak (the poor nations). They can then use the cloak of a 'multilateral' agreement and a new GATT/WTO-legitimacy to impose that burden with the aid of trade sanctions.

ENVIRONMENTAL PROBLEMS – SHARING THE BURDEN

The policy demand, often made, to alter the GATT/WTO to legitimise trade sanctions on Contracting Parties who remain outside a plurilateral treaty on a global environmental problem, is unlikely to be accepted by poor nations without safeguards to prevent unjust impositions. The spokesmen of the poor countries have been more or less explicit on this issue, with justification, and their concerns have been recognised by the rich nations.

Thus, at the Rio Conference in 1992, the Framework Convention on Climate Change set explicit goals under which several rich nations agreed targets for reducing emissions (returning, more or less, to 1990 levels), while the commitments of the poor countries were contingent on the rich nations footing the bill.

Ultimately, burden-sharing by different formulas related, for example, to past emissions, current income, current population, and so on, is inherently arbitrary; such formulas also distribute burdens without regard to efficiency. Economists will argue for burden-sharing dictated by cost-minimisation across countries, for the Earth as a whole: if Brazilian rain forests must be saved to minimise the cost of a targeted reduction in world CO_2 emissions, while the US keeps guzzling gas (petroleum) because it is too expensive to cut that down, then so be it. But this efficient 'cooperative' solution must not then leave Brazil footing the bill. Efficient solutions, only if combined with compensation and equitable distribution of the gains from them, make sense.

A step towards them is the idea of having a world market in permits: no country may emit CO_2 without having bought the necessary permit from a worldwide quota. That would ensure efficiency,[22] whereas distribution of the proceeds from the permits sold would require a decision reflecting multilaterally agreed ethical or equity criteria (for example, the proceeds might be used for refugee resettlement, UN peacekeeping operations, aid dispensed to poor nations by UNDP or the WHO fight against AIDS). This type of agreement would have the legitimacy that could in turn provide legitimacy for a GATT/WTO rule permitting the use of trade sanctions against free riders.

(ii) Labour Standards and the Social Clause

The question of labour standards – perhaps making them into prerequisites for market access by introducing a Social Clause in the WTO – offers both parallels and contrasts with the environmental questions just discussed.

The contrast is that labour standards have nothing equivalent to *transborder* environmental externalities since any country's labour standards are purely *domestic* in scope. It follows that the demand for 'social dumping' duties against lower labour standards that parallel the demands for eco-dumping, have the same rationale and hence must be rejected for the same reasons.

But a different aspect is that labour standards, unlike most environmental standards, are seen in moral terms. Thus, for example, central to American thinking on the question of a Social Clause is the notion that competitive advantage can sometimes be morally 'illegitimate'. In particular, it is argued that if labour standards elsewhere are different and unacceptable morally, then the resulting competition is morally illegitimate and 'unfair'.

When this argument is made about a practice such as slavery (defined strictly as the practice of owning and transacting in human beings, as for centuries before the Abolitionists triumphed), there will be nearly universal agreement that if slavery produces competitive advantage, that advantage is illegitimate and ought to be rejected.

Thus, there is here a 'values'-related argument for suspending another country's trading rights or access to our markets, in a sense similar to (but far more compelling than) the case in which the United States sought to suspend Mexico's tuna-trading rights because of its use of purse-seine nets.[23] Insertion of a Social Clause for Labour Standards into the WTO could therefore be a way of legitimising an exception to the perfectly sensible GATT rule that prohibits the suspension of a Contracting Party's trading rights concerning a product solely on the ground that, for reasons of morality advanced by another Contracting Party, the process by which that product is produced is considered immoral and therefore illegitimate.

The problem with the argument, however, is that universally condemned practices such as slavery are rare indeed. True, the ILO has many Conventions signed by different nations. But many have signed simply because they are not binding. The United States has signed no more than a tiny fraction of these conventions. It is doubtful whether a substantive consensus can be obtained on anything except well-meaning and broad principles without consequences for trade access in case of non-compliance.

DIVERSITY OF LABOUR STANDARDS

Indeed, the reality is that diversity of labour practices and standards is widespread and reflects, not necessarily venality and wickedness, but rather diversity of cultural values, economic conditions and analytical beliefs and theories concerning the economic (and therefore moral) consequences of specific labour standards. The notion that labour standards can be universalised, like human rights such as liberty and *habeas corpus*, simply by calling them 'labour rights' ignores the difficulty of making any easy equation between culture-specific labour standards and universal human rights.

The presumption in the United States that its labour standards are 'advanced' and that it is only providing 'moral leadership' on the question *vis-à-vis* developing countries, is problematic. In fact, the US logic on this issue could lead the US itself into a widespread and sustained suspension of its own trading rights if there was an impartial tribunal and standing to file complaints was given to concerned citizens and NGOs (rather than to governments which would be intimidated by the power of the United States).

Thus, for instance, worker participation in decision-making at plant level, a much more pertinent measure of true economic democracy than the unionisation of labour, is far more widespread in Europe than in the United States. Would we then condemn the US to denial of trading rights by the Europeans? According to numerous investigative television documentaries such as those on CNN and CBS's *60 Minutes* programme, migrant labour is ill-treated to the level of brutality and slavery in US agriculture due to grossly inadequate and at times even corrupt enforcement. Does this mean that other nations should prohibit the import of US agricultural products? Sweatshops exploiting female immigrants, with long hours and below-minimum wages, are endemic in the textile industry, as documented amply by several civil-liberties groups. Should not the right of the US to export textiles therefore be suspended by other countries, as surely as the United States seeks to suspend the imports of textiles made by exploited child labour?

Even the right to organise trade unions may be considered inadequate in the US if we go by 'results', as the US favours in judging Japan: less than 15 per cent of the US labour force in the private sector today is unionised. It is no secret, except to those who prefer to think that labour standards are inadequate only in developing countries, that unions are actively discouraged in several ways in the United States. Take strikes, for instance. In 'essential' industries they are restricted virtually everywhere, but the definition of such industries reflects economic structure and political realities, making each country's definition only culture-specific and hence open to objection by others. Should other countries have suspended US flights because President Reagan had broken the air traffic controllers' strike?

Since permanent replacements can be legally hired when workers go on strike, this evidently deters the ability to strike in the US. Should this make it possible for other countries to deny market access for any industry that so hires replacement workers in the United States?

CHILD LABOUR: PROTECTION NOT PROHIBITION

Lest it be thought that the question of child labour is an easy one, I must emphasise that even this raises complex questions, as has indeed been recognised by the ILO. The use of child labour, as such, is surely not the issue. Few children grow up even in the United States without working as babysitters or delivering newspapers; many are even paid by parents for housework in the home. The pertinent social question, familiar to anyone with even a nodding acquaintance with Chadwick, Engels and Dickens and the appalling conditions afflicting children at work in England's factories in the early Industrial Revolution, is rather whether children at work are protected from hazardous and oppressive working conditions.

Whether child labour should be altogether prohibited in a poor country is a matter on which views legitimately differ. Many feel that children's work is unavoidable in the face of poverty and that the alternative to it of further malnourishment and even starvation is a greater calamity. Eliminating child labour would be like voting to eliminate abortion without worrying about the needs of the children then born.

Again, insisting on the 'positive-right' to unionise in support of higher wages, for instance, as against the 'negative-right' of, for instance, freedom to associate for political activity, can be morally obtuse. In practice, such a right could imply higher wages for the 'insiders' who have jobs, at the expense of unemployed 'outsiders'. Besides, unions in developing countries with large populations and much poverty are likely to be in urban-industrial activities, with the industrial proletariat among the better-off sections of the population, while the real poverty is among the non-unionised landless labour. Raising the wages of the former will, in the opinion of many developing-country economists, hurt the prospects of rapid accumulation and growth which alone can pull up more of the landless labour eventually into gainful employment. If so, the imposition on poor countries of the culture-specific views of unions in developed countries about the right to organise for higher wages will only resolve current-equity and intergenerational-equity problems in ways that are (correctly) morally unacceptable to these countries.

My conclusion is that the idea of the Social Clause in the WTO is rooted generally in an ill-considered rejection of the legitimacy of diversity in labour standards and practices between countries. The alleged claim for the universality of labour standards is (except for such rare cases as slavery) unpersuasive.

Developing countries cannot then be blamed for worrying that major OECD countries' recent support for such a clause in the WTO derives from the desire of labour unions to protect their jobs by protecting industries that face competition from poor countries. These countries fear that moral arguments are produced to justify restrictions on such trade since they are so effective in the public domain. In short, the 'white man's burden' is being exploited to secure the 'white man's gain'. Or, to use another metaphor, 'blue protectionism' is breaking out, masked behind a moral face.

DOUBLE STANDARDS IN THE SOCIAL CLAUSE

These fears are reinforced when it is considered that none of the major OECD countries pushing for such a Social Clause expects to be a defendant, instead of a plaintiff, in any resulting trade-access cases.

The standards (such as prohibition of child labour) proposed for inclusion in the Social Clause are invariably presented as those that developing countries are guilty of violating, although transgressions are to be found also in developed countries.

Thus, according to a report in *The Financial Times*, a standard example used by the labour movement to garner support for better safety standards is a disastrous fire in a toy factory in Thailand where many died because exits were shut and unusable. I recall a similar example (but far more disconcerting since the fatalities occurred in the richest country in the world) in a chicken plant in North Carolina. Yet, the focus chosen has been on the poor, not the rich, country.

The standards chosen for attention and sanctions at the WTO also appear to be biased against the poor countries. None of the problems where developed countries would be found in significant violation – such as worker participation in management, rights of migrants and immigrants – is meant to be included in the Social Clause. Symmetry of obligations does not exist in the Social Clause, as currently contemplated, in terms of the coverage of standards. One might cynically conclude that the stones are to be thrown at the poor countries' glass houses by rich countries that build fortresses around their own.

As I argued at the outset, the salience which the Social Clause crusade has acquired in the USA and Europe, and the Clause's specific contents, owe much to the widespread fear, evident during the NAFTA debate in the United States, that trade with poor countries (with abundant unskilled labour) will produce unemployment and reductions in the real wages of the unskilled in the rich countries. The Social Clause is, in this perspective, a way in which fearful unions seek to raise the costs of production in the poor countries as free trade with them threatens their jobs and wages.

IF NOT SOCIAL CLAUSE, WHAT ELSE?

If this analysis is correct, then the idea of a Social Clause in the WTO is not appealing. The developing countries' opposition to its enactment is justified. We are not justified in condemning their objections and unwillingness to go along with our demands as depravity and 'rejectionism'. But if a Social Clause does not make good sense, is everything lost for those in both developed and developing countries who genuinely wish to advance their own views of what are 'good' labour standards? Evidently not.

It is open to them to use other instruments such as educational activities by non-governmental organisations (NGOs) to secure a consensus in favour of their positions. If ideas are good, they should spread without coercion. The use of the rack should not be necessary to spread Christianity; indeed, the Pope has no troops. Mahatma Gandhi's splendid idea of non-violent agitation spread, and was picked up by Martin Luther King, not because Gandhi worked on the Indian government to threaten retribution against others but because it happened to be morally compelling.

There is also the possibility of recourse to private boycotts, available under national and international law, as an occasionally effective instrument. They constitute a well-recognised method of protest and consensus-creation in favour of moral positions.

With the assistance of such methods of persuasion, a multilateral consensus could be achieved on the moral and economic legitimacy of a carefully defined labour standard. It could be formally agreed at the ILO in the light of modern thinking in economics and accumulated experience of developmental and labour issues, on the clear understanding that it is not just a matter of passing resolutions but that serious consequences may follow for signatory nations. The ILO is clearly the institution best equipped to create such a consensus, rather than the WTO, just as multilateral trade negotiations are best conducted at the WTO, not the ILO.

COMPLIANCE MONITORING

In turn, the annual ILO monitoring of compliance with its conventions is an impartial, multilateral process, undertaken with the aid of eminent jurists across the world. Such a process, with changes for standing and for transparency, would be the appropriate forum for an annual review of compliance by nation states of such newly clarified and multilaterally agreed standards. Such monitoring, the opprobrium of public exposure, and the effective strengthening therewith of NGOs in offending countries (many of which are now democratic and permissive of NGO activity) would often be powerful enough forces to prod these countries into corrective action.

In extraordinary cases where violations are such that the moral sense of the world community is outraged, existing international processes are available to undertake coercive, corrective multilateral sanctions against specific countries and to suspend their entire trading rights.

Thus, for instance, under UN embargo procedures, which take precedence over GATT and other treaties, South Africa's GATT membership proved no barrier to the embargo against it precisely because the world was virtually united in its opposition to *apartheid*. Even outside the UN, the GATT waiver procedure has permitted two-thirds of the Contracting Parties to suspend any GATT member's trading rights altogether, or for specific goods (and now services).

I add one final thought to reassure those who feel their own moral view in any specific instance must be respected at any cost, even if others cannot be persuaded to see things their way. Even they need not worry under current international procedures. Thus, suppose that (say) American or French public opinion on an issue (as in the Tuna-Dolphin case for the former and the Beef-Hormone case for the latter) forces the government to undertake a unilateral suspension of another GATT member's trading rights. There is nothing in the GATT, nor will there be in the WTO, which compels the overturning of such unilateral action. The offending Contracting Party undertaking the unilateral action can persist in a violation while making a compensatory offer of an alternative trade concession, or the offended Party can retaliate by withdrawing an equivalent trade concession.

Thus, unless we resent having to pay for our virtue (since the claim is, for example, that 'our labour standard is morally superior'), this is a perfectly sensible solution even to politically unavoidable unilateralism: do not import glass bangles made with child labour in Pakistan or India, but make some other compensatory trade concession. And remember that the grant of an alternative trade concession (or tariff retaliation) makes some other activity than the offending one more attractive, thus helping to shrink the offending activity. That surely should be a matter for approbation rather than impassioned dismissal.

North–North Issues

So far, I have discussed issues that touch primarily on North–South questions which emerge in the new world economy of freer trade and investment, cautioning against the proposals to modify the WTO to sanction and legitimise eco-dumping, social dumping and the inclusion of a Social Clause in the WTO.

But enhanced integration of the world economy, and sensitivity to 'unfair trade' of all varieties, have prompted increased friction and demands for harmonisation of policies among the developed countries as well.

Competition Policy

The principal area in which demands for such (predominantly) North–North harmonisation appear is competition policy. The main impetus behind this demand has been suspicion that the *keiretsu* and the *retail distribution* systems of Japan lead to impaired market access, in effect 'nullifying and impairing' the value of Japan's trade concessions.

These problems are not endemic only to Japan. For example, the EU also provides exemption from its competition directives to its auto industry so as to permit exclusive dealerships; that exemption was renewed last year. Besides, the *keiretsu* system is now widely recognised to be efficient and its side-effects on market access may be no more than those accruing from the vertical integration widely practised in the United States which works more directly against outside suppliers.

The WTO will have to bring these questions into its purview soon as they are beginning to prompt unilateral approaches and solutions.

My view is that, while the trading nations are engaged in doing this, it should be possible even under current rules to use Article XXIII 1(b) on 'nullification and impairment' to bring questions of competition policy before the WTO and to develop jurisprudence that will reflect some minimal commonly shared 'norms'. The tensions that unilateral actions bring would be soothed and the important principle would simultaneously be advanced that impartial rules must be deployed so as to apply symmetrically to all Contracting Parties instead of being invoked arbitrarily and only against others.

REGIONALISM VERSUS MULTILATERALISM OR FTAs VERSUS FT

If the matters above are broadly characterised as North–South and North–North issues, the one overriding phenomenon in the world economy today is the proliferation of inherently preferential Free Trade Areas. How should we view them? Do they detract from, or add to, multilateral free trade? As I asked several years ago,[24] are they building blocks or stumbling blocs to the ultimate goal of a world trading system ensuring freer trade to all?

In my view, there are only two compelling arguments for giving up the non-discrimination implied in all-embracing multilateralism in trade:

• If a smaller group of countries wants to develop a *Common Market*.

In this case, not only trade but also investment and migration barriers are eventually eliminated as in a federal state, so that the full economic and political advantages of such integration follow.

• If it is not possible to move to fully multilateral free trade (FT) for all through multilateral trade negotiations (MTN), at the GATT or now the WTO, the only feasible way to continue reducing trade barriers is to go down the route of open-ended, easy-to-join preferential free trade areas (FTAs) among as many willing nations as you can find.

The former argument underlay the European initiative for the Common Market. The latter argument provided a key motivation for the United States, a keen opponent of preferential trading arrangements (PTAs) and an avid supporter of multilateralism throughout the postwar period, to shift course and to embrace PTAs by initiating the Canada–US Free Trade Agreement (CUFTA) in 1983. The failure to secure agreement from Europe and the developing countries to start a new Round of MTN at the GATT Ministerial in November 1982 led Ambassador William Brock to this approach. The intention then was to use an ever-expanding set of FTAs, with the US acting as both catalyst and nucleus, to achieve the world-wide free trade that could not be reached via the GATT.

With Secretary James Baker, this open-ended approach, where the US-centred FTAs would be open to any nation anywhere (as was informally discussed with Egypt and the ASEAN nations), became captured by the proponents of 'regionalism' who linked it instead, and constrained it, to the Americas, as part of President Bush's Initiative for the Americas. Thus grew the fears that the world was dividing into three blocs: the EU, the Americas, and possibly a Japan-centred Asian bloc.

In the event, the US expanded CUFTA to NAFTA, and is now poised to go down the FTA route more energetically, promising to take Chile and then other South American nations on board. While the idea of regionalism is not dead, the Washington policy-makers, in response to criticisms (including mine),[25] have occasionally expressed the view that the earlier open-ended non-regional FTAs approach would be adopted instead. Thus, President Bush, in a major speech in Detroit at the end of the campaign for the 1992 Presidential election, promised that he would extend NAFTA to Eastern European nations and to the Far East. And recently, the Clinton administration has tentatively explored the possibility of extending NAFTA to South Korea and Singapore.

A NAFTA Common Market; APEC not an FTA

But we must ask: Is this infatuation with FTAs, including the pressure presumably being exerted by the United States to move APEC (the Association for Pacific Economic Cooperation) in the direction of an FTA, desirable when the multilateral trading system has already been jump-started with the ratification of the Uruguay Round and the birth of the WTO? Would it not be wiser for the world's only remaining superpower, and currently also its most robust economy, again to assume the leadership role on multilateral free trade? Should it not focus on converting NAFTA into a Common Market instead of seeking to extend it to more members and, given the inherently preferential nature of such FTAs, spreading what can be considered a stain on the now-realistic vision of a non-discriminatory world trading system? Should not the APEC be used as a platform for multilateral trade initiatives rather than as an FTA for more preferential trade liberalisation?

I should imagine this analysis and judgement are shared by many in Asia, even in Europe, and are certainly not without supporters within the United States, with its rich tradition of energetic and acute public debate. They also provide an opening for a leadership role for Japan and the Asian members of APEC in their own region, at the APEC and at the WTO.

Japan and the Far Eastern super-performers, often known as the 'new Japans', have produced supreme examples for the rest of the world by transforming their nations into world-class economies in just one generation of phenomenal growth. When economists talk of the 'Japanese miracle', I sometimes wonder whether ours is not after all truly a 'dismal science' if, every time an economy does strikingly well, we call it a miracle!

Many seek in this outstanding success the validity of their own pet policy prescriptions. Few things can be explained in terms of a single cause. My own pet theory (not too popular in the developing countries when I embraced it 30 years ago) is that outward-orientation produces major dividends for a country. I think there is now broad agreement that Japan and the new Japans have done tremendously well by going for world markets.[26]

Rooting for free trade where the intention is to go for the world's markets, instead of preferential free trade areas where sights are set low by thinking only of FTA-limited markets, has characterised this area. Even ASEAN, a regional grouping of political significance, had no economic dimension of substance for much of its life. Multilateralism came naturally with these attitudes which in turn were strengthened with economic success. Pro-FTA attitudes have often been associated with economic weakness: Imperial Preference went with Britain's fear of the newly emerging competition from Germany and the United States, whereas the NAFTA debate betrayed a similar desire of many business groups and politicians to keep Mexico's markets for themselves instead of sharing them with Japan and the EU.

But, while one may debate the many reasons for the desire of these Asian nations to go for world, rather than regional and sub-regional, markets, it surely provides them with a unique experience and potential to shape world trade policy in the direction of multilateralism.

The post-Uruguay agenda at the WTO will inevitably entail re-examining Article XXIV in a much more careful way than has been done to date. More than that, the new Director-General of the WTO will have to provide leadership to shape the emerging picture of exploding preferential trade groupings and to confront their impact on WTO-centred multilateralism, instead of simply accepting their emergence and agenda as a foregone political reality. In this task, Japan and other Asian nations, which have generally and properly kept away from preferential trade arrangements like FTAs, will have an essential role in providing support to the WTO leadership.

In the meantime, Japan and other Asian members of APEC can play a useful role at APEC itself by opposing its being turned into yet another FTA. They can set an example by rejecting the FTA model, using the APEC rather as a way of coordinating policies in the region on questions such as an Investment Code and, equally important, on the new issues before the WTO (such as the Social Clause) discussed in this paper. My informed guess is that, on those issues as well, Japan and the Asian nations have much to offer that is closer to what I have suggested. Since APEC straddles part of Asia and part of the Americas, it may well be the place for these remarkable Asian nations to bring their friends across the common ocean to greater wisdom on these new issues. They will thus assist the development of the WTO in more appropriate directions.

After the Indonesian meeting of APEC where free trade within APEC was embraced as a goal for the year 2020, this may seem a lost cause. But it is not. The stated goal is, in practice, unattainable without MFN extension of trade barrier cuts to other WTO members, unless APEC is turned into an FTA: but an FTA version of APEC has *not* yet been embraced as a goal. Equally, it is wholly improbable that this (or any) region would extend trade concessions within the region on an MFN basis to non-members automatically. That is simply not what trading nations do, especially those belonging to preferential trading areas. So, despite the rhetoric from Jakarta, the issue whether APEC will turn into another FTA or alternatively become a non-discriminatory institution stressing multilateralism that would buttress rather than rival the WTO, remains unsettled. The rhetoric of 2020 lacks the clarity of 20/20 vision. That is all to the good, for it means that there is still hope that the APEC will not turn into another FTA.

Japan's Leadership Opportunity in APEC

When APEC meets next year in Osaka, Japan will play the host and will thus have the opportunity to provide leadership on its future role and its relationship to the new WTO. I suggest four lines of progress.

- The *first* is to work with the United States and the European Union towards a new follow-up multilateral trade negotiation at the WTO.
- The *second* is to seek agreement among the Asian APEC members (including prospective new Asian members such as India) that APEC would not become a preferential FTA, while ensuring that American members of the APEC (led by the United States) are confronted clearly on the broader issue of the utmost importance, that is, whether multilateral free trade, not a spaghetti bowl of preferential free trade areas, is to be the centrepiece of the newly emerging world trading system.
- The *third* is to embrace an APEC agenda that includes coordination of policies and positions at the WTO and the new Round on such matters as the wisdom of including labour standards at all and the optimal method of including environmental matters in the WTO.
- The *fourth* would transform President Suharto's call for free trade in the APEC region by 2020 explicitly into a concerted effort to achieve this goal by a succession of focused APEC *initiatives* (not APEC-wide preferential liberalisations) in conjunction with G-7 (whose non-European members are members of APEC), to launch *multilateral* trade negotiations to reduce trade barriers worldwide on a *non-discriminatory* (MFN) basis.

This could be Japan's, and indeed Asia's, central contribution to the design of the new world trading system. It would be in keeping with Asia's commitment in the postwar period to a non-regional, non-preferential approach to world trade. It would reflect also her profound scepticism about illogical and misguided political demands to make 'fair trade' in environmental and labour standards a precondition for freeing trade.

The key issue is whether Japan can rise to the leadership role required on these central questions of the design of the new world trading system, by undertaking a *pro*-active policy, or whether she will continue to play a *re*active role that leaves leadership and hence the architecture of the new world trading system entirely to others. If the architecture of the new world trading system is left exclusively to the United States and the European Union (which too has proliferated preferential arrangements with other countries not in the core of the Common Market), I am afraid that dilution of the multilateral trading regime by the spaghetti bowl of preferential trading arrangements could well be our fate. Labour and environmental standards will also intrude as preconditions for, and indeed barriers to, free trade.

THE WTO: ARCHITECTURE, NOT ENGINEERING

The WTO thus stands on the threshold of a period of momentous new issues, requiring architecture not engineering. It requires *intellectual* leadership, not the skills of *political* fixmanship.

The qualities we must now seek in the leadership to be provided by the new Director-General of the WTO must include the ability to:

- put the WTO's new tasks in perspective, requiring an acute grasp of history;
- shape the solutions to these tasks in appropriate ways, requiring a deep familiarity with economics, an acquaintance with ethics and moral philosophy, intellectual integrity and a habit of independence from the crude pressures and exigencies of politics; and
- translate these solutions into policies acceptable to the member nations, while possessing the ability to communicate and articulate.

Instead, we observe the main trading nations battling to put *their* man in Geneva, with their choice settling on candidates whose chief virtue is that they are distinguished politicians, rather than the search being opened to a wider and richer range of candidates characterised by vision and intellectual strength. The chief desire of the central protagonists in this battle seems to be to pursue their narrow political advantage and to advance their preferred agenda by choosing a candidate who, if successful, will further their cause. What a pity!

NOTES

1. The text of this lecture has been slightly revised in the light of the sub-sequent APEC meeting in Jakarta and the ratification of the Uruguay Round by the US Congress.
2. Peter Sutherland has suggested that the introduction of biennial Ministerial Conferences at the WTO will mean that multilateral negotiations on trade issues 'will become a permanent event'; this need not, however, preclude a formal Round with a set agenda. (See John Whalley, 'The WTO and the Future of the Trading System', paper presented to the Conference in Honour of Jagdish Bhagwati, University of Lancaster, November 1994.)
3. The implementation period for the Uruguay Round agreements on textiles and agriculture extends up to 10 years so that Uruguay Round matters will continue to be manifest at the WTO in the next decade also.
4. The appellations 'North' and 'South' are used simply to describe the developed and developing countries.
5. These different economic-philosophical positions are discussed in depth in Jagdish Bhagwati (ed.), *The New International Economic Order: The North-South Debate*, MIT Press, Cambridge, Mass., 1977, Ch. 1.
6. This attitude extended to other areas too: the outward flow of skilled manpower was thus considered a 'brain drain' rather than an opportunity for one's citizens to train and work abroad that would lead to a beneficial impact as this diaspora expanded.
7. They were called the West, of course, then. The changing nomenclature of the poor and rich countries reflects a shift from an historical, cultural and imperial divide into East and West to a contemporary, post-colonial and development-related divide into South and North.
8. See, for example, Jagdish Bhagwati, *Protectionism*, Bertil Ohlin Lectures, MIT Press, Cambridge, Mass., 1988, on the question of free trade, and Bhagwati, *The World Trading System at Risk*, Harry Johnson Lecture, Princeton University Press, Princeton, NJ, 1991, on the issue of multilateralism.
9. The evidence in support of this phenomenon in the 1980s, both for the United States and for several other countries, is reviewed and synthesised nicely by Marvin Kosters in Chapter I of Jagdish Bhagwati and Marvin Kosters (eds), *Trade and Wages: Leveling Wages Down?*, American Enterprise Institute, Washington, DC, 1994.
10. Robert Lawrence, 'Trade, Multinationals, & Labor', Cambridge, Mass.: National Bureau of Economic Research, Working Paper No. 4836, August 1994.
11. See *Employment Outlook*, Paris, OECD, July 1993.
12. See Jagdish Bhagwati, 'Free Traders and Free Immigrationists: Strangers or Friends?', Russell Sage Foundation, New York, Working Paper No. 20, 1991.
13. This empirical work by Robert Lawrence and Matthew Slaughter is reviewed in Jagdish Bhagwati and Vivek Dehejia, 'Freer Trade and Wages of the Unskilled – Is Marx Striking Again?', in Bhagwati and Kosters, op.cit. A subsequent empirical study by Jeffrey Sachs and Howard Schatz,

'Trade and Jobs in US Manufacturing', in *Brookings Papers*, 1994, claims to overturn the Lawrence–Slaughter findings by omitting computers (a procedure that is debatable at best). Even then the coefficient with the changed sign is both small and statistically insignificant. So, while Noam Chomsky has educated us that two negatives add up to a positive in every language, it is wrong to claim that the two negatives of a statistically insignificant and small parameter of the required sign add up to a positive support for the thesis that trade has been depressing the real wages of the unskilled!

14. The work of Adrian Wood, *North–South Trade, Employment and Inequality*, Clarendon Press, Oxford, 1994, argues in support of the trade-hurting-real-wages-of-the-unskilled thesis but his arguments have been effectively criticised by Lawrence, op.cit. See also a review of the theory and evidence in Jagdish Bhagwati, 'Trade and Wages: Choosing Among Alternative Explanations', *Federal Reserve Bank of New York Economic Policy Review*, January 1995.

15. While I distinguish among 'North–South' and 'North–North' issues here, let me stress again that these descriptions are only broadly true, and reflect the principal historical origins of the issues; the issues are universal and now cut across nations in both groups. Thus, for example, the demands of eco-dumping duties (discussed below, pp. 192–6) have the potential of creating frictions among OECD countries, and not just between them and the countries of the South. Nor does my use of these shorthand labels imply that there are coalitions of the North and of the South to that effect on the issues being discussed. I was among the first to discount the enduring effectiveness of a coalition of the South when, in the flush of the OPEC success, so-called Global Negotiations were demanded by the G-77 countries at the United Nations: the developing countries were unsuccessful with these demands. Indeed, they have been substantially fragmented politically since then, as discussed in my 'Dependence and Interdependence: Developing Countries in the World Economy', Ernest Sturc Memorial Lecture, Johns Hopkins University, School for Advanced International Studies, Washington, DC, 1987; reprinted in Jagdish Bhagwati, *Political Economy and International Economics*, ed. Douglas Irwin, MIT Press, Cambridge, Mass., 1991.

16. John Wilson, in 'Capital Mobility and Environmental Standards: Is There a Theoretical Basis for a Race to the Bottom?', mimeo, September 1994, demonstrates that there can even be a 'race to the top'. This possibility is disregarded in the analysis above, as in the public discourse. The Wilson paper appears in Jagdish Bhagwati and Robert Hudec (eds), *Harmonisation and Fair Trade: Prerequisites for Free Trade?*, MIT Press, Cambridge, Mass., 2 vols, 1996.

17. The evidence has been systematically reviewed and assessed recently by Arik Levinson, 'Environmental Regulations and Industry Location: International and Domestic Evidence', mimeo, University of Wisconsin, September 1994; included in the 2-volume set of papers on *Harmonization and Fair Trade: Prerequisites for Free Trade?*, op.cit,

18. See Jagdish Bhagwati and T. N. Srinivasan, 'Trade and the Environment: Does Environmental Diversity Detract from the Case for Free Trade?',

July 1994, in Bhagwati and Hudec, op.cit. Their analysis is based on Levinson, op.cit.

19. There are other issues. One main class relates to the current GATT restrictions, as reflected in recent GATT Panel findings as in the two Dolphin-Tuna cases involving the United States, on 'values'-inspired restrictions on imports of products using processes that are unacceptable, which will have to be clarified and will be the subject of new negotiations. My own views on the best solution to this class of problems, as also to the other main class of problems raised by environmentalists who fear that it is too easy for countries to challenge the higher standards which they have enacted in their own countries (an issue that was at the heart of the latest GATT Panel finding, mostly in favour of the USA, in the EU–US case on differentially punitive US taxes and standards on higher-gasoline-usage cars) are developed at length in Bhagwati and Srinivasan, op.cit.

20. This, of course, does not apply equally to trade in highly differentiated products like autos where one can get fixated on specific countries, such as Japan.

21. See Bhagwati, 'American Rules, Mexican Jobs', *The New York Times*, 24 March 1993.

22. This efficiency is only in the sense of cost minimisation. The number of permits may, however, be too small or too large. Letting non-users also bid (and then destroy permits) is bedevilled by free-rider problems.

23. I talk of the United States 'suspending' Mexico's trade rights since the GATT Panel in the Dolphin-Tuna case upheld these rights for Mexico. If it had not, I should be talking simply of the United States 'denying' market access to Mexico.

24. Cf. Jagdish Bhagwati, *The World Trading System at Risk*, op.cit.

25. Cf. Jagdish Bhagwati, 'President Clinton's Trading Choices: Beyond NAFTA What?', *Foreign Policy*, Summer 1993. I advocated there the position taken above that the best course was to return now to multilateralism and to give up on further FTAs; but that, if FTAs were to be pursued, then non-regional FTAs were better than regional ones because, among other reasons, the regional approach would be more likely to promote fragmentation of the world economy into preferential blocs.

26. In regard to imports, there has certainly been 'controlled openness' in Japan; and the role of protection in her development, as of the other Far Eastern nations, is more complex than made out by ideologues on the side of either free trade or protection.

Index

Index entries relate to the Introduction and Chapters 1 to 10. Acronyms and initialised forms are treated as words. References to chapter notes are indicated by *n*.